The Nilgiri Hills

Ootacamund in 1830

Source: Lithograph by E. A. M'Curdy. Photo courtesy Paul Hockings.

The Nilgiri Hills

A Kaleidoscope of People, Culture, and Nature

Edited by

PAUL HOCKINGS

Orient BlackSwan

THE NILGIRI HILLS: A KALEIDOSCOPE OF PEOPLE, CULTURE AND NATURE

ORIENT BLACKSWAN PRIVATE LIMITED

Registered Office
3-6-752 Himayatnagar, Hyderabad 500 029, Telangana, India
e-mail: centraloffice@orientblackswan.com

Other Offices
Bengaluru, Chennai, Guwahati, Hyderabad, Kolkata,
Mumbai, New Delhi, Noida, Patna

First published by Orient Blackswan Private Limited 2023

ISBN 978-93-5442-396-3

041722

Typeset in
Minion Pro 11/13
by Le Studio Graphique, Gurgaon 122 007

Printed in India at
Avantika Printers Private Limited, New Delhi 110 020

Published by
Orient Blackswan Private Limited
3-6-752 Himayatnagar, Hyderabad 500 029, Telangana, India
e-mail: info@orientblackswan.com

Contents

Images, Figures, and Maps

Images

Figures

Maps

Plates

Between pages 220 and 221

Abbreviations

ASL	above sea level
BCE	before the Common Era, years BC
BLF	Bought-Leaf tea industry
ca	*circa*, about
CE	the Common Era, years AD
CLTM	Catharine Ling Toda Mission
CNRS	Centre National de Recherche Scientifique
FAO	Food and Agriculture Organization
ff.	following pages
INDP	Indo–German Nilgiris Development Project
IST	Indian Standard Time
IUCN	International Union for Conservation of Nature
km	kilometres
m	metres
MGNREGA	Mahatma Gandhi National Rural Employment Guarantee Act
mm	millimetres
NGO	non-government organisation
SC	Scheduled Caste
ST	Scheduled Tribe
UNESCO	United Nations Educational, Scientific, and Cultural Organization
UPASI	United Planters' Association of Southern India
VAO	Village Administrative Officer
WMO	World Meteorological Organization

A Timeline of Nilgiri Modernization

1572 First mention of the Nilgiri Mountains in Western literature, in the Portuguese national epic *Os Lusiadas* by Luis Vaz de Camõens

1600 Elizabeth I incorporated the East India Company

1603 First known visit by a European, when the Jesuit Father, Giacomo Fenicio, came to the Kunda area and reported on a meeting with Todas and Badagas

1799 Defeat and death of Tipu Sultan at the Battle of Seringapatam (Sri Ranga Paṭṭana) near Mysore

1801 Fruitless military incursion into the Wainad by a small British detachment under Colonel Arthur Wellesley

1811 Initial census and mapping of the Nilgiri Plateau area

1819 Arrival on the Upper Nilgiris of John Sullivan, who builds the first European house for himself near Kotagiri. First scientific research on the hills by a French botanist

1821 Sullivan starts developing Ootacamund as a new town, soon to have shops, roads, a market, a hospital, schools, and other facilities; he also encourages local farmers to adopt European seed and new commercial crops

1822 Sullivan opens the first school in a Badaga village

1823 First Roman Catholic chapel in Ootacamund

1825 Ooty Lake constructed by damming; hospital and market opened in Ootacamund

1829 St. Stephen's, the main Anglican church, founded; library started in Ootacamund

1830 First coffee plantation, in Kotagiri

1832 Sullivan tells a parliamentary commission in London that south Indians are capable of administering themselves; first ethnography of Nilgiri people published, by Henry Harkness

1834 T. B. Macaulay drafts the Indian Penal Code in the Ootacamund Club

1835 Tea planted experimentally in Kēti
1845 Arrival of Protestant missionaries from Basel, to start running schools in numerous Badaga villages
1847 First vaccination of 700 children against smallpox
1853 Military cantonment established at Wellington
1858 First Badaga man converted to Christianity
1859 First Nilgiri newspaper, *The Eclectic and Neilgherry Chronicle*
1863 First commercial tea estate, in Kotagiri
1866 Establishment of Ootacamund Municipality
1868 James W. Breeks becomes the first Commissioner of the Nilgiris
1873 Breeks writes the first account of five local tribes; first steam engines seen at Meṭṭupāḷayam
1877 Nilgiri Game Association established
1880 Madras government bans cultivation of opium poppies
1882 Nilgiris District established, with a Collector
1891 Nilgiri Planters' Association established
1900 Cordite factory started at Aravangāḍu; the formal opening was in 1904
1904 First cars arrive in the district; opening of India's first hydroelectric power station, at Kāṭēri; first Toda man converted to Christianity
1906 W. H. R. Rivers publishes his pioneering ethnography of the Toda people
1908 Walter Francis publishes the definitive *Gazetteer of the Nilgiris District*, and Frederick Price his history of Ootacamund
1908 Railway reached Ootacamund
1911 First Badaga co-operative society formed
1916 Timothy Mulley becomes the first Badaga man to graduate from a university
1923 First Badaga representative, H. B. Ari Gowder, elected to the Madras Legislative Council
1925 Kwaṛo·n becomes the first Toda to graduate from a university
1933 Completion of Pykara powerhouse
1947 Achievement of Indian Independence; departure of most British residents, and transfer of many tea estates to Indian ownership

1955 Initiation of Kunda hydroelectric scheme, with a large Canadian input

1962 Akkamma Devi becomes the first Badaga elected to the Lok Sabha in New Delhi; she was the first Badaga woman to graduate from a university. Intensive research on the Nilgiris, its peoples and resources, by numerous foreign scholars was now underway

1967 Indo–German Nilgiris Development Project initiated; opening of the Hindustan Photo Films factory (closed in 2018)

1986 Creation of the Nilgiri Biosphere Reserve

Preface

On 9 July 2018, Christiane Pilot-Raichoor wrote to me from a hospital bed in Paris that she liked the idea of preparing this book to commemorate two centuries of Nilgiri development and modernisation, and that she would contribute an article on 'Change of points of view on the status of the Badaga language in the last 200 years'. It would have been a really novel topic, but she passed away just a week later, after a long struggle with cancer. She was without doubt the world's leading authority on that language, and her special knowledge of Badaga, Kurumba, and Kannada make the loss to Dravidian scholarship irreparable.

The book in your hands was produced by its authors specifically to commemorate this Bicentenary of the opening-up of the Nilgiri Hills to the outside world by a Londoner named John Sullivan, but owing to the coronavirus pandemic, completion of the book was delayed by two years. The seventeen contributors have already published numerous more specialised books and articles about Nilgiri topics elsewhere, and in many cases have written articles for the 2012 *Encyclopædia of the Nilgiri Hills* as well. That volume's 600 entries richly document the panoply of people, places, nature, and social activities in a place that is barely 1,000 square miles in extent, yet presents us with a kaleidoscopic view of southern India today and yesterday.

That *Encyclopædia*, which we published some years ago, has been recommended here for further reading on many of the topics introduced in the present book, as most of its articles are fairly short, up-to-date, and quite accessible. Suggestions have otherwise been appended to most articles for further reading on the same topic.

The Nilgiris is the most heavily studied rural area anywhere in India, with a Bibliography of about 8,000 items, mostly in English. Despite the extensive literature that has accumulated over the past two centuries, every article in this book—whether it be on ancient metallurgy, the gathering of wild honey, or Toda relations with the British—represents an altogether fresh topic, and hence one that adds immediately to our understanding of this highly diverse region.

March 2023

Paul Hockings
Editor

Part I

Prologue

1

The Eve of the Modern

PAUL HOCKINGS

The first two decades of the nineteenth century saw three remarkable events in the previously silent, unnoticed, and undocumented history of the people living on the Nilgiri Hills, three events that quickly led to a radically different lifestyle for those same people.

The first event occurred in 1801, and was a very minor footnote in the history of south India. A local kinglet or warlord in the Wainad area, to the west of the Nilgiri Massif, had been trying to maintain his family's hold on a large tract of land there. The family was one branch of the Kottayam Rajas and was headed by Kerala Varma Raja; the East India Company called him the Pychy Rebel. His burning gripe with the British administration, which seems understandable enough today, arose from the fact that in 1787 his family had been made reluctantly to accept the suzerainty over their territory of Tipu Sultan and his government in Mysore. Between that time and 1799 there was a complex and shifting pattern of allegiances and attacks between Kerala Varma, Tipu, and the Company. The British had their own reasons for engaging in four short, localised wars with Mysore at that time, in the hope of dislodging Tipu from his paramount position. Ultimately the Fourth Anglo-Mysore War did indeed do this, and Tipu's death at the Battle of Seringapatam (Sri Ranga Paṭṭana), north of Mysore City, changed the situation altogether.

Now the British forces had conquered all of Mysore, and so a new dispensation came into being under the Subsidiary Alliance: the Mysore State was to be ruled by a dynasty of Hindu Maharajahs who were obligated towards the East India Company, while the more southerly fringes of Tipu's territories, which were not Kannada-speaking, fell under the direct administration of Madras Presidency. This meant that the lands of the unfortunate Kerala Varma did not revert to his family, as they had wished, but became a small corner of Madras Presidency. That was also true of all the land later to become the Nilgiris District.

Kerala Varma could not stomach this unfair situation, and so took to the Wainad jungles with a band of armed men to wage guerilla warfare against the British and their agents. This the Company's legislators were not willing to put up with, and so they sent a small detachment of soldiers in pursuit of Varma, but with little success. His band was so much more expert at jungle warfare that the British detachment, a handful of south Indian soldiers, never got a shot at him. This was in the spring of 1801.

One could hardly blame the commanding officer, a career colonel, for this failure to catch up with these 'rebels'. His men were not so used to the jungle environment; moreover, his detachment was too small for the task, and their muskets were slow to load. The officer himself was well-trained by the standards of the day, and had been given military control of the area. He was an Anglo-Irishman from Dublin, trained in a French military academy. This young officer (he was thirty-two) had been present at the Battle of Seringapatam, although he had probably had scant experience of the actual fighting. So, in short, this venture in the Wainad was perhaps his first real foray into military fieldcraft, and we might have forgotten all about him but for the fact that he is the first British person to have entered the Nilgiri region *whose name we actually know* (Hayavadana Rao 1908).

It was to be another five years before another military detachment managed to kill Kerala Varma and thereby finally resolve the festering issue. What is notable about this whole affair is that, contrary to an all-too-common image of Colonial Oppression, where foreign soldiers typically march into an area and bring the local populace to their knees by force of arms, there was no attempt in the Wainad to attack the local populace or establish British rule by force. And, more remarkably still, the officer who had first tried to assert the terms of the treaty learnt enough about strategy during this action to go on to lead a number of military triumphs elsewhere, culminating in 1815 when he defeated a much larger French army at the Battle of Waterloo, and was ever after celebrated as the Duke of Wellington. So the earliest memorable thing about the initial phase of modernisation of the Nilgiris is that the very first Briton to set foot there whom we can identify was to become a future Prime Minister of Great Britain.

This military escapade behind them, the British authorities showed little interest in the margins of their newly acquired territories. What we know as the Nilgiri Hills became, under the Subsidiary Alliance, a tiny part of Coimbatore District, while the Wainad was added to British territory in Malabar (Malapuram) District. We do know the names of several Britons who explored the foothills of the Nilgiris, including the botanist Dr L. G. Ford, who reached the upper Nilgiris, but none left any written account, so we really do not know what—if anything—they discovered.

That situation was to change in 1812, when the second remarkable event of the nineteenth century came in the form of an official investigation. This may not sound like a particularly interesting development, but it was unique. William Garrow, the Collector of Coimbatore and a resident of that city, was the person under whose jurisdiction the Nilgiri Hills had rested since 1804; not that it mattered. Every day, this man could see the distant hills from his office, without ever being prompted to go and take a look. But in 1812 he *did* order a survey with an accompanying map and census of the hills to be made, both produced by William Keys and an apprentice, C. McMahon, along with a few assistants. Keys, who was in charge, was a Sub-assistant in the Survey Department in Coimbatore.

A census—today a normal activity in many nations—occurred throughout Britain in 1811, and that was only their second decennial census. Ireland also attempted its first rather unsuccessful census in that same year. Otherwise the British Empire was expanding with sound and fury, but without any censuses. One has to look to Sweden, Austria, Finland, Norway, China, Japan, and the United States to find any censuses being made before the nineteenth century. So the taking of a census in the

Nilgiris in 1812, although such a restricted effort, was a pioneering endeavour, especially as India was not to hold a national census for another sixty years. It is even more extraordinary to realise that the officials took a census of the area that they were about to occupy some years *before* there was any European settlement whatever, even before some lowlanders had moved in to join the indigenous peoples of the hills—the Todas, Kotas, and Badagas, along with seven tribes of Kurumbas and four of Irulas (see Plate 4, this volume). Such a survey was surely unique in colonial history, and in social science too, for that 1812 census meant that we have a statistical description of the local population *status quo ante*—as it was before any changes took place. That census recorded 130 Kotas, 179 Todas, and 2,207 Badagas on the hills; but one suspects there was an under-enumeration of each group, perhaps omitting children, as a second census nine years later got considerably higher figures.

The map of the Nilgiris that was prepared in 1812 is invaluable because it adds so much to our knowledge of the pre-contact situation. It shows dozens of Badaga hamlets and six Kota villages, but no Toda ones. It also records some tracks between villages—there were no roads at all at that time. The map was never published. However, a resurvey by Captain B. S. Ward in 1822 produced a much improved map that is published in Price's book (1908, 4). It documents essentially the same local conditions, but with more placenames. The historian Frederick Price was rather dismissive of that early survey, saying that Keys and McMahon had not been in large sections of the Nilgiris. While this may be true, it should be mentioned that some other surveying of landholdings had already been done by 'native surveyors', whose data were presumably included. Moreover, the fact that Keys reported that the Badagas, the dominant indigenous group, had forty-one principal villages and 119 subsidiary hamlets shows that he had fully understood the extent of this, the dominant community, since the Badagas indeed had forty-one communes (*ūru*), each of which included a dozen or so small hamlets (*haṭṭi*; see Chapter 6, this volume).

The third and most consequential event for the Nilgiri people occurred in January 1819, when the Special Revenue

Commissioner of Coimbatore, a Londoner named John Sullivan, along with the Assistant Surgeon of Coimbatore and a small group of other men, ascended the eastern hills and arrived at the Badaga hamlet of Dimbaṭṭi, exactly as Keys and McMahon had done (see Image 5.1, this volume). Given the common stereotype that colonial interlopers always came with firearms to enforce their will, it must be emphasised that in this case, the only guns the men brought from Coimbatore were to ensure they had something good to eat along the way. Not one 'native' was shot in anger; rather, it was quite the opposite: folklore has it that these unexpected visitors received a civil welcome from Badagas and Todas alike (see Chapters 4 and 5, this volume). The Englishmen were impressed by the apparent fertility of the soil, by the many small villages they saw, and most especially by the mild January climate, which generations of visitors would liken to that in sundry parts of Europe. Although only 10° from the Equator, at night they actually felt too cold (see Chapter 3, this volume). On a second visit three months later, Sullivan brought a French botanist with him, thus launching the scientific study of the Nilgiri environment, and very soon he was busy building a European-style cottage for himself in Dimbaṭṭi. Sullivan looked like he was there to stay!

John Sullivan, one now realises, was a quite remarkable man and not just a paper-shuffling functionary, whose very common British name (and some might recall too the John Smith who first explored Ajanta) may belie his revolutionary intentions for the Nilgiris and their peoples. When I published an article about him in 1973, in the *Journal of Indian History*, he was all but unknown to anyone except local residents or specialists in south Indian history. Even today, the numerous books we have on the history of British India do not discuss him, tending instead to concentrate on the doings of viceroys, governors, and top military men.

Sullivan was in a different class. He worked in the civil service of south India for what was then a common reason: his relatives, for several generations, had already served in that civil service. His father (also named John) had been a Persian translator and sometime diplomat for the Company. The young man, his son, had never been to school, which is not as bad as it sounds since he had received private tuition in central London, his birthplace. At the age of fifteen he was sent out to Calcutta, where he laboured in the Writers' Building for months as he learned his pen-pushing trade. Advancement could be rapid in those days for those with the right family connections, however, as Sullivan had. He was born in 1788, an illegitimate child, but by 1815 was already the 27-year-old Collector of Chingleput (Cengalpaṭṭu).

It is rare indeed in colonial history to know so much detail about the man who started a new town from the rocks and earth upon which it now rests; but that is the case with Ootacamund (Udagamandalam in Tamil, or Ooty for short). When Sullivan was shown the centrally located vale where this town now stands, two years after his initial visit to Dimbaṭṭi, he realised that Dimbaṭṭi and what was to become the nearby town of Kotagiri were not so well-positioned, despite being closer to Coimbatore. So Sullivan mustered all available resources to develop the town that would, half-a-century later, become the district headquarters.

The prospect of developing this area was daunting, and one would have thought Sullivan hardly had the background to even get started. There were no roads anywhere on the plateau, no roads even from the Coimbatore Plain up into the hills. Instead there was a network of footpaths which at best could carry a horseman. There was no market anywhere on the plateau; indeed, almost no cash with which to conduct market relations. It goes without saying that there were no civic buildings, such as a law court, a hospital, a post office, a police station, a bank, or a school, and there were no shops at all. It was also fairly apparent that the local population could not be expected to construct any of these things, even if they had agreed they were worthwhile. The Todas had a dairying economy that allowed them to be self-sufficient. The Badagas and Kotas had a mixed farming economy, also with some dairying, and what few requirements these two groups lacked they got through barter from neighbouring groups. Nobody was in the habit of doing ordinary manual labour for other groups. And to make the social situation even more complicated for Sullivan and all his assistants, each of the indigenous groups—Kotas, Badagas, Todas, Kurumbas, and Irulas (see Plates 4 and 8, this volume)—spoke its own distinct language, despite their closeness to each other when measured in miles.

Nonetheless, within a decade or so the town had acquired all the civic buildings just mentioned (see Frontispiece). To suggest that Sullivan rolled up his sleeves and immediately got to work is a gross understatement. At a time when most villages in India and the non-Western world in general lacked a real school, Sullivan opened one in the Badaga village of Dēnāḍu, in 1821. This did not last very long, perhaps because it was in a remote village on the very margins of the plateau, but it was a sign of things to come, and soon many Badaga villages were ahead of Australia or America in this respect. Sullivan also was quick to invite a few Parsi shopkeepers to come and open stores in the new town, knowing that they understood commerce well, and as a small community of monotheists, were honest and intelligent people. Realising that a few shops were not enough, Sullivan also started a town market, where local farmers could bring their produce and transactions could take place using barter as well as cash, which was something new to them. In just a couple of years his innovations had transformed the economic situation, and Sullivan began to think about grander things (meanwhile abandoning his obligations in Coimbatore City). In view of the fertility of the soil and the fact that the mild climate allowed for a profusion of European vegetables and fruit to grow on the hills, he began to think of this as a possible area for the settlement of old soldiers and other Europeans or Eurasians who might spearhead the modernisation of the Nilgiris. In this he was not too successful, although wounded and retired soldiers did come and a rudimentary medical establishment was developed to provide healthcare for both European settlers and recuperating soldiers (with fifty patients in 1830).

Sullivan also got involved with two major civil engineering projects, even though he was obviously no engineer himself. One of these was the creation of a large artificial lake by damming a small valley within Ootacamund in 1825 (see Plate 3, this volume). This he thought might be used in an irrigation system, but that never happened. In 1830 and again in 1852, disaster struck when the dam burst and the lake emptied out totally. Each time it had to be repaired, as it had become a crucial place for water, laundry, boating, and scenic walks.

But even though the lake was a mile long in those days, the project was nothing compared with the other vast engineering project—the development of a system of new roadways up the ghats, the escarpments of the Nilgiris, and then across the hills to the main settlements. As the Collectorate in Coimbatore had no manpower for projects of such scale, the government arranged instead to use the men of the Madras Pioneers, a regiment of the Madras Army whose main activity was civil engineering. Throughout the 1820s and 1830s, these nameless workers improved half-a-dozen earlier trackways (see Image 5.1, this volume) so that they could take ox-drawn carts up the ghats, and then linked them with roadways crossing the plateau. It was a huge task because there was hardly any level land anywhere—as was realised once again when, in the late twentieth century, the possibility of a Nilgiri airport was broached.

The town of Ootacamund developed quite rapidly, as there was already a demand for housing and hotels for the numerous Europeans who were now arriving to rest or recuperate in south India's first hill station, a 'sanatorium', as they called it. Ten years after Sullivan first saw the site, Ooty had a population of about 500. John Sullivan himself made money out of private construction projects in the new town, including the first house, and he personally owned a large amount of land there, much more than anyone else (the town covered 3 sq. miles, and he farmed some 200 acres, about 10 per cent of it). Land acquisition in the hills was always a sore point with local people, as they had no idea at first that there could be a market in land, that one's field could have a monetary value. While some British personnel were no doubt avaricious and unscrupulous about getting hold of land, it has to be said that Sullivan, to his credit, arranged for the Toda tribe as a whole to be remunerated for their loss of grazing land to the growing town—albeit at rates that we would consider ridiculously low and exploitative (a rupee an acre within Ooty, for example).

The Badagas, however, were the main group to become involved in land transaction, especially once it was discovered that this area would support coffee plantations. Many Badaga farmers then sold tracts of land to Europeans, not understanding that such sales were final and they would never be able to get their land back later if they needed it. Over the long term, this led many Badagas into economic disaster, with the result that thirty or forty years later one began to see dozens of utterly impoverished Badagas, even women, breaking stones on the roadside or doing other gruelling manual labour. The advent of tea plantations, all owned by Europeans, only exacerbated this situation after the 1860s, although it began to employ Badaga labour.

It cannot be said, though, that Sullivan's efforts were solely directed towards the development of modern facilities for the benefit of European residents. He innovated in a variety of ways to benefit local people directly, too, and clearly had their welfare in mind from the start. He brought out a horticulturist from Scotland along with much European seed, some of which he gave to Badaga farmers to improve their wheat and barley. Aside from this, dozens of kinds of European vegetable and fruit were handed out to Nilgiri farmers. Sullivan and his assistants also experimented with hemp, flax, and even tea—which after 1865 became the major commercial crop on the hills. With the Todas, one can see he was ever protective of their grazing rights. In 1819 (being a Christian), he did decry their practice of female infanticide, yet it continued for another century and more, a 'functional prerequisite' for polyandry. His dealings with the Kotas were of a practical sort, too, for he tried to show them how to extract iron from local ore, at a time when they were the only blacksmiths on the hills (see Image 7.8, this volume) and were buying scrap metal from the plains.

John Sullivan had a number of intellectual interests too. As mentioned, he experimented with various commercial crops, including tea. He kept meteorological readings five times a day over the first four months he was in Ooty, with a view to demonstrating what a healthy climate it had (see Chapter 3, this volume). He opened two schools in Badaga villages, at a time when village schools were rarely to be found anywhere in south India (or indeed in places like Australia or America). He instituted the first lending library in 1829, and supported the construction of St. Stephen's church (see Plate 1, this volume) in that year too.

And in 1832, he argued in these words before a Select Committee of the House of Commons, in London, that south Indians were very capable of taking up administrative duties:

> *Parliamentarian*: 'How far do you think the native population in that presidency is in a state fitting it for employment in the higher stations of the country?'
> *John Sullivan*: 'I think them eminently qualified: all the business of the country is in fact now done by natives .... They must, in a great degree, occupy the places which are now filled by Europeans.' (Sullivan 1832, 5)

And after a century had passed, they were indeed doing so.

References

Hayavadana Rao, C. 1908. 'Political History'. In Walter Francis (ed.), *Madras District Gazetteers. The Nilgiris*, Vol. 1, 90–122. Madras: Superintendent, Government Press.

Price, J. Frederick. 1908. *Ootacamund. A History* (Compiled for Government). Madras: Superintendent, Government Press [reprinted, Calcutta: Rupa and Company, 2002, 2 vols].

Sullivan, John. 1832. 'Minutes of Evidence. Jovis, 9° die Februarii, 1832. The Right Hon. Thomas Frankland Lewis, in the Chair ... John Sullivan, Esq. called in; and Examined'. In *Minutes of Evidence Taken Before the Select Committee on the Affairs of the East India Company; and also an Appendix and Index. III.—Revenue. (Vol. IV.) Session 6 December 1831–16 August 1832*, Vol. XI. London: House of Commons, Paper 735 III, Vol. 11, 1–8. [Reprinted in *Irish University Press Series of British Parliamentary Papers, Minutes of Evidence Taken Before the Select Committee on the Affairs of the East India Company; and also an Appendix and Index [III Revenue] 1831–32. Colonies, East India, 9.* Shannon: Irish University Press, 1970.]

Further Reading

'History'; 'Ootacamund'; 'Pychy (Peechi) Rebel'; 'Sullivan'; and 'Wellesley'. In *Encyclopædia of the Nilgiri Hills*, Paul Hockings (ed.). New Delhi: Manohar, 2012.

Part II

Nature

2

Biodiversity and Conservation Challenges

R. J. Ranjit Daniels

Writing about the biodiversity and conservation challenges of the Nilgiris, one needs to first define the geographical area of the designated landscape. On the one hand there is the Tamil Nadu administrative area called the Nilgiris District, while on the other we have the much larger Nilgiri Biosphere Reserve spanning the hills of three states—Tamil Nadu, Kerala, and Karnataka. This latter Reserve is large, around 5,520 km^2 in extent. However, what was earlier described as the Nilgiris is a much smaller landscape and may more closely align with the present Nilgiris District.

The geographical area of the District as given in various sources of information varies. What nevertheless seems consistent is a total area of 2,552.5 km^2 (a figure taken from the Government of Tamil Nadu website, www.tn.gov.in). Nearly 73 per cent of this area has been classified as 'forest', the highest percentage among all districts of the state. The overall extent of forests within the District has made it rich in biodiversity. Other geoclimatic features that contribute to the rich biodiversity are the temperature, rainfall, and the elevation range. While the temperature averages around 15°C, during peak winter it drops to 0°C, creating a local temperate climate regime within an otherwise tropical range of hills. This low temperature is due to the high hills, which exceed 2,000 m ASL (above sea level), peaking at 2,636 m ASL in a place popularly known as Doddabetta.

The elevation range, which varies from under 900 m ASL to 2,636 m ASL, contributes to the heterogeneous temperature regime within the District. Complimenting the temperature regime is the varied rainfall. On average the Nilgiris receives 1,920 mm of rainfall annually. However, rainfall is lower than 800 mm in the eastern extremes (for example, the Moyar Gorge) but exceeds 3,500 mm in the high western hills that border Kerala. The geoclimatic variability has rendered the Nilgiris a heterogeneous landscape that offers diverse habitats for a very large number of species of plants and animals. The heterogeneity has also contributed to the high levels of endemism within the District. Endemism is a condition wherein species of plants and animals have restricted geographic ranges and are often confined to small areas of the world, such as an island, peninsula, mountain, river, or lake.

The geoclimatic variability is the primary reason for the diversification of vegetation types in the Nilgiris. While there are mosaics of scrub and tree savannah in the lower and drier areas, the vegetation changes to denser dry deciduous forests, moist deciduous forests, and wet evergreen forests along the elevation and rainfall gradients. At elevations above 1,500 m ASL, one finds the unique complex of sholas and grasslands. This vegetation type, which is characteristic of the higher elevation hills in the Western Ghats, is best developed and preserved in the Nilgiris.

Diversity of vegetation has underlain the richness of plants and animals in the landscape. Exactly how many species of plants and animals are found in the Nilgiris can at best remain a matter of guesswork. Much of the existing knowledge on the diversity and endemism in plants and animals concerns the larger Nilgiri Biosphere Reserve, with very little specific details available for the Nilgiris as such. The number of plant species in the Nilgiris may vary between 2,500 and 3,700. A comparable number cannot be provided for animals. However, a study of the birds of the Mudumalai Tiger Reserve by the Salim Ali Centre for Ornithology and Natural History listed 266 species. Yet another study by the Bombay Natural History Society of the birds of the Nilgiri Plateau suggests the presence there of 192 species. Consolidation of the results of the two studies has provided a comprehensive list of nearly 350 species of birds for the Nilgiris District.

Precise details of other groups of animals are not available. However, one can scale up the figures based on certain benchmark numbers available for the Mudumalai Tiger Reserve. That 321 km^2 Reserve is home to fifty-five species of mammals, fifty-eight species of fish, twenty-one species of amphibians, and thirty-four species of reptiles.

Despite the lacunae in the knowledge of biodiversity for the landscape, it is important to realise that the Nilgiris is biologically the most well-explored area in the Western Ghats. This claim can be substantiated by the fact that several species of animals endemic to the Western Ghats have been named in English using the title Nilgiri. Thus we have among birds the Nilgiri Wood Pigeon, Nilgiri Laughing Thrush, Nilgiri Thrush, Nilgiri Flycatcher, Nilgiri Flowerpecker, Nilgiri Shortwing, and Nilgiri Pipit. Among mammals, there are the Nilgiri Tahr, Nilgiri Langur, and Nilgiri Marten. Further, among the lower vertebrates, we have the Nilgiri Cricket Frog (amphibian), Nilgiri Salea (reptile), and Nilgiri Danio (fish). More importantly, the first Biosphere Reserve in India has been named after the Nilgiris: the Nilgiri Biosphere Reserve was established in 1986 to conserve the biodiversity and cultural diversity of the extended landscape.

The rich biodiversity of the landscape is of relevance not only to the Western Ghats, but also to the nation as a whole. As a result, we currently have two important protected areas of the landscape, the Mudumalai Tiger Reserve and the Mukurti National Park. They are not only representative of the landscape's heterogeneity and biodiversity, but are also home to a handful of endemic and endangered animals. The Mudumalai Tiger Reserve is home to around sixty tigers and some 800 elephants. It is also one of the last habitats in the state for the critically endangered White-rumped Vulture and the Indian Vulture.

The Mukurti National Park is representative of the high-elevation ecosystem complexes in the Western Ghats, and is one of the mainstays of the endemic and endangered Nilgiri Tahr. A 2004 census reported between 200 and 250 Tahr in this National Park. Besides, the protected area is home to endemic plants and other endemic animals, including birds, amphibians, and reptiles.

The need to conserve the rich biodiversity of the Nilgiris was first felt in the early 1870s. It was at this time that unregulated hunting of wildlife had led to a drastic reduction in the population of many species; and this was particularly true for the Nilgiri Tahr, which had reached the brink of extinction in the Nilgiris 150 years ago. To address the issue of wildlife conservation, the erstwhile Nilgiri Game Association was established in 1877. Soon after this, in 1879, the Nilgiri Game and Fish Preservation Act was passed by the then Madras government. Despite these early interventions, conservation challenges in the Nilgiris have only been on the increase.

Once the British established colonies in the landscape, vast areas of forest were cleared to accommodate commercial agriculture and plantations, especially tea. The British considered the grasslands as 'wastelands' and tried to 'improve' the productivity of these sensitive habitats by planting exotic trees. Eucalyptus and another Australian species, Wattle, were introduced into the grasslands in the 1840s, and by 1860, Cinchona was being cultivated locally too. Over the years, Pine and other non-native tree species were introduced into the landscape, upsetting the fragile ecological balance of the shola–grassland ecosystem.

The introduction of non-native plants did not stop with trees. Tea and coffee were introduced in the 1830s. Many other species of garden plants were brought in from Europe by the colonisers and planted. Most of these species naturalised in the landscape, thanks to the local climate. Some of the species have become invasive—for example, broom. Botanists estimate that there may be between 200 and 300 such exotic plant species in the Nilgiri landscape today.

Of all the introduced plants, the Wattle and Lantana have become devastating and have led to large-scale degradation of the natural hill ecosystem. While Lantana has emerged as a major cause for habitat degradation and fire in the drier habitats, Wattle has usurped extensive grasslands and has even invaded shola forests locally. Controlling the spread of these two species has cost the government huge sums of money annually for years now.

Centuries before the British set foot on the Nilgiris, there were tribes who had migrated into the landscape. It is generally accepted that the earliest of these immigrants were the Todas and the Kurumbas. Todas brought with them the water buffalo. Due to their religious beliefs, some individual buffalo were set free in the wild and they have since contributed to the now significant population of feral buffaloes in the Nilgiris. These feral buffaloes look almost like the Wild Buffaloes of Southeast Asia. While some ecologists consider the feral buffalo invasive, the actual impact of the species on the local ecosystem needs to be studied in detail.

Loss of grasslands has endangered a local bird, the Nilgiri Pipit. The Nilgiri Tahr, which is totally dependent on this habitat, is also endangered. Although their population recovered well from the bottleneck in the 1870s, the numbers are still fluctuating. The government has launched several programmes to restore the grasslands. Restoration of grasslands in the Nilgiris remains, however, one of the biggest conservation challenges of the twenty-first century.

In an attempt to address the conservation challenges in the District, the government established the two protected areas in Mudumalai and Mukurti, as mentioned. On a broader scale, the entire Nilgiri landscape has been brought into the fold of the Nilgiri Biosphere Reserve, with the two protected areas as a part of the 'Core Zone'. The Biosphere Reserve concept was first conceived and brought into practice by the United Nations Educational, Scientific, and Cultural Organization (UNESCO) in the 1970s under the banner of a 'Man Biosphere Programme'. It is a global programme wherein conservation, research, and people's livelihoods are simultaneously addressed in vast natural areas. There are currently eighteen Biosphere Reserves in India, of which the Nilgiri Biosphere Reserve was the first to be declared, and also the first one in India to be included in UNESCO's global list of Biosphere Reserves.

As many as ten hydroelectric projects are functioning in the Nilgiris. The dams have not only destroyed extensive forests and grasslands, but have also changed the character of the many streams and rivers that flow across the landscape. Dams and the associated infrastructure for conveying water to the power-generating units have led to the fragmentation of habitats, hindering the movement of wildlife like elephants and other large mammals. Dams have become a permanent blot on the Nilgiri landscape.

Urbanisation is a conservation challenge as well. The creation of urban infrastructure for the resident human population, now three-quarters of a million people, including the provision of clean water, has contributed immensely to the degradation of the hill ecosystem. The demand to improve road connectivity has resulted in road kills of rare and endangered wildlife. Urbanisation and the spread of invasive alien plants go hand in hand. Roads are the best conduits for the spread of these adaptive species of plants, which even colonise the edges of forests and grasslands. Safe systems of waste management are not in place in the district either. While sewage gets released into the natural aquatic habitats, solid wastes are dumped in landfills bordering natural areas. This is particularly the case in Ooty, where the municipal solid waste is dumped on the outskirts of the town. Due to its proximity to their natural habitats, wild mammals and birds frequent the solid waste dump. The danger of these animals getting killed due to ingestion of plastics and other hazardous wastes always remains. Also, since the dump is visited by domestic animals, the chances of the spread of parasites and diseases from the domestic to the wild are very high.

Yet another challenge to conservation in the Nilgiris is tourism. The area has had a long history of tourism, and has long been one of the most sought-after tourist destinations in southern India. This is particularly true for Ooty, the so-called 'Queen of Hill Stations', but the impact is felt by the entire landscape. Specific tourist seasons are devastating. Much of the associated infrastructure is illegal, yet flourishes in the form of jungle resorts, wildlife safaris, etc. Tourists bring with them plastics and other kinds of non-biodegradable waste. Although there has been a ban imposed on plastic bags in the district from time to time, observance of the ban is shoddy. Tourism and urbanisation work in tandem and result in heavy demands on water, accommodation, parking space, roads, sanitation, and other supportive infrastructure. These infrastructures in turn keep the natural ecosystems and biodiversity under constant pressure. There is, however, some hope, as the Supreme Court ordered in August 2018 the closure of all illegal infrastructures on elephant corridors in the Nilgiris.

Globally, the Western Ghats is listed as a 'Biodiversity Hotspot'. What this means is that this is a region of global significance for its rich biodiversity and endemism, while being under severe pressures from human-induced threats to the long-term survival of species. Apart from direct human threats, the Western Ghats are vulnerable to climate change; and the impact of climate change will be more acute in higher hill areas such as the Nilgiris. Fragile ecosystems such as the shola–grassland complex are severely threatened by climate change, as are the associated species of plants and animals. One iconic species of the Western Ghats that is severely threatened by climate change is the Nilgiri Tahr. Available estimates place the current population of the Tahr between 2,500 and 3,000 in the Western Ghats, and the Nilgiris is the northern limit of the species. About 10 per cent of the population of the entire species survives in this landscape. A recent study has reported that after 2030, there will be a 60 per cent reduction in the habitat of the Nilgiri Tahr due to climate change, which will further affect the already endangered species. Long-term conservation of the species is thus a serious challenge.

Climate change will pose a major conservation challenge also to the high-elevation vegetation types, such as the sholas and hilly grasslands. These already threatened natural habitats are likely to shrink further if the climate in the Nilgiris becomes warmer during coming years. One report states that only 10 per cent of the Reserved Forests in the district represent the shola type of vegetation. Grasslands have been lost to various kinds of exotic plantation and other infrastructure development. As with the rest of the Western Ghats, the shola–grassland complex exists precariously in the Nilgiris today.

Considering the biological diversity and conservation challenges in the district, it may be said that the landscape is a 'hotspot within a hotspot'. The conservation challenges need to be carefully addressed after prioritising them scientifically. The Biosphere Reserve concept provides opportunities for integrating biodiversity conservation with research and human livelihoods. The concept has to be fully implemented in word and spirit if the biodiversity of the Nilgiris is to be sustained. The scope of research has to be widened and sustained, and the onus cannot entirely be on the government either. Conservation of biodiversity in the Nilgiris needs to become a citizens' movement. Citizen–science initiatives should be encouraged. A model of sustainable ecosystem management should be developed for the Nilgiris, which can then be applied to the entire Biosphere Reserve as well as elsewhere in the Western Ghats.

Further Reading

Additional information about many of the topics discussed here may be found in the *Encyclopædia of the Nilgiri Hills* (Paul Hockings [ed.], New Delhi: Manohar, 2012). See the entries for Animal Life, Birds, Broom, Climate, Elephant, Environmental Degradation, Eucalyptus and Acacia, Fire, Forests, Grassland, Hydrology, Mudumalai, Mukurti Peak, Nilgiri Biosphere Reserve, Nilgiri Wildlife and Environment Association, Plantations, Sholas, Tahr, Tiger, Tourism, Silent Valley, and Wenlock Downs.

3

A Climatologist in the Nilgiris

HANS J. VON LENGERKE

Recording the Weather

The climatic conditions of the upper Nilgiris were a major attraction for Europeans to settle in and to develop the mountain area for their purposes, aside from any general curiosity to explore the unknown. The earliest account by a European of 'the wild and rugged mountains, where winds and climate are very cold' dates back to 1603, when the Italian priest Giacomo Fenicio, starting from Calicut, climbed the southwestern slope onto the plateau of the Nilgiris. But it was over two centuries before the cool climate of the elevated tracts, so different from the surrounding plateaux and plains, was really appreciated for its potential for European settlement and development; and then there followed the establishment of several hill stations (sanatoria, cantonments), commercial cinchona, tea, and coffee plantations, horticulture with European vegetables, and forest plantations with exotic, mostly Australian, tree species (wattle and eucalyptus).

Descriptions of climatic conditions soon became part of almost all written accounts by British and other European visitors, and in official documents pertaining to the Nilgiris. But it was not before the detailed botanical and phytogeographical research by ecologists from the French Institute in Pondicherry, published in the early 1970s, that climatological knowledge about the Nilgiris was substantially increased. At the same time, I too decided to study in detail the weather and climate of the Nilgiris Area (as a postgraduate geographer from the South Asia Institute of Heidelberg University). Spending over a year in south India (1972–1973), affiliated to the Tamil Nadu Agricultural University in

Coimbatore and residing in Ootacamund (now Udagamandalam, but still better known as Ooty), resulted in a doctoral dissertation (published as a book in 1976) and several papers in scientific journals.

The idea of this project was to conduct a detailed survey of available material and to learn as much as possible about the spatial (large-, meso-, and micro-scale) and temporal differentiation of weather and climate in and around this tropical mountain massif (of about 2,400 km^2), which rises by more than 2 kilometres (culminating in Doddabetta Peak at 2,636 m) into the seasonally changing, prevalent air flows and weather patterns over the Indian subcontinent. While the structure and seasonal dynamics of the Indian or South Asian Monsoon are the overriding large-scale climatic control, topographical and local features, such as relief, elevation, exposition, soils, vegetation and land use, are modifying factors determining atmospheric and related environmental conditions on the small and medium scale.

Information included qualitative and quantitative data, ranging from singular, chance observations to long-term systematic observations. They included phenomena only indicative of atmospheric features or they represented actual physical environmental properties. The latter could be obtained from meteorological or hydrological measurements with instruments, the former from field observations by the author or by farmers, foresters, and planters. Data from published as well as unpublished sources had to be considered too. Due to my attempt at identifying all possible relevant material, I was surprised by the wealth of available information and data for this region.

In the history of official meteorological observations, three periods can be distinguished: the period of isolated, mostly non-standardised local observations by administrative and medical officers (before 1865), the period of provincial but not yet standardised observation systems within the Madras Presidency (1865–1875), and the period of the India Meteorological Department (founded in 1875) with its administrative and data-collection headquarters in Delhi and Pune, respectively, and its Regional Centre in Madras conducting systematic, technically standardised, and routinely supervised instrumental observation systems with principal and ordinary surface observatories and later also upper air (aerological) stations. Over the years, many agencies established their own stations and thereby increased the density of the observational network and thus the accumulation and spatial coverage of data. Three categories of agencies could be tapped: Central government (India Meteorological Department, Indian Agricultural Research Institute, Indian Railways), state governments of Tamilnadu, Kerala, and Karnataka (Revenue, Public Works, Irrigation, Forest, and Agricultural Departments; Electricity Boards), and private agencies such as tea, coffee, and rubber estates.

Data collection was done personally by me, by two paid copying assistants in Madras, and by deputed staff members in numerous agencies, mostly using printed, formatted data acquisition forms that I supplied them with. These efforts resulted in the compilation of well over two million quantitative bits of information for over 400 stations, including 369 stations with rainfall records in the Nilgiris Area (approximately 24,000 km^2 when one includes the surrounding plains—see Map 3.1). Data homogeneity tests, conversion of British weights and measures into the metric system, and the actual analysis and interpretation of data started with simple manual calculations and were later facilitated by processing punched cards and magnetic tapes using computers in Heidelberg.

The personal inspection of stations, and enquiries about station records, revealed a host of possible reasons for missing, dubious, or erroneous data. Some examples: instruments had been stolen to be used for other purposes, or they were damaged (for example, by elephants in the Mudumalai and Moyar Canyon areas); interruption due to political disturbances (for example, the Malabar Rebellion in 1921 caused data gaps of eight to ten months at several stations in the Nilambur Basin); discontinuities due to change of proprietors or managers of estates; removal (privatising), neglect, or destruction of old files; rotting of files and damage by termites or other paper-loving insects; uselessness of wind and sunshine data where trees had grown tall next to measuring sites, slowing down air movement or casting shadows on recorders;

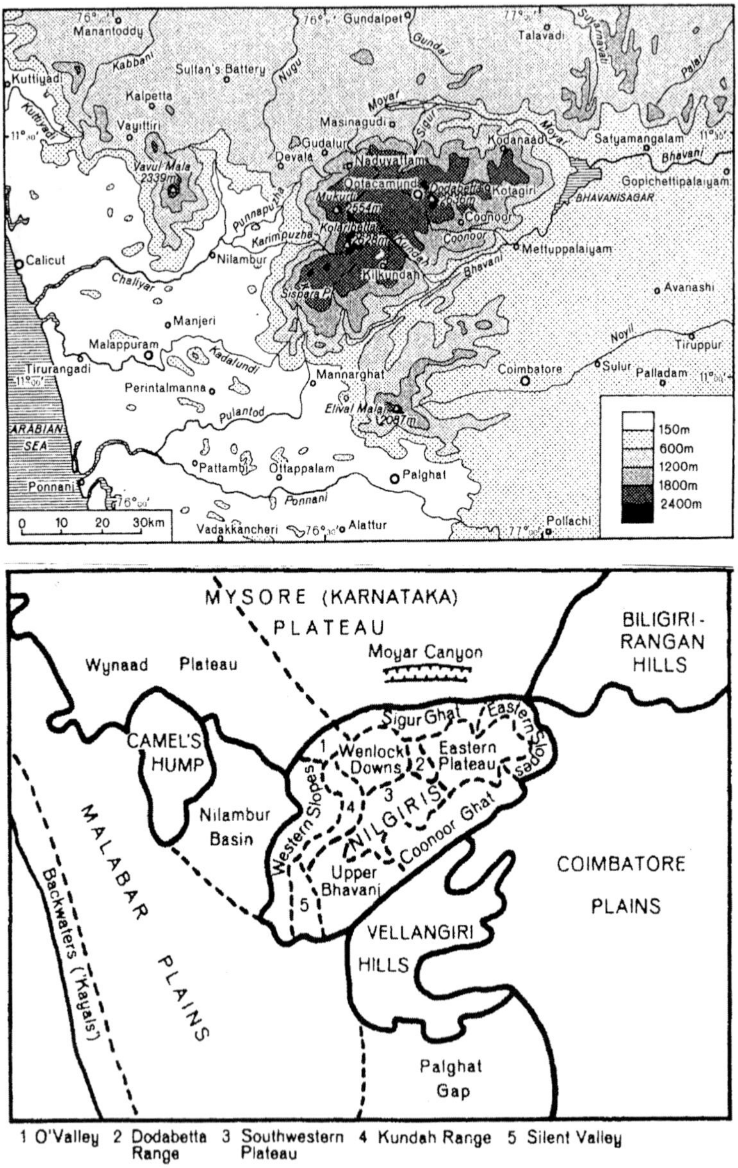

MAP 3.1: The Nilgiri Area: Topography and Physiographic Division

Source: Cape Comorin sheet of the Survey of India, scale 1:1 million Topographical Map Series; sketch maps by the author.

abandonment of a rain-recording station in the Upper Bhavani area in the mid-1960s after it was discovered that the person in charge had taken the instrument to his home in order to avoid the weekly inspection and walk to remove a chart several kilometres away—thus the 'artificial rainfall' under a water tap did not tally at all with rainfall recorded at neighbouring stations!

Main Elements of Weather and Climate

Atmospheric Pressure

There are regular diurnal and annual variations of atmospheric pressure (expressed in a mm mercury column or milibar), but with much smaller amplitudes than in mid-latitudinal regions (west wind zone), where travelling low pressure systems frequently alternate with high pressure cells. As everywhere, atmospheric pressure decreases with increasing elevation (from Calicut to Ooty by 10.25 mb per 100 m, on average). In the study area, very low pressure episodes of a few hours' duration only occur in the centre of strong local convection (for example, thunderstorms), deep depressions, or cyclonic storms, which form over the adjoining seas (mostly over the Bay of Bengal), and in a few cases move across south India.

Surface Winds

Surface winds, both their velocity and their direction, are important climatic factors, particularly with respect to plant growth, affecting natural vegetation as well as silvicultural trees and agricultural crops. Mechanical action and specific thermal and moisture properties of air flows influence physiological processes. While instrumental data of wind speed and direction could be collected for over twenty stations (of course with different periods of observation and at different heights above the ground) and provide a general idea of diurnal and seasonal, monsoonal changes of wind direction and speed, complementary field observations of wind effects (for example stunted, wind-shaped, or fallen trees) are necessary to get a realistic idea of extreme local wind conditions. The 'windiest' parts of the upper Nilgiris are the Doddabetta Range, the Wenlock Downs, the Upper Bhavani area, and particularly the Kunda Range.

Atmospheric Moisture

Atmospheric moisture was studied in terms of relative humidity, that is, the ratio (percentage) of actual to maximum possible water vapour content of the air at a given temperature and atmospheric pressure. This indicates the moisture exchange capacity between the land surface and the atmosphere in terms of precipitation (mist, dew, hail, or rainfall) or its uptake from the ground and vegetation (evapo-transpiration) that varies with the air's evaporative capacity or saturation deficit. Most data came from dry- and wet-bulb psychrometers kept in wooden, louvered (Stevenson) screens. The fact that most observations are done at 08:30 and 17:30 hours Indian Standard Time (IST) implies that extremes of relative humidity—maximum before sunrise (sometimes resulting in dew formation) and minimum (physiologically important) at midday or in the early afternoon—are not represented by such data.

Cloudiness, Mist and Fog, Visibility

The moisture content in the air in combination with air temperature and aerosol particles determines the condensation of water vapour into water droplets or icicles, and thus the formation of clouds, mist and fog, and visibility, all of which affect the amount of solar radiation reaching the ground. Cloud cover is noted in oktas or tenths of sky cover, visibility in horizontal distances. As in most tropical regions, thermal convection and associated cloud formation are most pronounced during late morning and afternoon hours, particularly over mountain slopes. During the Southwest Monsoon period (June–September), when moisture-laden air masses are transported from equatorial ocean areas and the Arabian Sea towards the mountain barrier of the Nilgiris, the Kunda Range, Wenlock Downs, Upper Bhavani Area, and Doddabetta Range can be 'misted in' for days or even weeks on end, with visibility remaining in the 'below 1 km' range.

Solar Radiation

Of all climatic elements, solar radiation is the most essential for the existence and functioning of terrestrial ecosystems. As far as instrumental records for the Nilgiris are concerned, there are hardly any total/global radiation (photometric) data available, so that bright sunshine duration (measured with Campbell-Stokes recorders working on the burning-glass principle, that is, bright sunshine burning traces or holes into special paper cards) have to be extrapolated for estimates of total radiation. In the field, it can be observed that there are periods when a lack of solar energy leads to the growth of fungi and certain plant diseases, whereas periods with excessive radiation show scorching of plant tissue and consequently reduced yields of agricultural and plantation crops. Around Ooty, the average sunshine duration varies between nine hours per day from December until March, and less than 4.5 hours/day from June to September (with a minimum of 2.8 in July), whereas Coimbatore experiences six hours/day of bright sunshine during the same four-month period.

Temperature

In extra-tropical regions, many people associate the tropics with warm or hot regions, overlooking the fact that snowfields and glaciers exist in very low latitudes and even at the equator in Latin America, Africa, and Asia. The vertical temperature decrease was already mentioned and in the Nilgiris area this thermal 'lapse rate' is within the range of 0.5 to 0.7°C per 100 m elevation. The average annual temperature—based on daily $^{(\text{maximum+minimum})}/_{2}$—for Calicut is 27.3°C, for Coimbatore 26.4°C, for Coonoor 16.9°C, and for Ooty 14.4°C. The author has elaborated extensively (forty-two pages of his book)[1] on temperature conditions in the Nilgiris area. A most fascinating aspect, not expected to that extent and significance, was the phenomenon of night/early morning frost in many parts of the upper Nilgiris, even as low as 1,400 m elevation. The study of frost frequency and intensity by means of air temperature measured in Stevenson screens, which are ideally installed in exposed locations, does not provide a realistic picture of actual conditions. Frost, however, which in the Nilgiris lasts only for a few hours after strong night-time long-wave re-radiation of energy during the dry Northeast Monsoon period (December–March), causes damage to crop plant tissue and necroses and so leads to financial losses for farmers and planters. Most tea plantations with frost problems keep detailed records about the dates and extent of hoar-frost and of damages to their leaf-producing crop. Normally, frost first occurs in hollows of the undulating terrain, where cold air accumulates and stagnates, and where individual tea plants may even die if bark-splitting due to recurrent very low sub-zero temperatures occurs. In some estates, whole fields may go out of production for several months, because the 'bushes' (actually tea, *Camellia sinensis*, is a tree plant) need time to replace the necrotic/brownish 'two leaves and bud' that become the best tea. On some tea estates frost is so frequent and severe that rather costly frost protection techniques (covering with mats, smoke-screening, water sprinkling) were tested and continue to be carried out in critical locations and seasons. Two of the most frost-affected tea estates in the Nilgiris appeared to be Dunsandle (near Sholur) and Korakunda, beyond Kilkunda, with over twenty and over forty frost nights on an average, respectively, per year; one frost night on Korakunda Estate occurred as late as 3 April.

Precipitation

In my monograph, I dealt at length (across seventy-three pages) with rainfall, for which more stations could provide data than for any other element; a few more pages dealt with other forms of precipitation, namely hail, mist and fog, and dew. For the Nilgiri mountain block, the density of stations for which data could be collected worked out to be, quite remarkably, one station per 10 km^2, whereas for the surrounding plateaux and plains it was one rain-gauge per 180 km^2, which was good enough for drawing isohyetal (rainfall distribution) maps. Eighty per cent of all rainfall stations had been maintained by the Hydro-Metric Survey of the Tamil Nadu Electricity Board in Madras (Chennai), and by private companies and planters. Averages of rainfall for all stations were calculated or adjusted for the standard period 1941–1970; data for observations before this period and until December 1972 were also used, but for other statistical analyses and interpretations. The 'rainiest' station on record within the Nilgiri area is Mukurti Ridge Top (2,545 m) in the Kunda Range, with an average annual rainfall of 6,330 mm on more than 140 rainy days; the station with the lowest average during the same reference period was Mangalapatti in the Lower Bhavani–Kedarhalla confluence area, with only 468 mm on less than forty rainy days. These statistics are quite exceptional, if not record-breaking, for peninsular India. When looking at individual years, one finds that averages can be surpassed considerably both upwards and downwards. Regarding the seasonal pattern of rainfall, a clear distinction can be made between stations to the west of a line—Pollachi–Kilkunda–Ooty–Gundlupet—where July is the rainiest month, and stations to the east of this line, where in the plains October and in the mountains November experience the peak amounts.

Cyclones

An extraordinary weather phenomenon is the tropical cyclones (cyclonic storms), which are associated with very strong winds and high amounts of preciptation falling within brief periods. Near the Nilgiri area, most cyclones form over the warm surface waters of the Bay of Bengal and move in a northwesterly direction. Rarely do they reach the Nilgiris with their full force, because while passing over the Tamilnad land surface they weaken into deep depressions which are less fierce. Nevertheless, even these may bring heavy rainfall. Such an event—remembered as the 'Cuddalore Cyclone' crossing south India and reintensifying over the Arabian Sea—was experienced by me and my family during the first week of December 1972. Kodanad Estate registered more than 900 mm and

Burliar over 600 mm of rain within a week, and many landslides blocked the Coonoor and Kotagiri Ghat roads as well as the Nilgiri railway track.

Water Balance and Hydrology

Crucial for applied climatology and most certainly for hydrology and water management is the relationship or balance between precipitation and evapo-transpiration, that is, the return of precipitated water as evaporation from the soil or other surfaces and transpiration by plants into the atmosphere. Two approaches to studying this were employed: indirect assessment of the water balance at a meteorological station by subtracting from rainfall amounts the estimated evapo-transpiration (both in mm) using measured atmospheric elements—such as temperature, relative humidity, radiation, wind speed, or open water-pan evaporation—in formulae based on experience made in experimental stations throughout the world and recommended by the World Meteorological Organization (WMO) and the Food and Agriculture Organization (FAO) of the United Nations. On that basis, humid and dry months, that is, months with positive and negative water balances, respectively, were determined. Fortunately, due to the interest in tapping the hydroelectric power generation potential of the Nilgiris, the Hydro-Metric Surveys of the State Electricty Boards had carried out direct water flow measurements in many catchment areas over long periods. These runoff or discharge data (in volumes of water passing through a geometrically defined weir in m^3 per second) were collected and analysed. Converting volumes of water into depth of water evenly covering the catchment area (areal runoff in mm) allowed a comparison with indirect water balance results. Apart from deforestation and the introduction of exotic crop plants and the resultant land-use changes, the control and utilisation of the copious but greatly fluctuating water resources through storage reservoirs and river diversions was another fundamental manipulation of the environment by the British. The first damming-up of a natural water course by the colonialists in the Nilgiris was the Ooty Lake—as early as 1825! Many more reservoirs were to follow, serving as drinking-water storage (for example, Doddabetta and Marlimund for Ooty in 1870) or for hydroelectric power generation (the first scheme was at Kateri in 1904, supplying the Aruvankadu Cordite Factory with energy). Later, even relatively small catchments in the Kunda Range (the so-called Western Catchments) were tapped by diverting streams through tunnels towards the complex Pykara–Moyar (started in 1932) and Kunda Schemes (started in 1956), because these tracts receive enormous amounts of precipitation (well over 2,500 mm every year), making the technical effort and investment pay off after a few years of operation.

A Summary

My climatological survey revealed a remarkable diversity of atmospheric and hydrological conditions within the Nilgiris area, although in its entirety and irrespective of elevation, it clearly belongs to the tropical climatic realm, in that diurnal temperature amplitudes exceed seasonal and annual variations and seasons are dominated by variations of precipitation during the course of the year and not by temperature. Five hydro-thermal climatic types are distinguishable (for physiographic units, see Map 3.1):

(1) warm and wet (10–12 humid months): The lower Coonoor Ghat and southern Eastern Slopes;
(2) warm and semi-humid (7–9 humid months): The Malabar Plains, the escarpment and western part of the Mysore Plateau, the lower western slopes of the Nilgiris and Vellangiri Hills, the Kerala Bhavani catchment and the lower western Sigur Ghat:
(3) warm and semi-arid (6–10 arid months): The Coimbatore Plain, the eastern Mysore Plateau, the lower eastern Sigur Ghat and northern Eastern Slopes, and the Biligiri Rangan Hills;

(4) cold and humid (10–12 humid months): The upper Coonoor Ghat and Eastern Slopes, the southern tracts of the Eastern and Southwestern Plateau;
(5) cold and semi-humid (7–9 humid months): The northern part of the Eastern Plateau, the Doddabetta Range, the Wenlock Downs, the Southwestern Plateau, the Kunda Range, the elevated parts of the Vellangiri Hills, and Vavul Mala (Camel's Hump).

Probably the most outstanding examples of the temporal and spatial climatic diversity are:

- the close proximity of very humid conditions (twelve humid months) along the Coonoor Ghat and of semi-arid conditions (8–9 arid months) on the adjoining Coimbatore Plains within a distance of a few kilometres only;
- the steep west–east gradient of rainfall during the Southwest Monsoon period (June–September) due to the uplifting, cooling, and precipitation of the moist equatorial westerlies on approaching and reaching the mountain barrier and their foehn-like descent to the leeward, resulting in excessive rainfall and runoff on the westward exposed mountain slopes and ridges (Mukurti ridge top, June–September, 5,480 mm on average for the period 1941–1970), and dry winds and severe drought conditions on the eastern Mysore Plateau (Mangalapatti, 100 mm) and the Coimbatore Plains (Sulur, 102 mm) during the same season;
- the large vertical temperature contrasts during the Northeast Monsoon period (December–March) with temperature averages—daily $^{(\text{maximum+minimum})}/_{2}$—on the Arabian Sea coast of 28°C in Calicut versus 10°C on Korakunda Estate at 2,240 m elevation, where, during one particularly harsh 'winter', sixty-seven nights with early morning hoar-frost and damage to tea plants were observed, and a minimum of –6.7°C in the weather screen is on record.

The image of the upper Nilgiris as a cold tropical 'island' rising above the warm tropical 'sea' suggests itself. And just as oceanic islands are known to have evolved special faunistic and floristic characteristics, the upper Nilgiris also show a high degree of endemism (that is, species not found anywhere else; *cf.* Chapter 2, this volume) or species that are only found again in far away, disjunctive areas with similar ecological conditions (for example, *Rhododendron arboreum* in the Himalayas and the highlands of Sri Lanka). But these phenomena cannot be elaborated in the present context.[2]

Notes

1. Hans J. von Lengerke. 1977. 'The Nilgiris. Weather and Climate of a Mountain Area in South India'. *Beiträge zur Südasienforschung* 32. Wiesbaden: Steiner. The book is available for reference in the Nilgiri Library; some copies are still with the author.
2. For more details, including a list of endemic plants, see Lengerke and Blasco (1989).

Acknowledgements

A scientific project such as mine cannot succeed without the support of many persons and institutions, some of them already mentioned here. I am particularly indebted to my wife Hedi and son Thomas for coming along to south India, sharing the 'Southmere' bungalow on the shores of Ooty Lake, attending Elkhurst Prep School (run by Ms. Momot from Canada), and uncomplainingly travelling on a Mysore-built Java motorbike, even in bad weather and after encountering a rogue elephant (or tusker) in Mudumalai, who did not like the two-stroke engine sound and charged us. (The editor of this book had a similar experience at the same place, and was able to clock an elephant chasing his motorcycle at 37 km/hr.)

Besides, many other individuals—the German horticulturist Klaus Wiedemann and his late Toda wife Evam (née Piljain), the anthropologist Paul Hockings, the late Badaga K. Lakshmanan, the tea planter N. K. Rawlley (Dunsandle Estate), and staff members of the United Planters Association of Southern India (UPASI), Coonoor, deserve much gratitude for their assistance in the early stages of the venture. The Indian government and the German Academic Exchange Service (DAAD) extended financial support (travels, scholarship for fifteen months), which is once again gratefully acknowledged.

Further Reading

'Climate', in *Encyclopædia of the Nilgiri Hills*, Paul Hockings (ed.). New Delhi: Manohar, 2012.

Lengerke, Hans Jürgen von, and François Blasco. 1989. 'The Nilgiri Environment'. In *Blue Mountains: The Ethnography and Biogeography of a South Indian Region*, Paul Hockings (ed.), 20–78. New Delhi: Oxford University Press.

Part III

Communities

4

John Sullivan and the Toda *Monegars*

Anthony R. Walker

Around the world the Western imperial enterprise, it seems, was ill-at-ease with administering communities that, unlike Europe, had no formal leaders: these were societies without kings, princes, or local lords—indeed, no chiefs at any territorial level, be it region, district, or just a village. They were the 'stateless societies', the 'tribes without rulers', as so many Africa-focused British social anthropologists, in particular, knew them in the years immediately before and after World War II (Fortes and Evans-Pritchard 1940, 5; Middleton and Tait 1958). Faced with the absence of formal leadership, the imperial response was frequently to create chiefly offices, bestowing them on male individuals deemed capable of acting as intermediaries between the administration and their local communities. Sometimes this strategy was successful, otherwise, it was problematical at best (see Mair 1962, especially pp. 254–259 for East African examples).

In the Nilgiris prior to British annexation, indigenous headmen were by no means altogether absent. There were local Badaga chiefs, whose authority was widely recognised—not only among all Badagas but also by the other communities of traditional Nilgiri society, including the Todas (Hockings 2012a, 681–682; also 2013, 25–26, 192–194). Moreover the new British administration, as Hockings (2013, 195–196) has written, 'perpetuated the existing [Badaga] hereditary headmen, certain of whom received the title of *maṇegār*', even though, at the same time, the indigenous '*hierarchy* of traditional headmen did not enter into the British scheme for local government'.

Turning specifically to the Toda community (see Plate 8, this volume) as it was prior to British annexation early in the nineteenth century, so far as we can tell the Todas had no system like the Badaga one (Hockings 2013, 192–193), with headmen or chiefs at village, commune (in Hockings's usage [ibid., 11 n.2], a congeries of hamlets), divisional, and entire community levels. Traditional Toda society functioned without formally-appointed judges, headmen, or decision-makers at any level, except perhaps that of the individual household. Here, the *pater familias*, in this formerly polyandrous society (Peter 1963, 240–300), the eldest among the co-resident brothers, formally dominated the affairs of his domestic unit. And if a Toda hamlet (*mund*, or in Toda, *mod̲*[1]) comprised the separate residences of men who, as was most often the case, were either actual or clan brothers, but with each having his own wife or wives, then the eldest of these men held authority, not unlike that of a village headman elsewhere; but the number of people over whom this elder exercised authority in the usually tiny Toda hamlet of two or three households (see Image 12.3, this volume) obviously was not large. Moreover, a weak or disabled elder brother (whether actual or clan) would likely lose whatever authority he held in favour of a stronger sibling (actual or classificatory).

There is some—albeit debatable—evidence that Toda headmanship might have been more formally structured around 1900, when Rivers was in the Nilgiris. This Cambridge anthropologist, who studied Toda social institutions during the cool months of 1901–1902, reported that:

> Each clan has a headman or *etudol* [*ïtwïḍ o·ḷ*, lit. 'big man'], usually, it seemed to me, one who had come to the top by virtue of his character and ability ...; [i]t was quite clear ... that the leading man of a clan might lose his position in old age or as a result of an illness, and at the time of my visit there were several men who had been the heads of their clans but no longer occupied those positions. (1906, 556–557)

Certainly there is support, even in recent times, for the scenario Rivers describes here, although any particular patriclan—though seldom one hamlet—might be home to more than one such charismatic leader. But Rivers's description goes further: he speaks of the nature and function of Toda headmen, beyond their being simply charismatic clan leaders.

When Rivers was with the Todas, membership of their caste council, the *no·ym*, seems to have been more rigidly prescribed than has been the case in recent times, or indeed was likely to have been the situation during the preceding several decades—perhaps even earlier centuries. This is what Rivers had to say (his orthography corrected):

> The *naim* [no·ym] should have five members, or, if more … they should be drawn from five sources. Four of these sources are the Tarthar [To·r̠θas̠] clans of Kars [Ka·s̠], Nòdrs [No·ṣ], and Taradr [To·r̠o·ṛ] and the Teivali [Tö·fiḷy[2]] clan of Kuudr [Kï·wïṛ]. The fifth source is the Badaga village of Tuneri [Tūnēri, seat of the Badagas' paramount chief] …. (1906, 550; *cf.* Hockings 2013, 22, 193) ….
>
> The Toda representatives should be drawn from *certain families of their respective clans*. The Kuudr [Kï·wïṛ] representative should belong to the family known as the *manikudupel* [*moṇy kwiḍbïl*],[3] and the representatives of Kars [Ka·s̠], Nòdrs [No·ṣ], and Taradr [To·r̠o·ṛ] to the families known as *tinkanikudupel* [*tingoṇy kwiḍbïl*].[4] (emphasis mine)

But whether those men specifically designated to be council members in Rivers's time were indeed hereditary Toda 'chiefs' in a political sense remains very debatable. He himself admitted (1906, 551) that some of the specially-assigned clans were not in fact represented on the council while others, not among the selected few, were active participants.

From what I was able to glean from Toda informants over half-a-century later, the situation witnessed by Rivers in 1901–1902 was seemingly an aberration, an outgrowth of the overpowering personalities of just a few elders at that time. They told me about four men, all still well-remembered by elders in the early 1960s, as being men who had usurped the judicial authority properly belonging to the collectivity of male adults. Rivers mentions (1906, 550–551) two of the four names given to me sixty-odd years later, viz., Kwï·s̲yaḷf of Kï·wïṛ patriclan (Rivers's spelling, Kuriolv; see Walker 2012b) and Panïs̲ of To·r̲o·ṛ patriclan.

It is also clear that, among all the politically influential Todas at the start of the twentieth century, Kwï·s̲yaḷf headed them all. Rivers himself noted: 'there is no doubt that ... [Kwï·s̲yaḷf] almost entirely dominated the Toda people' (1906, 552–553). In the early 1960s, informants who still remembered him told me that Kwï·s̲yaḷf used to be carried in a bamboo chair, borne on the shoulders of fellow Todas, to meetings of the *no·ym*. No other Toda leader they remembered had ever commanded such a demonstration of respect and authority.

The situation, which probably prevailed even before British annexation is that, although some patriclans can boast outstanding men whose voices are always pre-eminent in debate, no single man holds *formal* clan, subcaste, or caste headmanship, (that is, apart from the external government's appointee, to be discussed below).

Despite this absence of formal office-holders, the Todas had (and still have) well-defined procedures for ensuring that community members observe traditional social norms; also for settling disputes, as well as for deciding upon united community action when such was (or is) deemed necessary or desirable. Traditionally Todas have looked to their caste council for the dispensation of justice within their own community, just as other Indian communities look to their caste or village *panchayat*s (Mandelbaum 1970, 269–310). In their disputes with other indigenous peoples, Todas sought—as they were still doing in the 1960s and 1970s—the occasional mediation of Badaga headmen, representatives of the politically dominant caste in traditional Nilgiri society.

* * *

John Sullivan's appointment of a government-recognised Toda headman did not radically change the functioning of political leadership within the Toda community. Not too long after Sullivan established his first residence on the hills in 1819, at Dimbaṭṭi, it is told among Todas, even today, that he chose the Kï·wïṛ patriclansman Te·ty (a man named after a pool of water called Te·tyxö·r at the clan's Mü·ny hamlet: Maruḷemandu in Badagu) to become the first government-recognised headman or *monegar* (in Toda, *moṇyxo·r̲n*) for the Toda community. (As a matter of fact, this appointment was as sub-*monegar*, not *monegar*, as we shall see.)

According to the Toda account of this event, as recorded by the American linguist Murray Emeneau (1963, 189), it was while on his *first* visit to the site of what is now Ootacamund (see Frontispiece) that Sullivan chose Te·ty as Toda *monegar*. This most likely would have been in April 1822 (Hockings 1973, 865; Price 2002 [1908], 18–21), although the year of Sullivan's first visit to this place is sometimes given as 1819 (thus Bennett 1940), or else as 1821 (Gopalakrishnan 1995, 224).

The story of Te·ty's appointment that Emeneau recorded in 1938 (1963, 189) was related by his informant-interpreter Kaṇfis̲ody (Walker 2012a), a Christian Toda convert born to Ka·s̲ patriclan. Kaṇfis̲ody, in turn, had heard it from Piḷya·r̲ (Walker 2012c),[5] the *monegar* at that time, who was Te·ty's grandson (the second son of Mutefïn, Te·ty's fourth son; see Figure 4.1). Emeneau suggests that Piḷya·r̲ had a vested interest in telling this story, since it provided the background to the appointment of his family as office-holders. This is how it went:

> Te·ty, Piḷya·r̲'s grandfather … was building a new mund [hamlet] and began to make preparations for the ceremony of giving salt to the buffaloes and its accompanying feast.[6] He had to go to the plains for rice, salt, sugar, etc., to a place called Pe·ṭ [meaning, in Toda, simply 'market', but Emeneau suggests it may have been Meṭṭupāḷaiyam]. As he and his companion were going down, they met Sullivan coming up. They asked with gestures, since they spoke no Tamil, where he was going, and said that they would carry loads for money. He promised money if they would carry him up the mountains. They made a stretcher with cloaks [*pu·txuḷy*] and brought him up. When they reached what is now Stonehouse Hill [within today's Ootacamund Municipality], he asked shelter in the Toda mund that was situated there [this was the Ka·s̲ patriclan settlement-cum-male funeral place, subsequently demolished, named Patïrmod̲ or Patmod̲ for short]. They

> gave it [that is, shelter] in a small tent.[7] After a few days he paid Te·ty three rupees and appointed him *monegar*.

It is a nice story, but its historicity is very questionable, particularly in the light of what follows in Emeneau's text, suggesting that it belongs more to legend than to history, viz.,

> He [Sullivan] asked all the Todas to be called and made with them an agreement for as much ground as could be covered by a sheepskin [since, in Toda, the same word is used for both sheep and goat and no sheep were reared on the hills at that time, this would have been a goatskin]. Then he cut the skin round and round into a long strip as thin as hair. It was ten miles long. He measured ground with it and said that all this ground was his, and the Todas kept their agreement.

This account of 'the sheep/goat skin and the tricky bargain', as Emeneau (1963, 190) immediately realised, is a variant of a widespread folktale (one told by the poet Virgil in connection with Queen Dido's [879–759 BCE] acquisition of the site of Carthage). Emeneau saw the incorporation of this 'tricky bargain' episode as 'the chief point of interest in the story' of Sullivan's acquisition of the site on which he built his famous 'Stone House', thereby initiating a train of events that would result in constructing from scratch south India's premier hill station and the summer capital of the Madras Presidency. Declaring he had never been able to discover a record of this incident 'anywhere [else] in the accounts of Sullivan and the founding of the town', Emeneau claims nevertheless not to have been particularly surprised the Todas had a variant of this tale as it recurs so frequently in Asian and European folk literature.[8]

The Swedish historian Gunnel Cederlöf, in her book *Landscapes and the Law*, has an interesting take on the story of 'Sullivan's tricky deal'. She asks rhetorically (2008, 20), 'Is this not … a mocking story told among British settlers who were highly critical of Sullivan's quick move in the 1820s to secure for himself a government grant of almost 2,000 acres: a colonial tale of the … [champion of Toda rights] cheating poor tribals'[!]

One might reasonably suppose that an altogether less fanciful scenario lay behind Sullivan's appointment of Te·ty, namely the

Commissioner's institution in the mid-1820s of local *monegar*s throughout the Nilgiris. As the British historian Deborah Sutton writes in her book *Other Landscapes: Colonialism and the Predicament of Authority in Nineteenth-Century South India*, 'John Sullivan instituted the position of *Monegar* as a pivot between state and cultivators as part of his reorganisation of the revenue administration of the hills' (2011, 91). Moreover, Sutton (ibid.) specifically mentions '[t]he first *Monigars* ... [being] recruited from the hill communities' (presumably the indigenous inhabitants), although it seems that as early as the 1830s some '*Monigars* had come from the plains'. Sutton adds (ibid.) that the *monegar*s, apart from 'collecting revenues, ... were expected to organise, or more often coerce, labourers for government works or to carry travellers' baggage; supply information when disputes arose, and perform sundry duties such as "supplying Gentlemen that go about on hunting parties."'

Nonetheless, against the seemingly sensible proposition that Te·ty was appointed Toda *monegar* as part of John Sullivan's more general reorganisation of the District's administrative order, and lending some (if not total) credence to the special circumstances in which he was appointed, such as are propagated in the Todas' 'sheep/goat skin and the tricky bargain' tale, there is the 1940 report to the Presidency government in Madras by the then District Collector, J. Bennett, which states in part:

> The orders governing the appointment of the Teivali [Tö·fiḷy] chief [that is, Te·ty] as the first Toda *sub-monegar* [N.B., not *monegar*] are not traceable in this office. Enquiries by the Deputy Tahsildar [a deputy sub-district head], Ootacamund, go to show that the family of the Teivali [chief] held the appointment even before the original settlement [presumably he refers to the Revenue Survey and Settlement of 1878?] was introduced and the family was so selected *for the help rendered by them to Mr. Sullivan* when he first came to the Nilgiris in the year 1819, while others got frightened and ran away. [emphasis mine]

And to this, Collector Bennett adds (ibid.): 'in recognition of this appointment' of Te·ty as Toda sub-*monegar*, the Nilgiri

Commissioner James Breeks (1830–1872; see Plate 6, this volume), 'during the Neilgherry exhibition' presented a silver medal with Queen-Empress Victoria's image engraved upon it to 'the [then] present *monigar*' (probably Mutefin; see Figure 4.1). (The Neilgherry Exhibition to which Bennett refers would have been that organised in 1869 by the Agricultural and Horticultural Society of the Neilgherry Hills, a body that Breeks had formed that same year; Hockings, pers. comm.; Price 2002 [1908], 247).

* * *

Here we need to digress from the story of the Toda *monegar*ship in the hands of Te·ty and his lineal descendants so as to introduce two anomalies, neither of which is easily explainable.

In January–February 1882 the Italian polymath Paolo Mantegazza (1831–1910), a physician, surgeon, physiologist, neurologist, psycho-pharmacologist, and physical anthropologist, and the man who founded the Italian Anthropological Society, visited the Nilgiris (Mantegazza 1888, 137–164). This was particularly because of his interest in the Todas, about whom he had read extensively in the English literature—most notably the two books of Marshall (1873) and Breeks (1873). He put up at Sylk's Hotel (now the Savoy) and was thus able to establish particularly close contacts with the Todas of Ka·s̱ (Kandalmund), the nearby chief hamlet of the patriclan of the same name.

Among the most fascinating of the data Mantegazza recorded among the Todas was his meeting, probably at Sylk's Hotel (to which he would summon Todas, in return for a fee, to be photographed and to undergo physiological tests), with a Ka·s̱ patriclan elder whom he names as 'Karudi'[9] and calls 'the chief or king of the Todas'. Moreover, Mantegazza (1888, 152) tells how this Karudi, 'seeking esteem and respect, drew out from his cloak a large sheet', confirming that 'Queen Victoria recognised him as head of all the Todas'. It read (and Mantegazza transcribes the original English):

> In command of his Excellency the Viceroy and Governor General this certificate is presented in the name of Her Gracious Majesty Victoria, Empress of India, to Pathathothee

> of Kandalmund [= Ka·s̲], Head of the Toda Tribe, son of Kandoothoovand, in recognition of his services as Monigar and general good character.
>
> Jan 1, 1877
>
> Buckingham Chandor[10]

Mantegazza notes the discrepancy between the name of the man who produced this document for him (that is, 'Karudi') and that on the document itself, viz., 'Pathathothee son of Kandoothoovand',[11] but writes that: 'There were those who explained to me the enigma, telling me that he ("Karudi") was only the son of the king who, old and feeble, never left his hut' (1888, 153).

In a major publication on the Todas, Mantegazza (ibid., 406, n.1) recalls his meeting with 'Karudi' (although he omits the name): 'I will never forget the air of sovereign complacency with which a Toda showed me an official document, which declared him to be the head of the whole tribe, although I had many reasons to believe that this document belonged to somebody else.' Unfortunately Mantegazza says nothing further on this matter.

So the enigma remains. The administrative history of the Nilgiris, as we know it, relates that the first British-appointed Toda *monegar* (or more correctly sub-*monegar*) was Te·ty of Kï·wïṛ patriclan—thus a member of the opposite subcaste to that of 'Karudi' of Ka·s̲ patriclan. We know also that the office remained in Te·ty's family line until its abolition in the late twentieth century. True, the anthropologist Prince Peter of Greece and Denmark, in his report to Lord Erskine, then Governor of Madras Presidency (Peter 1939, 5), claimed that it was a Ka·s̲ man, Ö·knïs̲, not Te·ty's descendant Piḷya·r̲, who was the legitimate chief of the Todas. But while the prince certainly believed the British regime had erred in appointing Te·ty, he did not challenge the historicity of that appointment nor the subsequent descent of the office in Te·ty's family. Furthermore, there is no evidence that might link Ö·knïs̲ to Mantegazza's acquaintance 'Karudi'. While we cannot simply dismiss Mantegazza's 'document in the name of the Queen-Empress', the enigma of the Italian scholar's 'king of all the Todas' remains unresolved.

The second anomaly is occasioned by Paul Hockings's entry on Sullivan for the *Encyclopædia of the Nilgiri Hills* (2012b, 886), in which he records that, due to Piḷya·ṟ being without offspring, 'the institution [of the Toda *monegar*] … was transferred … [to] Te·θyxe·n … [of] To·ṟo·ṛ, a patriclan in the opposite moiety [= subcaste]'.[12] Te·θyxe·n unfortunately is long since deceased, but a recent communication from Tarun Chhabra (investigating on my behalf) suggests that he did indeed hold some form of official position, although whether it was that of *monegar* Chhabra's informants were unable to say (Chhabra, personal communication, 2019). Certainly, I never heard from a Toda informant that another man held the office of Toda *monegar* after Piḷya·ṟ's resignation but before Piḷyxuḍ, Piḷya·ṟ's younger brother's son (see Figure 4.1), inherited the office; yet we cannot be certain that no such situation arose. What can be confirmed is that, in late 1962, when I began fieldwork with the community, the office of Toda *monegar* was held by Sinfa·twï· (now also deceased), who was the great-great grandson of the original appointee.

* * *

The office of Toda *monegar*—potentially a position of considerable sociopolitical power, involving as it did the collection of the annual tax that the community was obliged to pay on its grazing grounds,[13] along with keeping a record of births and deaths in the community—never realised its potential, and its abolition three or so decades back had quite minimal impact on the functioning of the community, despite this institution having existed for over 150 years. The reason, almost certainly, was because the office lacked any traditional base in this inordinately tradition-conscious society.

Whatever the actual reason for Sullivan's choice of Te·ty to become the first Toda *monegar* (Rivers plausibly suggested [1906, 556] that it might have reflected the fact that Te·ty, at that time, happened to be one of the most influential members of the Toda community), the fact remains that Sullivan made the appointment, doubtless without realising it, with scant regard to the principles of Toda social organisation. Te·ty, as a Kï·wïṛ patriclansman, was from the numerically smaller and ritually inferior Tö·fiḷy subcaste.

The anthropologist Prince Peter, in his confidential report (1939) to Lord Erskine, the last Governor of the former Madras Presidency, on the condition of the Toda community, among other matters seized upon this appointment of a Tö·fiḷy subcaste man as Toda *monegar* as one of the reasons for his perception that the Todas' body politic was on the verge of collapse. The prince voiced the opinion that the British authorities, *ca* 1820, had made a fundamental error in appointing a Tö·fiḷy subcaste man to this office. 'I am of the opinion,' Prince Peter told Lord Erskine, 'that should the government correct their mistake and … invest … [a To·ṟθas̱ 'chief' instead] a definite turn for the better would take place.' Prince Peter (1955, 106, addition no. 6 [to Rivers 1906]) had identified—mistakenly, I believe (Walker 1986, 91, n.31)—a man of Ka·s̱ patriclan, who was the *tingoṇy* holder of his patriclan (see Section I, above), as the legitimate hereditary chief of the entire Toda community. He was now canvassing the government authorities, through the Presidency's governor, to invest this man with the office of Toda *monegar* in place of the current holder, Te·ty's grandson Piḷya·ṟ.

The aforementioned Nilgiri Collector, E. Bennett, was deputed to respond on behalf of the Presidency government to this and other of Prince Peter's suggestions. (The prince's close blood ties with the British royal family [Mandelbaum 2012; Pedersen 2005]—he was an uncle of Philip, Duke of Edinburgh—doubtless compelled the Madras authorities to consider his suggestions more carefully than they might have done for those of some run-of-the-mill academic anthropologist who happened to be doing a spot of fieldwork among the Todas!).

It was in his response to the prince's suggestion concerning the re-allocation of the *monegar*ship that Bennett reported the Nilgiri authorities' understanding of the background to Te·ty's appointment, already examined here. But Bennett went a step further: he positively rejected any move to re-allocate the *monegar*ship to Prince Peter's preferred candidate, declaring the Collectorate's satisfaction with the present *monegar*'s legitimacy, and noting 'the present incumbent' (in 1939–1940 it would have been Piḷya·ṟ; see Image 4.1) still retained the medal his father had received from James Breeks some seventy years before. Bennett agreed that the prince's candidate for the office was the acknowledged 'chief of his own mund', but went on to say that 'every mund has its own chieftain' and that '[a]ll these chiefs join together and hold their own panchayats and carry on their administration'. Finally, to clinch his argument, Bennett declared that the prince's candidate 'has lost his eye-sight and is not fit to hold the post of a monegar'. Consequently, Bennet wrote, '[t]here is no justification for replacing the present … [office holder].' Thus the office of government-recognised (sub-)*monegar* remained in Te·ty's family until the Tamil Nadu authorities abolished the institution in the late 1970s.

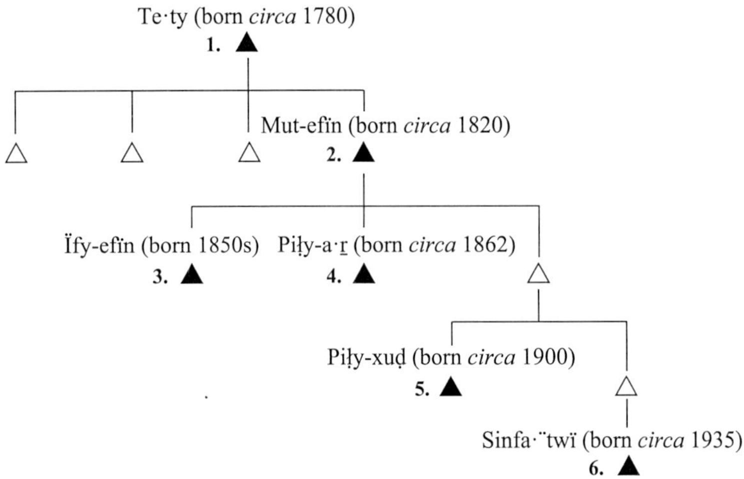

FIGURE 4.1: The descent of the office of Toda *monegar*

The esteem of Todas for the *monegar* has varied, from its inception in the 1820s until the office was done away with some 150 years later, according to the personal charisma (or lack thereof) of any particular office-holder. Te·ty surely must have been an influential man to catch Sullivan's attention, but there is little on record to suggest that his fourth son and successor, Mutefïn, was a particularly influential leader. Mutefin got the office because the first two of his elder brothers died young, while the third, as Rivers learned, 'was said to be weak-minded' (1906, 556). By the time Rivers was with the Todas, Mutefin was already 'about eighty years old' (ibid.), and had been succeeded in office by his eldest son Ïfyefin (in Rivers's Ivievan).

Whether or not Ïfyefin was particularly charismatic is likewise not recorded. What is certain, however, is that his importance was quite eclipsed by that of his (classificatory) brother (father's brother's son), Kwï·s̱yaḷf (Walker 2012b). He too was a direct patrilineal descendant of Te·ty, his father being Te·ty's third son, Pes̱efin (in Rivers's Persevan). It is instructive to note that Kwï·syaḷf himself never became the *monegar* despite the legendary authority he wielded in the community. When Kwï·s̱yaḷf died, Piḷya·ṟ (Walker 2012c), his classificatory brother, who did inherit the *monegar*ship, lamented the great man's passing with these words (Emeneau 1971, 124–125, Song 34):

> O my elder brother!
> O child that was born [as my brother]!
> O clever man!
> You were born as a tiger [a strong man] to Kï·wïṛ hamlet ...!
> You settled disputes as were not settled before; you discussed disputes that were not settled before!
> [a reference to Kwï·s̱yaḷf's dominant role in the caste council]

And Kwï·s̱yaḷf's daughter, Pu·pi·ẕ, lamented in similar vein:

> O my father!
> O important man! ...
> You acted powerfully, seizing the bow. /You spoke, seizing the sword. //
> ... [a reference to Kwï·s̱yaḷf's powerful personality and leadership]!
> You were responsible for the families of the three divisions of the Nilgiris./
> You paid for all three directions. //
> [a reference to Kwï·s̱yaḷf's political supremacy over all Todas]! (adapted from ibid., 129, Song 35)

Piḻya·ṟ (Image 4.1), the fourth *monegar*, was Te·ty's grandson through the latter's fourth son, Mutefin. Todas relate that Te·ty mystically bestowed this name—derived from *piḻy*, 'silver', with the common suffix *-a·ṟ* (Emeneau 1974, 43)—on his grandson by announcing it in a dream to Piḻya·ṟ's father, Mutefin. Piḻya·ṟ must have been born around the early 1860s, as he was already middle-aged in Rivers' time (1901–1902). He inherited the headmanship from his elder brother, Ïfyefin (who died *ca* 1927). Piḻya·ṟ was still functioning as Toda *monegar* in 1939, when Prince Peter was first with the Todas, but by the time the prince returned to the

IMAGE 4.1: Piḻya·ṟ, the fourth Toda *monegar*, with Sinmal, his opposite-subcaste consort

Source: Ootacamund studio portrait, *ca* 1938.

Nilgiris in 1949 Piḷya·ṟ had resigned as *monegar* in favour of his son Piḷyxuḍ (Peter 1963, 252). In the event, Piḷya·ṟ outlived his son, the fifth and penultimate Toda *monegar*, by a year. Piḷya·ṟ died on 2 June 1962, very likely over 100 years old. Paul Hockings and I attended his second funeral rites in January 1963.

Both Piḷya·ṟ and Piḷyxuḍ—particularly the former—were robust leaders of the community, even if not quite as autocratic as was Kwï·s̱yaḷf. But this may hardly be said of the sixth and last Toda *monegar*, Sinfa·θwï·, whose father was Piḷyxuḍ's younger brother, and who took up the position of Toda *monegar* on the death of his 'elder father' (father's elder brother) in 1961. In the 1960s and 1970s, it seemed that Sinfa·θwï· commanded very limited authority, being quite overshadowed in public debate by the then most powerful man of his Kï·wïṛ patriclan, Pïnoy, a son of Sodyxwï·ṛ (Emeneau 1974, 76, no. 641).

* * *

We may conclude that, notwithstanding Sullivan's appointment of a headman for the Toda community and the retention of that office in the same family for some 150 years, it never evolved into an autocratic chiefly institution. Rather, the Todas continued to look to their *no·ym* or caste council—as they still do—for the dispensation of justice within their own community. In disputes with other indigenous peoples they sought the mediation of Badaga headmen, representatives of the politically-dominant caste in Nilgiri society at the time of British annexation and possibly for at least the previous two centuries as well, if we are to believe the Italian Jesuit Giacomo Fenicio's 1603 observation that the Todas 'have no vassals ...; on the contrary, they are subject and pay tribute to the Badaga chiefs' (de Alberti, trans. in Rivers 1906, 727). Appeals to British lawcourts were for many decades rare or non-existent, and summonses issued to Todas to appear before these judicial bodies were very infrequent.

Throughout the era of British rule here and for the first three decades of independent India, due to the strength of its caste council Toda political life ran more or less satisfactorily, whether or not a strong, charismatic *monegar* held office. But while the Todas, it seems, could manage without a recognised 'high chief', government administrators needed such an official through whom to liaise with the community. Consequently, in 2006 the authorities requested that Todas elect a new community leader, who would serve a five-year term (Parthasarathy 2008, 85). At the present time, this first community leader has served his term and his successor has been voted into office.

In addition, in 2008 the Tamil Nadu government reconstituted the Tamil Nadu State Tribal Advisory Council, to which body the orthodox community's first university graduate, a woman, has been appointed as member for the Toda community (ibid.). Whether these newly-created positions of political authority will evolve into a more characteristically Toda-style political leadership—where the former *monegar* institution failed—it is still too early to determine.

Notes

1. For the most part in this chapter, I follow Murray B. Emeneau's orthography for Toda words (but see n2 below); see, in particular, Emeneau (1958; 1984, 5–49).

2. To reflect Toda pronunciation, on the expert advice of Tarun Chhabra, I have modified Emeneau's transcription of the name of this subcaste from Töwfiḷy to Tö·fiḷy.

3. This title, I was told in 1963, refers to the family of the *moṇyxo·rn* (see below).

4. The *tingoṇy kwïḍbïl* were families, I was told, which had received small coins from the Tūnēri headman, paramount chief of the Nilgiris, presumably in recognition of their superior political status within their patriclan.

5. Piḷya·ṟ died in 1962, aged around 100 years (Hockings and Walker 1983).

6. Whether there is any connection between these two events is unclear: building a new settlement and giving salt to the buffaloes are said to be two quite separate ritual events.

7. As Todas are not known to make or use tents, it is unclear what sleeping quarters the Patmoḏ people offered Sullivan—perhaps a rough shelter made from cloaks?

8. Yet another variant—purporting to explain how an American Baptist missionary acquired his ecclesiastical headquarters on land then ruled by the Shan prince of Menglian, in southwest China—is still told by Lahu people living there, much to the delight of the Party faithful (Walker 2003, 606–607)!

9. No matching name appears in Rivers' genealogical charts (1906, Charts 6–15).

10. Presumably a misprinting of 'Chandos', as Buckingham Chandos was the title of Richard Grenville (1823–1889), Third Duke of Buckingham & Chandos (full name: Richard Temple Plantagenet Campbell Nugent Brydges Chandos). He was the Governor of Madras in 1875–1880 (Boase 1890, 131–132). Probably Grenville, as Governor, was responsible for despatching, on behalf of the Viceroy, the document that Mantegazza copied.

11. Again, none of these names matches those given in the genealogical tables for Ka·s̱ patriclan (Rivers 1906, Tables 7–15).

12. Hockings claims the transfer of the office from Piḷya·ṟ to Te·θyxe·n was arranged by the famous Kwï·s̱yaḷ̣f of Kï·wïṛ patriclan, grandson of Te·ty and son of the second *monegar,* Mutefïn. But against this contention we must note, first, that Kwï·s̱yaḷ̣f died *ca* 1933–1934 (Emeneau 1971, 109), while Piḷya·ṟ still held the office of Toda *monegar* in 1939, when Prince Peter was first studying the community (1939, 5). Second, Hockings claims Kwï·s̱yaḷ̣f sought the succession of the office from Piḷya·ṟ to Te·θyxe·n because Te·θyxe·n's mother, Pu·pi·ẓ, was his daughter and, as such, a direct descendant of the first Toda *monegar*, Te·ty; moreover, Hockings claims Pu·pi·ẓ was 'formally married to a To·ṟo·ṛ man [that is, Te·θyxe·n's father]'. But if by 'formally married' Hockings refers to formal marriage within the endogamous subcaste, this could not have been the case, since Te·θyxe·n's father (a To·ṟθas̱ subcaste man) and Pu·pi·ẓ (a Tö·fiḷy subcaste woman), as members of opposite endogamous subcastes, were unable to be formally married. Even if Pu·pi·ẓ was indeed Te·θyxe·n's biological mother through the formal inter-subcaste institution, he could not have been a To·ṟo·ṛ patriclansman, since his socially-recognised father would necessarily be the Tö·fiḷy subcaste man who gave her a symbolic bow-and-arrow during the prenatal paternity rites.

13. Two annas per acre (0.4 ha) per annum (Francis 1908, 212).

References

Bennett, E. 1940. 'Letter from E. Bennett Esq., I.C.S., Collector of the Nilgiris to the Secretary, Board of Revenue, Madras. Sub. Village Officers–Headman–Sub-Monigar–Toda–Ootacamund Taluk–Appointment–Authority–Report. Confidential R. Dis. No. 931/40, dated 6 April 1940'. Chennai: Tamil Nadu State Archives.

Boase, George C. 1890. 'Grenville, Richard Temple Plantagenet Campbell Nugent Brydges Chandos'. *Dictionary of National Biography* 23, 131–132. London: Smith, Elder & Co.

Breeks, James W. 1873. 'The Todas'. In *An Account of the Primitive Tribes and Monuments of the Nīlagiris*, 5–39. London: India Museum. (Reprint, Delhi: Cultural Publication House, 1983).

Cederlöf, Gunnel. 2008. *Landscapes and the Law: Environmental Politics, Regional Histories, and Contests over Nature.* Ranikhet, Uttarakhand: Permanent Black.

de Alberti, A. (trans.). 1906. 'The Mission of Todamalâ' (Trans. of *Missão de Todamalâ*). London: British Library. Add. MS 9853, MS 40 vol., 479–483). Published in Rivers 1906: 720–730.

Emeneau, Murray B. 1958. 'Toda: A Dravidian Language'. *Transactions of the Philosophical Society* (London), 1957, 15–65. (Reprinted in M. B. Emeneau. 1967. *Dravidian Linguistics, Ethnology and Folklore: Collected Papers*, 1–36. Annamalainagar: Annamalai University Press, Linguistics Dept. Publication No. 8.)

____. 1963. 'Ootacamund in the Nilgiris: Some Notes'. *Journal of the American Oriental Society* 82 (2), 188–193. (Reprinted in M. B. Emeneau. 1994. *Dravidian Studies: Selected Papers*, 405–413. Delhi: Motilal Banarsidass.)

____. 1971. *Toda Songs*. Oxford: Clarendon Press.

____. 1974. 'Ritual Structure and Language Structure of the Todas'. *Transactions of the American Philosophical Society* (n. s.) 64 (6), 1–103.

____. 1984. *Toda Grammar and Texts.* Philadelphia: American Philosophical Society.

Fenicio, Giacomo. 1603. 'Missão de Todamala'. [Letter to Revd. Fr. Albert Laerzio, S. J., Vice-Principal of the Society of Jesus in Malabar at Cochin, dated 1 April 1603. British Library Add. MS 9853, MS 25–26 Vol., 464–465 (Translated into English by A. de Alberti in Rivers 1906, 719–730.)

Fortes, Meyer, and Edward E. Evans-Pritchard (eds). 1940. *African Political Systems*. London: Oxford University Press, for the International African Institute.

Francis, Walter (ed.). 1908. *Madras District Gazetteers: The Nilgiris*, Vol. I. Madras: Superintendent, Government Press.

Gopalakrishnan, M. (ed.). 1995. *Gazetteer of India, Tamil Nadu State: The Nilgiris District*. Chennai: Government of Tamil Nadu, Commissioner of Archives and Historical Research.

Hockings, Paul. 1973. 'John Sullivan of Ootacamund'. *Journal of Indian History* 50, 863–871.

———. 2012a. 'Law, Justice and Decision Making: Badaga Practice'. In Paul Hockings (ed.), *Encyclopaedia of the Nilgiri Hills*, 524–525. New Delhi: Manohar.

———. 2012b. 'Sullivan, John'. In Paul Hockings (ed.), *Encyclopaedia of the Nilgiri Hills*, 881–888. New Delhi: Manohar.

———. 2013. *So Long a Saga: Four Centuries of Badaga Social History*. New Delhi: Manohar.

Hockings, Paul, and Anthony R. Walker. 1983. 'Toda Secondary Funeral Ritual'. In Giri Raj Gupta (ed.), *Main Currents in India Sociology, Vol. 5: Religion in Modern India*, 313–342. New Delhi: Vikas.

Mair, Lucy P. 1962. *Primitive Government*. Harmondsworth: Penguin Books.

Mandelbaum, David G. 1970. *Society in India*. Berkeley and Los Angeles: University of California Press.

———. 2012. Peter (H.R.H., Prince of Greece and Denmark). In Paul Hockings (ed.), *Encyclopaedia of the Nilgiri Hills*, 697–698. New Delhi: Manohar. (First published 1981, as 'Prince Peter of Greece and Denmark 1908–1980'. *American Anthropologist* 83, 616–617.)

Mantegazza, Paolo. 1883. 'Studii sull' Etnologia dell' India, Parte Seconda: Le Tribu Selvaggie e Semielvaggie del Nilghiri' [Studies in Indian Ethnology: The Wild and Semi-wild Tribes of the Nilgiris]. *Archivio per l'Antropologia e la Etnologia* 13 (3), 379–504.

———. 1888. *India*. Milan: Fratelli Treves, Editori, Ch. 6–7, 137–81.

Marshall, William E. 1873. *A Phrenologist amongst the Todas or the Study of a Primitive Tribe in South India. History, Character, Customs, Religion, Infanticide, Polyandry.* London: Longmans, Green.

Middleton, John, and David Tait (eds). 1958. *Tribes without Rulers*. London: Routledge and Kegan Paul.

Parthasarathy, Jakka. 2008. *The Toda of the Nilgiri District, Tamil Nadu: A Study of a Pastoral Tribe and its Development.* Ootacamund [Udhagamandalam]: Hill Area Development Programme.

Pedersen, Poul. 2005. 'Out of India: Prince Peter of Greece and Denmark and the Greek Royal Family'. *Folk* (Copenhagen) 46–47, 181–200.

Peter, Prince of Greece and Denmark. 1939. Confidential Report to Lord Erskine, Governor of Fort St. George, from H.R.H. Prince Peter of Greece (7 pp. typescript, dated Coonoor, 3 August 1939).

____. 1949. 'Report on the Todas: With Special Reference to the Rate of their Extinction and with Suggestions to Check this Trend' (12 pp. typescript, dated 23 August; summarised in Peter 1953).

____. 1953. 'The Problem of Toda Survival'. *Vanyajati* 1, 59–68.

____. 1955. 'The Todas: Some Additions and Corrections to W. H. R. Rivers's Book, as Observed in the Field'. *Man* 55 (106), 89–93.

____. 1963. 'The Polyandry of the Todas of the Nilgiris'. In *A Study of Polyandry,* 240–300. The Hague: Mouton.

Price, J. Frederick. 2002 [1908]. *Ootacamund: A History.* Chennai: Rupa & Co.–Dukshin. (First published, 1908, Madras: Superintendent, Government Press.)

Rivers, W. H. R. 1906. *The Todas.* London: Macmillan & Co.

Sutton, Deborah. 2011. *Other Landscapes: Colonialism and the Predicament of Authority in Nineteenth-Century South India.* Hyderabad: Orient BlackSwan.

Walker, Anthony R. 1986. *The Toda of South India: A New Look.* Delhi: Hindustan Publishing Corp.

____. 2003. *Merit and the Millennium: Routine and Crisis in the Ritual Lives of the Lahu People.* New Delhi: Hindustan Publishing Corp.

____. 2012a. 'Kanfisody'. In Paul Hockings (ed.), *Encyclopaedia of the Nilgiri Hills,* 462–463. New Delhi: Manohar,

____. 2012b. 'Kwï·s̱yaḷf'. In Paul Hockings (ed.), *Encyclopædia of the Nilgiri Hills,* 509–510. New Delhi: Manohar.

____. 2012c. 'Piḷya·ṟ'. In Paul Hockings (ed.), *Encyclopædia of the Nilgiri Hills,* 708–709. New Delhi: Manohar.

____. Forthcoming. *The Todas and their Buffaloes: Secular and Sacred Dimensions of a South Indian Community.* New Delhi: Manohar.

5

Innocent Times

A Glimpse Back into Sullivan's Nilgiris

Philip K. Mulley

Sir Frederick Price, well-known as the chronicler of the history of Ootacamund town, strangely enough rejects the idea that Sullivan was the 'discoverer' of Ootacamund (1908, 29). This is quite a myopic view, considering that Sir Frederick was only concerned with a topographical perspective of Ootacamund's history, one, moreover, that focused almost exclusively on the actions of British people there (see Chapter 13, this volume). However, I believe that, but for Sullivan, Ootacamund would not have been 'discovered' at all, in the sense of what it has become and how it has evolved across the two centuries since the advent of this one official. To put it bluntly, Sullivan not only discovered Ootacamund, but he also created the place and began the whole process of etching the saga of the modern Nilgiri Hills, which for him was a perfect replica of the Finest Country somewhere in Western Europe. As Hockings once said (during a personal conversation), his memorial is in a sense everywhere, throughout the district.

Sullivan, guided by Muddah and his energetic band of Badaga scouts, had reached the Nilgiris for the first time in January 1819: this is a well-known fact. Muddah hailed from Mīdēṇu, a Badaga hamlet very near Kotagiri. His name and that expedition are actually inscribed on the back of a venerable orthostat standing on the village green in Mīdēṇu (Images 5.1–5.3).[1] Sullivan and his retinue decided to camp at Kannērimukku, another Badaga hamlet a couple of kilometres away, on an attractively located spur. What remains a great mystery even to this day is how Sullivan ever managed to acquire a building site at Kannērimukku (in the neighbourhood of what those early Britons called the Dimbaṭṭi Valley).

IMAGE 5.1: The road up to Kotagiri from Meṭṭupāḷayam
Source: M'Curdy (1830).

The ancestral site of my forebears lies a mere ten-minutes' walk from there, hence this constant inquisitiveness about Sullivan's sojourn. Although the Kannērimukku folk recall a very early tradition of a white man from the West Coast turning up in this locality (not, however, any of the three mentioned by Hockings [2012], under 'History'), Sullivan came from Coimbatore and had a forward-looking influence. Intriguingly enough, his chosen site was situated very close to the sacred precincts of the hamlet. The sacred grove lies on one side and a large *kraal* for the sacred herd of Badaga buffaloes is on the other. While the sacred grove is still there, the buffalo-pen (*tō*) has been converted into a community hall. The sacred buffalo herd, it is said, came to be relocated at the most sacred Bēragēṇi site some miles to the north, and soon after Sullivan's arrival, allegedly because Sullivan's camp followers started polluting the water channels (which had been

IMAGE 5.2: Inscription on an orthostat standing on the village green in Mīdēṇu

Photograph courtesy: Letizia Trinco.

hāge nīru—unpolluted water) used only on ceremonial occasions, dedicated to the use of sacred buffaloes and for the milking ritual.

Whatever that story may be, Sullivan seemed to have made some earnest efforts at the site he had acquired by August 1819 and towards erecting a real building there. Francis (1908) says, 'It was once an excellent little building ... well and substantially built.' Another writer, Alexander Morrison (2004), refers to its Doric pillars. Without going into more details, suffice it to mention that this abode of brick and mortar thereafter became a local landmark. Badagas started calling it Peddukal, a 'prominent landmark'. For

IMAGE 5.3: Reverse side of the orthostat

Photograph courtesy: Letizia Trinco.

them, it was a mansion of sorts. But unfortunately, there is no evidence whatsoever of Sullivan himself having nurtured any interest in this earliest European edifice in the district. Sullivan, as we know, soon established his base at Ootacamund in 1822, while his Kotagiri residence with its fine kitchen garden was gradually abandoned. This bungalow on the 'fine lawn-like piece of ground' and the 'handsome wood adjoining on the 5.25 acres of property' (Francis 1908, 325) were sold (*sic*) in 1880 to Badagas! How such a swapping of land and transaction thereof occurred is an unstudied factor in the history of the British-introduced land tenure settlement system in the District.

Sullivan's encounter with the Badagas was a fascinating one. The first official Medical Report in the hills appeared in June 1822 (Grigg 1880: 284–285). This identifies convenient Dimbaṭṭi (Kotagiri), prettier Kodamuḍi (Tūnēri Valley), and Sōlūru (possessing both these advantages) to the west of Ootacamund as suitable places for the settlement of Britons, and indeed to become the 'capital' of the Nilgiris. Shrewd administrator as Sullivan was, he evidently did not want to get into trouble meddling with these ancient Badaga habitations, instead opting for a long-abandoned dancing ground of the Todas and its vicinity in what is now popularly known as Ooty (see Frontispiece, this volume). Badagas called it 'Ottegemanda', to mean perhaps the common green intended for the performance of a particular dance, *otege*. This special Toda dance featured the 'swinging of the foot' in its performance (and is now largely forgotten). All early British records have almost correctly transcribed the name as something close to 'Whotokaymand'. But apocryphal versions of the original name continue to haunt the etymology—Utakamand, Hottegemund, Oatacamund, Otacamund, Oatakamund, Ootakumund, Whatakaimand, Whotakamund, Whotakay, Whotakaymund, Whotokaymund, Wootaycamund, Wotacamund, Wotokymand, Wuttacamund, Wotay! And the most ghastly version is the Tamil one: Udhagamandalam—when there was never a *maṇḍalam* here! Can anything be done to recover the original name in this Bicentenary period?

The actual dance meadows lay on the slopes of the present-day Breeks School, just above the Adam's Fountain (where Toda figurines can still be seen) at Charing Cross. It was right at the centre of a circuit of at least eight Toda hamlets of the past, although presently only two of them exist. The *kwasm* and *kon* in the ritual language of Todas, referring to this venue of dances, may be recalled here. More than just a dancing ground, the broad extent of Toda land in the Ootacamund basin was available to Sullivan, literally for a song!

Sullivan, now with great alacrity, began to envisage using the green expanses of this 'grand valley'. An evaluation of the land-tenure measures that Sullivan sought to introduce in the matter of what is called 'the proprietary rights of the Todas' is not intended in this chapter (see Chapter 4, this volume). But Sullivan, since then and throughout his career as the first administrator of the Nilgiris and later on as the Senior Member of the Board of Revenue of Madras Presidency, saw to it that Todas would not lose out on their traditional possession of land. He ensured persisting measures to safeguard their rights despite colonial inroads, trying to accommodate most of the Toda claims to the best of his discretion and authority. Apart from their ethnic and cultural uniqueness, the Todas also registered many benefits from landownership measures that Sullivan undertook on their behalf.

Sullivan's special ties with Badagas, cited earlier, caused a new kind of transformation in the socioeconomic realms of the area. He called their farming lands his 'Promised Land'. The readily available workforce that they represented and the appreciable skills they displayed in their small-scale agricultural enterprises, and above all, the vast extent of cultivable land, made Sullivan their great benefactor. Commercial farming, especially of European fruits and vegetables of all sorts, was promoted by Sullivan; more than that, modern husbandry methods that he introduced to Badaga livelihoods brought about an augmentation of the market economy which had now been fostered by the British. Potato and cabbage, with their Badaga names, made a remarkable entry into Badaga vocabulary, for while potato was simply called by a traditional term to mean a 'tuber', cabbage lacked any nomenclature. Innovative as the Badagas are, they coined a pair-word for 'cabbage', so that while potato was *gāsu*, cabbage was euphoniously called *gōsu*. Badaga cuisine without *gāsu–gōsu* became unthinkable, even till a mere generation ago.

Sullivan tried to argue effectively the case of Badaga land-use. In a note dated 3 July 1827, he stated very forthrightly, '… the first objects of my care and attention are the Native inhabitants of the Hills. I am extremely anxious that they should have no reason to regret the settlement of Europeans in their country….' He went on to demand magisterial powers for the revenue administration, '… effectually to prevent them from oppression'. In a similar vein, but in a more detailed manner, Sullivan, appearing before a select committee of the House of Commons in London (9 February 1832), made the same kind of representation. Expert buffalo-herders and swidden cultivators for centuries, many Badagas were now turning into commercial farmers who needed a boon—and Sullivan granted it. But within the next generation, later administrators had attempted to curb Badaga rights. A form of revenue settlement foisted on them caused no less a person than the Secretary of State, Sir Charles Wood, to issue a dispatch, dated 23 November 1864, in which he expressed his gratification at the result of this settlement and acquiesced in the restrictions now imposed on the Badagas (Grigg 1880, 324).

As the vagaries of their history would have it, the Badagas seemed to have slipped into a state of 'structural amnesia' during the British Imperial era. After abandoning their great pastoral past, as expressed in many of their ballads, for want of grazing areas, Badagas now started to construct a new worldview. Sullivan also probably had a role in the evolution of this new Badaga ethos. According to Ouchterlony's survey (1848), Badagas now had a total of 936 buffalo pens and 484 breeding huts, whereas Todas, a smaller community, had only ninety-two pens and ninety breeding huts. But since those days, the Badaga village landscape has totally lost both structures. Another vanished feature was their engagement in some sort of long-distance trade. Thomas H. Baber, the Collector of Malabar, in a note dated 7 June 1823, offered the interesting information that he had re-opened the road between the West Coast (at Calicut) and Nambalākōḍu (near Gudalur) after more than two decades of its closure. Considerable trade between Moplahs and Badagas had formerly been carried on via this road; however, that activity came to a halt when a Badaga trader was killed by a Moplah and, for fear of retaliation by Badagas, this road remained closed.

Frederick Price (1908, 294) also alludes to this trade route, as well as that of the Kannērimukku folk (mentioned above). Hockings has also referred to faint political ties that had once existed between the West Coast and the Nilgiris (1980, 43). Many such long-lost ties lay behind the grand metamorphosis of the Badaga culture that emerged in the aftermath of Sullivan's reforms and improvements, their early steps towards modernisation.

Sullivan's interaction with other indigenous people, like the various tribes of Kurumbas and Irulas, has neither become sufficiently known nor well-documented. Only the Revd. Hough (1829, 105) noted that the Kotas had already refused to forge any liaison with Sullivan, and this may have been so. There used to be a senior Kota priest and their chief of protocol, Kanagraj, who had been my classmate at the Mission School in Kotagiri for eight long years. He has always asserted that, unlike the Todas and the Badagas, the Kotas were never subservient to Sullivan. I have tried to share with him Kota insights from David Mandelbaum's research, but he could not care less about that. Instead, he used to insist with subtle humour that the Todas and Badagas were always mere greenroom boys for British performances! But I guess Kotas were able to perform their best in their own way too, perhaps with minimal regret because their various crafts were already crucial.

Among many other ardent enterprises of Sullivan, his obsession with having a lake at Ootacamund (see Plate 3) calls for some mention (although it was never properly evaluated). He dared to dream of carrying the Nilgiri waters down to Erodu in the Kongu plains. That dream came to fruition only after about a century and quarter, for the Bhavanisagar reservoir now remains as a grand monument to Sullivan's far-sightedness. (Badagas and Irulas had christened the confluence of these waters Rangasamudra, with the apex hill of the god Ranga towering above this sheet of water.) Why could we not name the dam Sullivan Reservoir?

The paths Sullivan tried to promote for the Nilgiris and their various communities were varied and many. Although ostensibly a colonial bureaucrat, he prophetically set his eyes beyond this orbit. While all roads led to Rome in its imperial times, all roads actually built under Sullivan's supervision led into the Nilgiris nearly two centuries ago (and have we embarked yet on any newer roads?). What does the future hold in store for the Nilgiris? Certainly there is ongoing sea-change in the demographic profile of the district. Would the Badaga cliché of yesteryears—'innocent times' (reminiscent of the dreamtime of many a preliterate society)—vibe with the new moral heterogeneity in our worldview? So, could a future anthropology of the Nilgiris chart a new destiny for its peoples?

Note

1. The original orthostat itself betrays some archaeological and anthropological significance. There is also an ancient rock art site nearby. The photos are courtesy of Letizia Trinco.

References

Francis, Walter (ed). 1908. *Madras Gazetteers—The Nilgiris*. Madras: Supdt., Government Press.

Grigg, Henry B. (compiled and ed.). 1880. *A Manual of the Nílagiri District in the Madras Presidency.* Madras: E. Keys, Government Press.

Hockings, Paul. 1980. *Ancient Hindu Refugees.* The Hague: Mouton Publishers.

—— (ed.). 2012. *Encyclopædia of the Nilgiri Hills*. New Delhi: Manohar Publishers.

Hough, James. 1829. *Letters on the Climate, Inhabitants, Productions, &c. &c. of the Neilgherries, or Blue Mountains of Coimbatoor, South India*. London: John Hatchard & Son.

M'Curdy, Edward A. 1830. *Views of the Neilgherries, or Blue Mountains of Coimbetoor,—Southern India. Drawn from Nature and on Stone by Captn. E.A. M'Curdy, 27th Reg. M.N.I.* London: Smith, Elder and Co.; lithograph by W. L. Walton

Morrison, Alexander. 2004. '"White Todas": The Politics of Race and Class amongst European Settlers on the Nilgiri Hills, c.1860–1900'. *Journal of Imperial and Commonwealth History* 32 (2), 54–85.

Price, J. Frederick. 1908. *Ootacamund. A History.* Madras: Superintendent, Government Press.

Shortt, John, and John Ouchterlony. 1868. *An Account of the Tribes on the Neilgherries, by J. Shortt… and a Geographical and Statistical Memoir of the Neilgherry Mountains, by the Late Colonel Ouchterlony*, John Shortt (ed.). Madras: Higginbotham & Co.

Further Reading

'Kotagiri', 'Ooty Lake', and 'Sullivan', in Paul Hockings (ed.), *Encyclopædia of the Nilgiri Hills*. New Delhi: Manohar Publishers.

6

Through Badaga Eyes

The Social Construction of a Cultural Landscape

Frank Heidemann

Viewpoints

When I was a teenager, I watched a sketch by a comedian on TV. He mimicked answers to a question about how to go from A to B in some fictive town. In sequence, he slipped into the roles of a car driver, a drunkard, a girl, and an elderly housewife, and described the route according to specific landmarks. The first one used petrol bunks, the second pubs, the third boutiques, and the last supermarkets. Later, as a student of social and cultural anthropology, I recalled this sketch and also tried to see the world from the point of view of my counterparts. Thus, as a postdoctoral anthropologist, I was not surprised that Badaga people saw things differently from what I was perceiving. This different view cannot, however, be presented as easily as that comedian managed. When Badagas see a particular temple, the narrative of the deity, her/his characteristics, and the relationship to other deities and the history of the temple will likely come to their minds. In Badaga-land there are many invisible boundaries, villages form named clusters, formal marriage patterns connect them, and a hierarchical system of councils and jurisdictions creates a distinctive order. In the next few pages, although I cannot go into details of this cultural totality, I will try to offer a glimpse of the logic behind what Badagas see when they move around the plateau. My focus will be on the Gauḍa (or Gowder), the largest sub-group (or phratry) in the more easterly part of the plateau, which I have visited annually since the 1980s (Heidemann 2006). Let us begin with an outsider's view.

A visitor to the Nilgiris can easily identify Badaga villages by their visual form (Heidemann 2017). The house lines of this peasant community look different from settlements that the state government has built for Scheduled Castes and Tribes (SC/ST), or from the labourer colonies of plains-people. Badaga villages, totalling about 400, appear as large bright spots in the middle of green tea fields or terraced vegetable gardens, and they contribute to the distinct appearance of the plateau. Usually, if the topography permits, entrances to the houses face the rising sun in the east, as it can be rather cold at an elevation of 1,800 to 2,200 m ASL. The houses are built in several long rows and are separated from their neighbours by an unbounded terrace that looks like a street. The old homes have a small veranda, although most of these roofed spaces have been turned into entrance rooms or bedrooms. Refurbished houses have often modified the construction, from a one-and-a-half-floor house with tiled roof to a two-floor residence with a flat roof. Former kitchen gardens have become construction sites, and also on the edges of many villages free-standing houses have risen, usually with two floors and an external staircase up to the flat roof. In spite of these recent changes, Badaga villages retain their distinct form.

From viewpoints and from roadsides overlooking any valley one can see several villages at a time. Often the distance between the villages is barely a few hundred metres, or at most a couple of kilometres. A visitor will see the difference between large and small villages, but the links between those villages, meaningful to Badaga people, will remain quite invisible. Conceptually the villages are linked by archaic kinship relationships, by a precolonial political system, by sacred rituals, as well as by a modern clustering of administrative wards and urban agglomerations. It is impossible to view these valleys and their villages through Badaga eyes, then, and for at least two reasons. First, the concept of *dārshan*, common throughout South Asian cultures for untold centuries, suggests an almost physical yet magical contact between viewer and object, and is of great importance in the religious context and beyond, especially when a worshipper is in the presence of a deity. Second, an outsider does not share the social, religious, and mythical concepts that Badagas have in their minds. Even within their communities there are many differences, so that the view of one person does not always match another's. But the knowledge of their myths, their old boundaries and jurisdictions, their kinship ties and religious institutions will help to see the world in a different way. The attempt to see the Nilgiri plateau through Badaga eyes might be intellectually unattainable, yet the attempt itself is worth the effort.

Legend

When I began research on the Badaga society in the 1980s, some friends told me on a bus trip from Kotagiri to Ooty: 'Now we come to a new region. Behind us is Poranganāḍu and this is Todanāḍu.' Later I learned that these were two of the four precolonial *nāḍus* (divisions), each having their own hierarchy of councils, their own jurisdictions, and specific rules for religious worship. In the eyes of local Badagas, their villages form clusters, each representing ancestral groups and kinship relations, while now overlain by modern administrative units like taluks, wards, or electoral divisions. Here, I shall summarise some of the precolonial dimensions that have been the foundations of Badaga society and give meaning to village clusters, from the people's point of view. I would like to demonstrate that status groups among the Badagas, kinship groups, marriage patterns, village and divisional councils, temples, and inter-ethnic relationships form a very complex yet coherent totality. There is no privileged point to begin with, but for convenience we might start with Badaga mythology. The myths are complex and exist in numerous localised variations. I shall stick to an abbreviated form in speaking of myths, which I recorded in Poranganāḍu during the 1990s (Map 6.1).

The Gauḍas, by far the largest group within the community, are descendants of 'Seven Brothers' who, it is said, came with their sister to the plateau. Their story begins in the eastern plateau, the

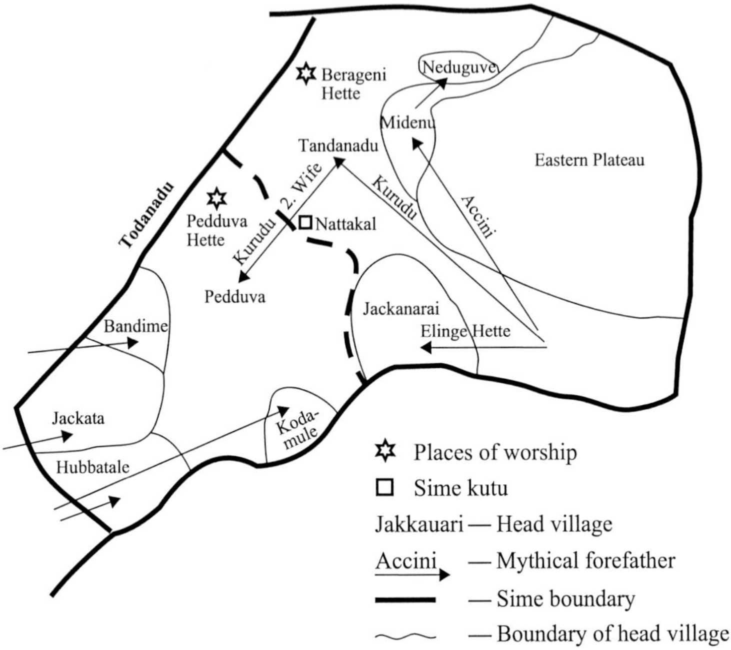

MAP 6.1: Map of the legendary migration in Poranganāḍu
Source: Author.

region which became Poranganāḍu. From Bēṭḷāḍa, where they camped, men went for a hunt, followed a deer, slept in various locations, and in their dreams learned about good places to build their homes. The eldest brother, Acciṇi, established Mīdēṇu, and from there the villages Kērukambe, Baṭṭakore, and Koṇakore were founded. The story of the second brother, Kuruḍa, who was blind but regained his sight after a prayer, is more complex. He went to Hāyūru, built a house and a Mahālingasāmi temple, and moved on to become the founder of Tandanāḍu. He left his first son behind near the temple, since a god could not be moved easily. Therefore, the Mahālingasāmi temple of Tandanāḍu remains near Hāyūru until today. The second son, Hāli, married three times. With his first wife he had three sons, Balajja, Dūmajja, and Mugilajja; they became the founders of twenty-seven villages in total (Map 6.1). With his second wife he had three sons, Guruajja, Hāliajja, and

Uppajja, whose successors founded eighteen villages around Pedduva, a separate territorial unit. The second wife died after the birth of her third son and Hāli married Māsi. She had three daughters and no male children, but looked after the sons from the second wife. In the myths, she is depicted as an ideal woman, and later was worshipped as Pedduva Hette, a Badaga goddess.

These and many other tales present a common theme: the first settlers brought a holy item, founded a temple, and built a ritual gateway, an *akka bakka*, which we find today in Mīdēṇu and Tandanāḍu, for example. These first settlements became the head villages (*ūru*) and their offshoot settlements are hamlets (*haṭṭi*) that depend ritually and politically on the head village. The male village founders are considered historical personages and are venerated as village gods, usually called Hiriyadēva. Therefore, each *ūru* has a Hiriyadēva temple and an *akka bakka*. Pedduva, however, seems to contradict this logic, because it was the home of Māsi, the third wife. A closer look at the legends offers some clarity, though. Hāli's second wife, whose existence was not known to the first wife in Tandanāḍu, had to come to Hāli's village for a ceremony. After a dispute with the first wife, she stole a sacred item from the temple and took it to her home near Pedduva. The third wife, Māsi, looked after her children and after the holy item; and therefore in Pedduva there was no male village founder, but an ideal woman has been worshipped. Māsi became one of the important Badaga goddesses; quite often she is said to be 'the sister of Bēragēṇi Hette', the most respected Badaga goddess (Heidemann 2021).

Bēragēṇi Hette's story links up with that of Kamajjāl, Hāli´s elder brother. Kamajjāl was in search of a bride, and found a family with two daughters but no son. He was promised to marry the elder one when she reached puberty, and meanwhile worked in the fields of his prospective in-laws. That elder daughter, however, eloped with a different man and so a conflict about the proposal arouse. The second daughter then offered to fulfil the promise of her elder sister, but Kamajjāl died before the marriage could be conducted. This is the basic plot of the first part of the Hette story, and there are numerous versions for the second part, in which she drowned or otherwise died, committed suicide or sati, or vanished in the jungle (Hockings 2012, 410–414). Common to all versions is that she embodied a perfect character and died as a virgin. Nowadays she is worshipped as the highest Badaga deity, Bērагēṇi Hette, in the village of Bērагēṇi, which is a part of the Tandanāḍu village cluster. Her temple lies in the eastern part of Tandanāḍu, and that of her 'sister' Māsi in the western part of the region, called Kaigāru. Other legends tell about the founding of those villages which established marriage relationships to the 'Seven Brothers'. I shall come back to them later. Beyond Poranganāḍu the story of the Seven Brothers continues, following the same themes of sacred items and Hiriyadēva temples and *akka bakka* ceremonial gateways. The former, the temples, stand for religious autonomy, the latter for an independent council with its own jurisdiction.

Councils

On the bus trip from Kotagiri to Ooty, or in Badaga terms, from Poranganāḍu to Todanāḍu, the main road passes Horasōle on the right side and Naṭṭakal on the left. These villages lie near the boundary between Tandanāḍu, where Hāli's first wife lived, and Kaigāru, where his second and third wives lived. Most Badagas consider Kaigāru, with its *akka bakka* in Pedduva, as a fully independent unit and pay little attention to the fact that the third wife, Māsi Hette, raised 'children of Tandanāḍu' there. When passing Horasōle, the last village of the Tandanāḍu cluster, there is a lawn on the left side of the road. My co-travellers hastened to tell me that this is the meeting-point of the nineteen head villages, or nineteen *ūru kūtu* (village councils). When I asked them for the names of all the head villages, their answers included the Gauḍa villages founded by the Seven Brothers: Mīdēṇu, Tandanāḍu and Pedduva, but also Neḍuguve as an autonomous offshoot of Mīdēṇu, and Hubbatale, an offshoot of Pedduva, and Jakkata, Bandime, and Kōḍamūle, all of which were founded by migration processes shifting from Todanāḍu towards Poranganāḍu, a kind of re-migration. The list of 'nineteen *ūru*' is still incomplete, though, because the head villages of Lingayats, the highest-status group, and Toreyas, formerly the lowest-status group, should be added. The only Lingayat *akka bakka* is in the east of Porangaṇāḍu, in Tūnēri, and four *akka bakka* of Toreyas are found in Sakkata, Bāmuḍi, Kengare, and Doḍḍamanehaṭṭi. Even so, the count does not reach nineteen. Some Badaga elders explain that once the other ethnic groups, Toda, Kotas, and Kurumbas, had *akka bakka* too, but all are forgotten now.

More than once, my Badaga friends told me that the nineteen-village council is the parliament and the 'high court' of Porangaṇāḍu. The 'supreme court' is in Todanāḍu, however: it is called the *nāku beṭṭa kūtu* ('four hills council'), in reference to the four regions (or *nāḍu*) of tradition. But almost all disputes in the eastern hills are settled here in the nineteen *ūru kūtu*. It is a historic place and one of high importance, but all that a visitor can see is a slightly sloping lawn and an old tree with a whitewashed stone revetment. Not all headmen can call for this meeting, but only those of the head villages where one of the first forefathers settled with a sacred item and where an ancestor temple and an *akka bakka* signify their religious and political autonomy. Before mobile phones became common, a crier used to walk from village to village to inform people about a meeting, which usually takes place on a Sunday afternoon. On such occasions, men in white dress and turbans get down from the bus at Naṭṭakal and walk up the steps to meet on the lawn. But such meetings are rare occasions nowadays.

More often than at the nineteen *ūru kūtu*, men meet at the council of a head village. Travelling on the plateau, visitors might see men debating in an open space under an old tree. The headman of the village and the main priest sit at a higher elevation while other men sit on the lawn. They discuss the organisation of temple festivals or solve probate disputes or take up family issues after a divorce. Women are conspicuous by their absence. The Badagas take pride in the fact that they do not claim dowry and allow remarriage for both men and women after a divorce, and maintain that they treat sons and daughters alike, that they vote for female candidates in public elections (thus Akkamma Devi was elected as the first Badaga Member of Parliament in 1962); nevertheless, they do not invite women to these *kūtu*. If a woman is called as a witness, she has to talk to a man, who repeats her words for the gathering. Usually, therefore, requests or complaints from women are presented by their male relatives.

Religion

Most Badaga women who pass the villages of Horasōle and Naṭṭakal might not think of the male-dominated council but of the female goddess Hette. She is the highest deity of all Badagas (except among the Lingayat subgroups) and is often called the foremother of the Badaga people. The term *hette* (foremother, grandmother, old lady) is no impossible contradiction for a childless person, since that term includes father´s mother's sister and mother's mother's sister. Unlike most goddesses in the Hindu pantheon, she is not ambivalent but only good, understanding, charitable, mild, and always helpful. The goddess Hette (irrespective of her particular form or location) is venerated in over ten temples in the Nilgiris, but Bēragēṇi Hette is pre-eminent. Her annual festival takes place in December or January and involves several processions. The meeting place of the nineteen villages becomes a religiously-loaded place, where Bēragēṇi Hette and her 'sister', Pedduva Hette, appear together. In the 1980s, I never heard mention of feminist ideas being associated with Hette, but in more recent years this connection could be sensed in the conversations of younger Badaga women.

The festival for Bēragēṇi Hette begins on a Monday and in the first few days, visitors come to her temple for worship. The visit of her 'sister' and the devotees from the Kaigāru area is scheduled for Wednesday. Thursday is reserved for a collective rest. All over Poranganāḍu people know the particular paths or roads that form the Hette trackway, and the annual processions create visible links between villages. They recall mythical motives and manifest a lived tradition of Badaga unity in a culturally diverse environment. On Friday her procession leads off via several villages of the Mīdēṇu and Tandanāḍu clusters to the nineteen-village meeting place, where coffee and snacks are offered. The 'two sisters' unite the areas that were divided in mythical times, Tandanāḍu and Kaigāru. This message is echoed in many small rituals at symbolically loaded places (although many details are not known to all participants). The main message and the division of Kaigāru and Tandanāḍu, however, are shared knowledge among Badagas.

The male deity Hiriyadēva has his temples in all head villages, and embodies success, authority, and power. With his strength and assertiveness he created head villages, it is said. Festivals for the first sowing of seeds and for the first harvest of field crops are celebrated in his name. His temple is connected to the *akka bakka*, and both confer on the head village its ritual, judicial, and political autonomy. Hiriyadēva is a man of action, while Hette is a woman of morality. He creates conflicts, territories, and boundaries, she pacifies and unites. Hiriyadēva and Hette stand for a complementary dichotomy of power and status. As in many national constitutions, the most powerful position, the Prime Minister, faces a higher authority, the President, who owns a higher status yet has less power. In the Nilgiris, the small group of vegetarian Todas have—in comparison to Badagas—a higher status, and yet the large group of peasants appears more powerful in secular matters. In such a way, Hette is benevolent and pure, she bridges the boundaries created by Hiriyadēva, and now is often mentioned as an emotional anchor for emigrated Badagas in the diaspora. As a Badaga who had been living in Chennai for three decades put it, 'Thinking of Nilgiri is thinking of Hette.'

Haṭṭi or Satellite Villages

One of the oldest roads in the Nilgiris leads down from Kotagiri on the plateau to Meṭṭupāḷayam (see Image 5.1) on the southern plains, to the final station of the Blue Mountain Express coming from Chennai. All visitors arriving from Tamil Nadu towns will pass through this riverside town towards the hills. From Kotagiri, there are frequent buses down this road, which descends slowly from Johnson Square to Donnington, first passing shops, offices, and hostels, and later tea gardens on either side of the road. After about ten minutes the local bus stops at Aruvēṇu, a polyglot bazaar with banks, local administration offices, bakeries, teashops, and a Gandhi statue. This little yet lively township is surrounded by residential houses, workshops, and industrial units. Several tea factories process the leaves delivered by Badaga small growers. Local people knew that in the valley east of Aruvēṇu there was a former British tea estate, Rob Roy, later owned by the Indian Spencer Company, that was bought by a Badaga and re-sold in small allotments to the local farmers—a postcolonial victory over the British past. West of Aruvēṇu, several hundred houses were built by Tamil labourers around three decades ago, in Badaga eyes a new development. Today, Aruvēṇu no longer appears like a Badaga village—despite being an offshoot of the head village of Jakkanāri (Figure 6.1).

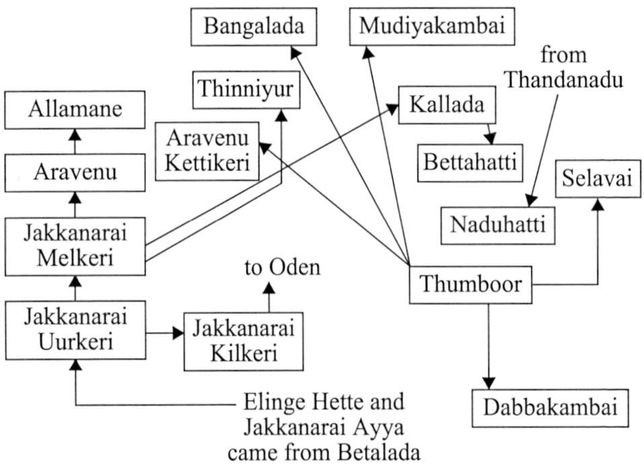

FIGURE 6.1: Migration within the territory of Jakkanāri head village

The story of Jakkanāri begins with the arrival of the Seven Brothers in Bēṭḷāḍa, their first campsite. They came along with their sister, Ēlingi Hette. Her husband was a stubborn man who quarrelled with the brothers. So when they decided to spread out, he preferred to stay on a nearby mountainside. His settlement became Jakkanāri, a head village with an *akka bakka* and a temple devoted to him, called, like other forefather shrines, the Hiriyadēva temple. The temple is in central Jakkanāri (on *ūru kēri*), and from here the upper village (*mēl kēri*) and lower village (*kīe kēri*) emerged. Today all form one physical village, although still with three parts. From the upper village the hamlets of Diṇṇiyūr, Kallāḍa, and Beṭṭaṭṭi, and also the hamlet of Aruvēṇu, were founded. From the villages of the Seven Brothers, a forefather built Naḍuhaṭṭi. Other families from the Todanāḍu region founded Tumbūru: thus Bengaḷāḍa, Muḍiakambe, Sēlavare, and Dabbakambe originated from this village of in-laws. One part of Aruvēṇu is still named after its village of origin, Kēti *kēri*. All these villages come under the jurisdiction of the Jakkanāri *akka bakka*. For the convenience of the visitors, its council meets near Aruvēṇu, as that is more centrally located than the head village on the ridge.

Once a year the people of Jakkanāri celebrate their unity on the occasion of a grand religious festival, with fire-walking. The smaller festivals for the village founder take place in the head village, while the festival for the god Jeḍeyasāmi is celebrated by all hamlets. Each year in February devotees form a procession and walk from village to village. They wear white clothes and walk in a long line headed by Ālu-Kurumba musicians (see Image 9.4, this volume), who live on the slopes towards Meṭṭupāḷayam town in the forested area. The procession is something to be heard and seen, and it marks the villages belonging to the *akka bakka* of Jakkanāri. Villages compete in offering a tea-break for the devotees or a supper, the only warm meal of the day when the devotees may eat. They sleep in local temples or schools, abstain from polluting activities, and keep to a minimal, always vegetarian diet. They walk to a stream in the former Rob Roy estate, the boundary of the village cluster, make a *puja* there, and then return to their hamlets. In Aruvēṇu bazaar, they perform a major dance. Traffic comes to a standstill; with the Ālu-Kurumba musicians in the centre, the devotees in their white dresses and white turbans, with ritualistic bamboos in their hands, form a large circle and dance. This aesthetic experience, a perfect dance demonstrating the presence and unity of the local people of Jakkanāri, comes to the mind of many Badagas when they reach the Aruvēṇu bus stop after a trip to the plains.

Kinship

In the late 1980s, I visited all 133 Badaga *ūru* and *haṭṭi* in Poranganāḍu and made a survey of the demography and the sociopolitical, religious, and legendary links of these residential units (listed in Heidemann 2006, 118–126). I was trying to find out about the migration of legendary forefathers, the connectivity of religious festivals, hierarchies of the council systems; but what my contemporaries were most interested in was their own kin relationships. I used to travel around then with my friend and field assistant, T. K. Mathan of Tumbūru. In the villages, the headmen and priests would ask him his father's name: he was a prominent Communist politician, and in most Gauḍa villages they knew about a sister of his grandmother, a cousin of his father, or a sister-in-law of one of his nine sisters, all of them married to different villages. In most instances there was more than one relationship traceable, and in a competitive way they might try to find a more direct family link. After this was done, we could begin with my census work. On the way back to Kotagiri, Mathan sat on the back of my motorcycle and pointed out the houses of his remote relatives in villages near the road. In the beginning, I was highly interested and impressed, but later became confused and finally lost in our question-and-answer game about who married whom. I needed a chart to follow his comments.

In Badaga eyes their mental map of the Nilgiri plateau is made up of such family links. But marriage relations are more than an individual matter: affinal relationships connect villages and structure the village clusters of the plateau. Badagas follow the basics of south Indian (or Dravidian) kinship rules. They should not marry the descendants of father´s brothers, but can marry from the paternal group of their mothers. In other words, marriage with parallel cousins (that is, children of father´s brother or mother´s sister) is banned, but alliances are permitted with cross-cousins (that is, children of mother´s brothers or father´s sisters). Therefore, the villages descended from the Seven Brothers cannot engage in affinal relationships with each other, but they can marry with the group of their sister, who founded Jakkanāri.

Further, potential marriage partners come from other regions of the Nilgiri, for example the founder of Tumbūru, who came from Kēti. T. K. Mathan is classified as a 'Kēti man' because this identifies his position within the marriage system. He and his sisters can marry 'from Jakkanāri' and with their 'fictive brothers'. It must be added that each status group of Badagas, that is, Gauḍa, Lingayat, and Toreya, marry among themselves (only the Hāruvas make a rather complicated exception, as they are an exogamous clan). A diagram can show the basic pattern of marriage alliances (Figure 6.2).

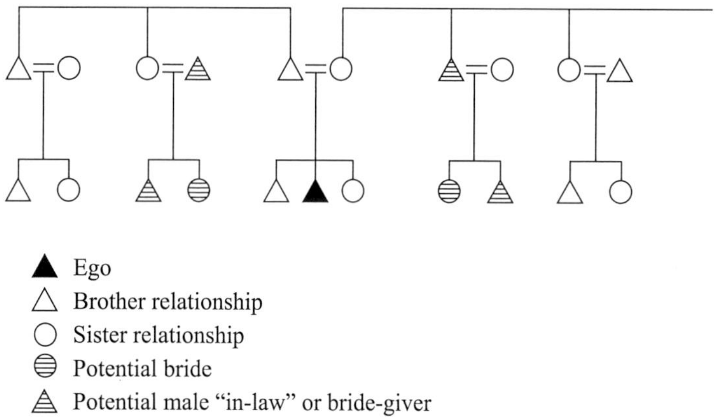

FIGURE 6.2: Badaga kinship relations

A Badaga person who travels on the plateau will make a distinction conceptually between those villages having either 'brothers' or potential marriage partners, and others belonging to groups without a family relationship. In their memories, there are a great number of ceremonies that people have attended, mostly weddings and funerals. On such occasions, kin relationships get performed and visualised. At weddings, participants line up for photo-shoots and create sociograms to be manifested with a camera. At funerals, male and female relatives of the bereaved line up and move in anticlockwise circles around the corpse to honour the deceased, but with meticulous recognition of the sequence of male generations. These events all happen in public places, sometimes even visible from the seats of a public bus. Like the legendary migration, religious festivals, and the structured councils, these acted-out kin relationships contribute to a mental order of the built landscape, an understanding of the social structure, and serve as a constant reminder of everyone's position in society.

Today's Landscape

Today, many details of the cultural landscape that I learned from elderly Badagas thirty years ago are scarcely known to the younger and often English-educated generation. Thus, a person from Tumbūru might not know whether the Seven Brothers actually camped in his village or in Bēṭḷāḍa. Nonetheless, the social system continues to operate in many fields. A young man from Tumbūru knows that he cannot marry a girl from the Kēti group, but can marry one from Jakkanāri. Moreover, he knows that a civil dispute can be handled by his village council, and that his case must be dealt with in the Jakkanāri head village before it can be discussed in the (superior) nineteen-village council. Every person in Tumbūru knows his village cluster, because the procession of the god Jeḍeyasāmi visits all those hamlets. And every Badaga knows that the temple of the most eminent Hette is in Bēragēṇi.

Over the last 200 years of colonial and postcolonial integration of the Hills into modern Indian life, much has changed (Hockings 2013, 192–210). The veneration of the god Jeḍeyasāmi began in the nineteenth century and his festival was celebrated on a grander scale from 1903. In the Aruvēṇu area, the main crops shifted from being grain and vegetables to commercial tea in the middle of the twentieth century. New systems of administration, taxation, communication, transportation, education, health maintenance, etc., were established. But the basic structures of the legends and of village councils, the veneration of Hette and Hiriyadēva, and the marriage rules remained little changed in all those years. The cultural landscape, sketched above, is just one side of the coin. The other side was created by modern state institutions.

The state's administrative system makes a distinction between private land and revenue land held by the state. There are special categories like forest, highway land, territories for wildlife, cemeteries, or areas protected for water reservoirs. For long the Nilgiris was divided into three taluks, but later, this became six. Public signposts inform residents about boundaries, town limits, distance to particular destinations, or direct them to a police office or the central Collectorate. Each piece of land is numbered and classified. A village administrative officer has access to the files, and it is his duty to update them. Thus, landownership is documented on paper. Today the administrators in the taluk office, the lawyer in the magistrate's, the engineer in the electricity board, policemen and medical doctors, and other 'modern' professionals and stakeholders are all more powerful than the 'traditional' headmen and priests back in any village. But the dichotomy of 'modern' and 'traditional' does not really reflect today's social complexity: many institutions and offices are neither one nor the other! The Young Badaga Association and numerous other *sangams*, most of them represented in the Federation of Badaga Associations, organise events, celebrations, and rallies and contribute to the public image of the lived space. Owners of bought-leaf tea factories put up the largest buildings in rural valleys and create singular, rather unsightly landmarks there (see Chapter 11, this volume). In the lower parts of valleys, where open water flows and wells never dry up, greenhouses emerged—sponsored by government loans. All these visible constructions and remembered events contribute to the cultural landscape of the Nilgiris. I wonder where the Seven Brothers would camp and what they would dream of were they to arrive here today.

Note

The author would like to point out that the many place names in this chapter, and throughout the book, all conform to the phonetic spellings given in the *Badaga-English Dictionary*; yet over the years, there have been many other spellings in local and administrative use that do not conform to Dravidian phonology, for example, Jackanare, Jackanairy, Jackawary, Jackanary, Jackanarai, Juckanairy, Jucnaury, etc. The etymology in this particular case is actually ‹ *jakkaḷu+(n)āre*, 'Nilgiri barberry+rocky hilltop', and was clearly descriptive of the place at the time of its initial settlement.

References

Heidemann, Frank. 2006. *Akka bakka. Religion, Politik und duale Souveränität der Badaga in den Nilgiri Süd-Indiens*. Berlin: Lit.

———. 2017. 'Social Aesthetics, Atmosphere and Proprioception'. In Alexandra Grieser and Jay Johnson (eds), *Aesthetics of Religion. A Connective Concept*, 457–464. Berlin/Boston: de Gruyter.

———. 2021. 'Ritual as Performed Constitution. Badagas in the Nilgiris District'. In Henry Albery, Jens-Uwe Hartmann and Himanshu Prabha Ray (eds), *Power, Presence and Space. South Asian Rituals in Archaeological Context*, 83–99. London: Routledge.

Hockings, Paul. 2013. *So Long a Saga. Four Centuries of Badaga Social History*. New Delhi: Manohar Publishers and Distributors.

Further Reading

'Badaga Family and Kinship', 'Firewalking', 'Seven Brothers' and 'Society. Badaga'. In *Encylopædia of the Nilgiri Hills*, Paul Hockings (ed.). New Delhi: Manohar, 2012.

Part IV

Arts & Crafts

7

Ancient Nilgiri Metallurgy

Sharada Srinivasan

The Nilgiris in the Iron Age

Although the Nilgiri region has received much attention for its natural heritage as a bio-diversity hotspot and for being the home of over a dozen indigenous groups, it also forms part of a remarkable, ancient cultural landscape which has yielded intriguing finds of metal artefacts that deserve looking at in terms of the history of technology. This chapter will explore some archæo-metallurgical insights from this region, based on finds of high-tin beta bronzes, and on the ancient local gold- and iron-working.

The Iron Age of peninsular and southern India is not thoroughly understood, yet the landscape is dotted with traces of stone circles, cairns, dolmens, and menhirs (see Plate 5, this volume), often with burials with rich finds of iron in them. Usually described as 'megalithic' (that is, big stones), it has been hard to gain insights into their chronology because only rarely have habitation sites been uncovered near cairns or burials. However, it is generally thought that the south Indian Iron Age or Megalithic dates from about the beginning of the first millennium BCE, continuing into the early Christian Era (ce).

Sundry nineteenth-century accounts by British collectors and surveyors in the area, such as Sir Walter Elliot and Commissioner Breeks (1873; see Plate 6, this volume), throw some light on finds of the so-called cromlechs and cairns of this region. The material culture unearthed from Nilgiri cairns not only included pottery, often with lively animal (Image 7.1) or bird finials, and iron

IMAGE 7.1: Terracotta vessel with dog finial, from a Nilgiri cairn

Source: Government Museum, Chennai; photo by Sharada Srinivasan.

implements, but also several examples of bronze bowls (Image 7.2) and occasional gold jewellery of a marked sophistication.

This chapter looks at some intriguing insights into the metallurgy of Nilgiri finds, particularly those of high-tin bronze. Insights can sometimes also be gleaned from the surviving crafts

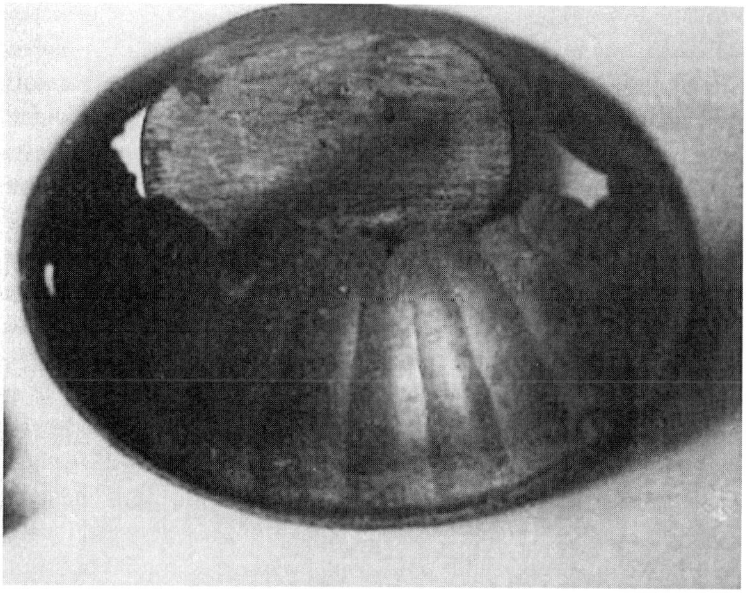

IMAGE 7.2: Fluted high-tin bronze vessel from a Nilgiri cairn
Source: Photo by Sharada Srinivasan.

and artisanal traditions in the area, such as the high-tin bronze-working traditions of the Kammalar people of Kerala, which were first documented archæo-metallurgically by me (with the late Ian Glover; see Srinivasan 1994, 1997a, 2016; Srinivasan and Glover 1995). The distinctive cultural landscape and aspects concerning metalcraft and metal usage have been the subject of recent anthropological and archaeological work by such scholars as Hockings (1975, 2013) and Kapp (1985). Preliminary field observations that I made recently, along with Digvijay Mallah, a native of the Nilgiris, on the relevant practices of several local communities are integrated here, as certain of their cultural traits seem reminiscent of the Megalithic remnants on the one hand and the trajectories of past migrations on the other. The archaeology of the Nilgiris nonetheless remains a complex and opaque field that immediately calls for more systematic study and excavations.

Megalithic High-Tin Bronzes: An Enigma of Prehistory

The bronze bowls and artefacts uncovered from Nilgiri cairns by Breeks and Metz one-and-a-half centuries ago were divided between the British Museum and the Government Museum in Chennai (some also went to Berlin). They comprise quite a sizeable collection, one that shows skill and a fair amount of diversity, ranging from deep concave and convex pottery shapes, with very thin rims (see Image 7.2), sometimes with a knob-base with rings and sometimes decorated with scroll patterns or floral or lotus motifs.

Some of the bronze has been analysed in a laboratory. In retrospect, the analyses by Breeks (1873, 63) of a few vessels from the Nilgiri cairns, showing them to be of 20–25 wt per cent tin-bronze, were in fact the earliest identifications made of high-tin bronze. Binary high-tin beta bronze refers specifically to an alloy of copper with a tin content approaching 23 per cent, which underwent heat treatment followed by quenching or rapidly cooling by plunging the item in water, thereby serving to optimise the formation and retention of a high temperature beta phase which is an inter-metallic compound with an equilibrium composition of 22.9 per cent tin in a martensitic transformation. The desirable properties of this alloy included increased tensile strength and tonality. Image 7.3 shows an extremely thin-rimmed fluted vessel made in Payangadi in 1991, with a typical structure of hot forged and quenched beta bronze, with the needle-like quenched beta martensitic phase matrix interspersed with islands of alpha phase with annealing twins. The microstructure of this vessel is shown in Image 7.4.

High-tin bronze came to scholarly notice after the archæo-metallurgical studies of finds of vessels and bracelets from Thailand. Rajpitak and Seeley (1979), who reported micro-structural investigations on Thai vessels from Ban Don Ta Phet to show that they were of high-tin beta bronze of about 23 per cent tin, pointed to the compositional similarities with vessels analysed by Breeks (1873, 63) from the Nilgiri cairns. Given that Southeast Asia has rich alluvial cassiterite or tin ore reserves, they speculated that such

IMAGE 7.3: Wrought and quenched high-tin bronze bowl made in Payangadi in 1991 with 23 per cent tin

IMAGE 7.4: Microstructure of wrought and quenched high-tin bronze vessel from Payangadi, with quenched martensitic beta phase and alpha islands with annealing twins (magnified 400X)

Source: Photos by Sharada Srinivasan.

examples might have had Thai origins, being items of maritime trade that reached the Nilgiris via the Palghat Gap. Leshnik (1974, 156) pointed out that such vessels were reported in association with other Megalithic sites in southern India, such as Mauli Ali, but postulated that they may have been imports from western Asia.

However, even if the questions of chronology and provenance remain unresolved, more recent archæo-metallurgical research and compilations by other scholars and I have shed new light, suggesting that not only were finds of high-tin bronzes fairly widespread in the Indian subcontinent, but that there have in fact also been robust surviving traditions for making beta high-tin bronzes, in southern India and in Kerala especially, with such marked similarities as to suggest long-standing continuities and a conclusion that Indian finds should not necessarily be regarded as imports (Srinivasan 1994, 2010, 2016; Srinivasan and Glover 1995).

Wrought and Quenched High-Tin Bronzes from Nilgiri Cairns, and Continuing Traditions of the Kammalar

My field and archæo-metallurgical investigations into vessel-making by the Kammalar community in Kerala began in the 1990s

(Ramaswamy 2004; Thurston and Rangachari 1909, 3, 106–140). As especially observed in the surroundings of Palakkāḍ (Palghat), at sites such as Payangadi and Pattambi, Kammalar were making vessels known as *ottupatram*, *odu*, or *talavettu* by a process of first casting a 23 per cent tin beta bronze blank and then extensively annealing and hot-forging the circular blank or ingot in alternate cycles; it was finally water-quenched, resulting in the retention of the beta phase (Image 7.5).

IMAGE 7.5: Quenching of a hot forged high-tin beta bronze bowl, Kerala

Source: Photo by Sharada Srinivasan.

The craftsmen used huge hammers known as *cērangulam* with five or six people hammering together, one of them holding the blank down on a bowl-shaped depression in a massive stone anvil (Image 7.6). They were thus able to forge extensively a vessel of 30 cm diameter, 1 mm rim thinness, and 8 cm depth, from a flat ingot of diameter 15 cm and 1 cm thickness. The micro-structural features prominently showed a two-phase structure of beta bronze with the retention of the needle-like martensitic beta phase interspersed with a few islands of alpha phase, showing annealing twins that bore evidence of hot forging (see Image 7.4). What was remarkable was the close similarity with the micro-structural investigations and ICP-OES analysis on half-a-dozen metal fragments from artefacts I sampled from the Nilgiri cairns and Adichanallur burials in the Government Museum, Chennai, originally from the collections of Breeks and Rea (Srinivasan and Glover 1995), which indicated that they were also made by a very similar process of extensively hot forging 23 per cent high-tin beta bronze, followed by quenching.

IMAGE 7.6: Hammering of annealed ingot, Pattambi, Palakkāḍ, Kerala
Source: Photo by Sharada Srinivasan.

As observed in 1990, after quenching, the surface of the vessels was finished in various ways by cold working, by heavily polishing to reveal a golden lustre, sometimes leaving portions of the blackened quenched surface for contrast, or sometimes finishing the surface of a vessel by mounting it on a hand-turned lathe and making concentric rings; which is remarkably reminiscent of the Nilgiri vessels (Image 7.7). In fact, the south Indian Megalithic examples

IMAGE 7.7: Decorations of concentric rings on beta bronze bowls made on a hand lathe, Payangadi, Palakkāḍ, Kerala, 1990

Source: Photo by Digvijay Mallah.

rank amongst the most heavily hot-forged high-tin bronzes found anywhere, as indicated particularly by three examples that were analysed and found to be of hot-forged and quenched beta bronze of around 23 per cent tin bronze. One is a fluted convex-shaped Nilgiri vessel in the Government Museum, with rim thinness at a fraction of a millimetre (Image 7.2); the second is a strainer with patterned perforations from Adichanallur, southern Tamil Nadu, in the same museum; and the third is an extraordinary piece excavated from Kodumanal by the State Department of Archaeology, with perforations in floral and bird motifs. The beta inter-metallic compound is found to be quasi-superplastic (Sherby, personal communication), that is, approaching the property of super-plasticity whereby it can take a high degree of hot formation, which may explain this degree of malleability at high temperatures. Craddock and Hook (2007) reported on some more martensitic quenched beta bronzes from Nilgiri cairns in the British Museum. They acknowledged the significance of my ethnoarchaeological explorations, pointing to the connections between the surviving tradition of making wrought and quenched beta bronzes in Kerala and the Nilgiri high-tin bronzes (ibid.), as against the earlier presumption that the Indian subcontinent would have been receiving its bronze technology or trading tin or bronze items from tin-rich Southeast Asia (Craddock, et al. 1989, 23).

Although tin ore deposits are scarce in India (Chakrabarti 1979), pre-modern exploitation of even these minor reserves cannot be ruled out. Indeed, the smelting of hard rock cassiterite in a secretive way by tribals of Hazaribagh was reported by Mallet (1974). Some early observations of Foote (1874, 140) pointed to minor finds of tin ore in the streams of the Dambal area in Karnataka, an area where alluvial gold washing was known to have been practised by communities of Jalagarus; there were unexpected finds too of old bronze smelting slag from Kalyadi in Karnataka (Srinivasan 1997b), all of which suggest that exploitation in antiquity of what might today be uneconomical deposits cannot be precluded. As pointed out below, I observed that the Beṭṭa Kurumbas near Gudalur were managing to extract gold from very minor reserves there.

It may be noted that the finds from the Adichanallur burials seem to include the most archaic shapes, with metal closely imitating terracotta prototypes, as seen in a well-rounded metal vessel with an elaborate finial with four animal figurines, similar to rounded terracotta jars with bird and animal figurines, including birds and animals such as leopards, cheetahs, dogs, and boars, that are found in Nilgiri cairns (refer to Image 7.1).

Finds of rounded terracotta jars with animal and bird finials seem to continue well into the first millennium CE, as seen in the excavation from a cinerary burial on the Paikara summit in the Nilgiris by Hockings (1975), which he dates to the eighth century, with finds of finials with a leopard and hoopoe. He also found a fine convex fluted vessel there (ibid., pl. VI, no. 45), which is very similar to another in the Breeks Nilgiri collection in the British Museum, both having the distinctive appearance of hot forged and quenched high-tin bronze. This Pykara 'bowl' appears, however, to have been the inverted ring-base cut from a much larger bronze jug—a piece of waste metal, in fact. The few links of a gold chain also suggest it was a 'token' offering of no real value.

While there is, on the one hand, a keen sense of observation of the flora and fauna of the forest environment, there is, on the other hand, evidence of links with a more cosmopolitan, urbane world. An intriguing dimension of the Nilgiri bronzes lies in some parallels to the material culture of the Gandharan region of the northwestern subcontinent, which suggest Hellenistic, Bactrian, or Persian influences. A high-tin beta bronze vessel with 21 per cent tin from the Iron Age Gandharan grave-culture, attributed to the early first millennium BCE, was analysed by me (Srinivasan and Glover 1995). Marshall (1951, 567) reported eight bronze vessels and mirrors with more than 20 per cent tin from the early historic Gandharan Buddhist Bhir mound at Taxila, datable broadly from the fourth century BCE to the first century CE. A granite vessel with a knob-base with rings, from Taxila, in the British Museum, was been compared by Glover (1990) to a Southeast Asian example from Ban Do Ta Phet with a knob that had been separately cast and added on, although this feature is best formed in two Nilgiri vessels that had been intrinsically hammered out from the ingot itself.

It may be mentioned here that even if some stylistic aspects came in from the Sassanian, Bactrian, and Hellenistic worlds, such as the fluted shapes and vessel stands, probably through a broader influence from northern India or via maritime Alexandrian–Roman contact, these need not preclude the possibility of an earlier familiarity with the working of the high-tin bronze alloy itself. In fact, there is an intriguing clue that suggests that the Greeks may have encountered the high-tin beta bronze alloy on the Indian subcontinent. Rajpitak and Seeley (1979) pointed to an account in Strabo's *Geography* (1950–1961, Book XV, 1.67) where Nearchus is said to have mentioned that Indians used vessels that broke like pottery when dropped on the ground: this may well relate to the intrinsic fragility of high-tin bronze. In the Hellenistic and Roman world, low tin bronze was more in vogue; it was of no more than 8–10 per cent tin, which was heavily worked into sheets (Welter and Guibellini 2004).

The Communities of Todas and Kotas, and Metal Usage

The important excavation by Hockings (1975) of a burial on Paikara hilltop yielded a likely date of the eighth century CE with similar finds of pottery and material culture, which he suggested showed the imprint of Toda and Kurumba culture. This could perhaps indicate longstanding continuities and practices of the hoarding of material culture. A Toda priest from a nearby *mund* with a temple (Taranāḍumandu) close to a cairn also showed me numerous examples of high-tin beta bronzes in his possession. A photograph by Tarun Chhabra (2015, 203) shows a Toda lady with a high-tin bronze vessel filled with honey. There are also examples in the Kota village of Kunda Kotagiri (Me·na·ṛ) and in Badaga homes that were used, for example, in wedding rituals. As I observed, high-tin beta bronze vessels were being made in Palakkāḍ as recently as 1998, and could well have come to the Nilgiris via the Palghat Gap or from the plains of Tamil Nadu. However, as seen in the Kammalar workshops, the *ottupatram*, *kinnam*, *odu*, and *talavettu* made of high-tin beta bronze undergo large-scale and organised recycling for remelting and reshaping of old vessels, and in fact survive in this way, since copper and tin have now become too expensive to allow the creation of the alloy afresh. This may also offer one explanation for why so many examples of high-tin bronze are found in the Nilgiris, where they may have been preferentially hoarded, or were better preserved due to burial or other cultural practices. Indeed, Kelly (2017) argued that communities such as the Todas may not have been as culturally isolated from neighbouring tribes or from the states on the plains as was previously assumed.

The Kotas are known for their blacksmithing skills, but there seem to be no memories now of their ever having worked with bronze. However, it was observed in Kollimalai (Kolmel), a Kota village, that they were at any rate able to do heavy smithing using massive hammers to make hoes, hammers of the kind that forging high-tin bronze would also require (*cf.* Image 7.6). The types of curved iron sickle that were still in use and locally made do recall shapes from Nilgiri Iron Age cairns. Hockings (2013, 137–140) showed that traditionally, the Badagas had depended completely on Kotas for their metal goods, artisans who were also their goldsmiths and silversmiths. One Kota blacksmith, Mr Kollan (Image 7.8), told me that in the past they would collect iron ore from the hilltops to smelt. This fitted with the account from Thurston and Rangachari (1909, 4, 8) that the Kotas initially used local iron ore, and only later imported scrap metal, that is, that they had previously smelted their own iron. John Sullivan had reportedly given them advice about this.

IMAGE 7.8: The blacksmith Kollan with a Kota priest in the Kollimalai smithy

Source: Photo by Digvijay Mallah.

Whereas blacksmithing is an all-male preserve (Image 7.8), pottery is exclusively a female domain amongst Kotas, unlike elsewhere in India (see Chapter 8, this volume). Past scholars have pointed out that the coarse wares of Kota pottery are not dissimilar to the pottery found from Nilgiri cairns (Hockings 1975; Naik 1966, 149).

Gold Finds from Some Nilgiri Cairns

The prehistory of the Nilgiris is intriguing, having yielded some of the earliest surviving specimens of gold jewellery from the subcontinent in the post-Harappan period. The rich but rare finds of gold jewellery from some Nilgiri cairns, demonstrating skills of stone setting, filigree, and granulation, items now housed in the British Museum (Naik 1966, 227–229), may date from the early or mid-first millennium BCE to CE, according to some commentators such as Knox (1985). The gold granulation technique in some of the earrings from the Nilgiris (Image 7.9), where tiny gold spheres were formed due to surface tension, may suggest Hellenistic influences, and it is found, for example, in jewellery discovered at Taxila. However, the use of gold micro-beads was also noted at much earlier Harappan sites such as Lothal and Mohenjo Daro. Hockings (1975) also reported the excavation of a tiny fragment of a loop chain from the Paikara cinerary burial (mentioned above), similar to the Nilgiri example in the British Museum.

Numerous nature motifs also seen in these gold finds from the Nilgiri graves and cairns include an intricate pendant with crescent moon motifs, a granulated flower motif (Image 7.9), and a peepul leaf motif. There has been speculation that the sophisticated finds from the Nilgiri cairns were imports (Leshnik 1974). Knox (1985), however, surmises that there is enough that is distinctive in them to suggest 'local' styles, and that they could probably have been made of local gold.

Certainly minor auriferous quartz deposits did occur in the Nilgiris and Wainad, as also attested by numerous old workings and evidence of gold prospecting in the Gudalur region. Hockings

Image 7.9: Earring with granulation, from a Nilgiri cairn

Source: British Museum (through Richard Blurton); photo by Sharada Srinivasan.

(2013, 18–19) points to evidence of old gold workings also between Ooty and Nanjenāḍu, along with references to a medieval town of gold or iron miners that was once protected by a mud fortress. Sewell (1882, 224) pointed to the evidence of old gold workings in the Nilgiri Wainad, with remains of slopes honeycombed with shafts and remains of old aqueducts. He also pointed to the gold workers of the Korumbar castes who confined themselves only to alluvial washings. I noticed the skill of Beṭṭa Kurumbas in gold washing in 1990, on a visit to the old Rosenmalai gold working near Gudalur, which has heavily worked auriferous quartz veins (visited with the help of S. Thekekara and geologist Dr Purushottam; see Image 7.10). According to hearsay, these were worked in the late eighteenth century. Here, beside a stream in 1990, some young Beṭṭa Kurumba children were rather skillfully extracting alluvial gold using large concave wooden pans (Image 7.11), and then using

Image 7.10: Old mine at Rosenmalai, near Gudalur, 1990

Source: Photo by Digvijay Mallah.

Image 7.11: Panning of stream gold by Beṭṭa Kurumba children, using mercury amalgam, near Gudalur, 1990

Source: Photo by Digvijay Mallah.

mercury to form an amalgam with the heavier gold particulate matter, which then settled into the bottom of the pan, the lighter material getting washed away in the stream. They then proceeded to extract the tiny pellet of mercury and gold amalgam from the pan, and put it on a leaf, which was then burnt away as the mercury sublimated, to thereby leave behind a tiny gold globule (Image 7.12). This activity was done illegally, the mercury was dangerous, and they were paid a pittance by gold shopkeepers for their efforts.

It is also interesting that Kurumbas mentioned that, according to tradition, it was the hill-tribes of the 'Veddahs' who had undertaken gold quarrying (Hockings 2013, 18; Sewell 1882, 224). The enigmatic Veddas are known to have been an archaic community who were also found in Sri Lanka and parts of southern India (but their name just means 'hunter'), and one might speculate that they were associated with the shared Megalithic cultures of the region.

IMAGE 7.12: Beṭṭa Kurumba children retrieving gold by burning amalgam, 1990

Source: Photo by Digvijay Mallah.

Pliny's first century CE account of 'gold from the country of Naris' might have referred to the land of the traditional Nair community of Kerala, that is, the region of the alluvial gold tracts of the Nilambur Valley below the Wainad Hills (Radhakrishna and Curtis 1991, 23). Hockings (2013, 18) suggested that the finds of Roman coins in a few burials of the Wainad and the Nilgiri plateau, as well as on the Coimbatore Plain, may indicate that traders were exploiting the local goldmines in the area.

The Hoysala kings of Karnataka were said to have 'ruled' the Nilgiris from around 1116 CE to the early fourteenth century, and may have been mining for gold in Wainad under Vishnu Vardhana (1108–1152 CE; Balasubramaniam 2009, 9). More concerted investigations into the old gold-mining activity of the region (Image 7.10) could illuminate these intriguing aspects.

Acknowledgements

The author is grateful for the support of the Institute of Archaeology, London; Government Museum Chennai; Dr Richard Blurton at the British Museum, London; Stan Thekekara and geologist Dr Purushottam during visits in Gudalur; and the support of Digvijay Mallah in exploring the Nilgiris.

References

Balasubramaniam, B. 2009. *Paame: The History and Culture of the Badagas of the Nilgiris*. Bangalore: Elkon India.

Breeks, James W. 1873. *An Account of the Primitive Tribes and Monuments of the Nilagiris*. London: India Museum.

Chakrabarti, Dilip K. 1979. 'The Problem of Tin in India'. *Man and Environment* 3, 65–74.

Chhabra, Tarun. 2015. *The Toda Landscape: Explorations in Cultural Ecology*. Hyderabad: Orient BlackSwan (Harvard Oriental Series).

Craddock, Paul, Ian Freestone, Lalit Gurjar, Lynn Willies, and Andrew Middleton. 1989. 'The Production of Lead, Silver and Zinc in Early India'. In Andreas Hauptmann, Ernst Pernicka and A. Gunther Wagner (eds), *Old World Archaeometallurgy. Proceedings of the International*

Symposium 'Old World Archaeometallurgy', Heidelberg 1987, 51–69. Bochum: Selbstverlag des Deutschen Bergbau-Museums.

Craddock, Paul, and Duncan Hook. 2007. 'The Bronzes of the South of India: A Continuing Tradition?' In Janet Douglas, Paul Jett and John Winter (eds), *Scientific Research on the Sculptural Arts of Asia,* 75–90. London: Archetype Publications.

Foote, Bruce R. 1874. 'The Auriferous Rocks of the Dambal Hills'. *Records of the Geological Survey of India* 7 (7), 133–142.

Glover, Ian. 1990. 'Early Trade between India and Southeast Asia—A Link in the Development of a World Trading System'. Occasional Paper No. 16 (2nd revd. ed.). Hull: University of Hull, Centre for Southeast Asian Studies.

Hockings, Paul. 1975. 'Paikara: An Iron Age Burial in South India'. *Asian Perspectives* 18 (1), 26–50.

——. 2013. *So Long a Saga: Four Centuries of Badaga Social History*. New Delhi: Manohar Publishers & Distributors.

Kapp, Dieter. 1985. 'The Kuṟumbas' Relationship to the "Megalithic Cult" of the Nilgiri Hills (South India)'. *Anthropos* 80, 493–534.

Kelly, Gwendolyn. 2017. 'Not Isolated, Actively Isolationist: Towards a Subaltern History of the Nilgiri Hills before British Imperialism'. *Modern Asian Studies* 51 (4), 1035–1069.

Knox, Robert. 1985. 'Jewellery from the Nilgiri Hills: A Model of Diversity'. In Janine Schotsmans and Mauricio Taddei (eds), *South Asian Archaeology, 1983,* 523–533. Instituto Universitario Orientale, Dipartimento di Studi Asiatici, (Series Minor XXIII). Naples: Instituto Universitario Orientale.

Leshnik, Lawrence. 1974. *South Indian 'Megalithic' Burials. The Pandukal Complex*. Wiesbaden: Franz Steiner.

Mallet, Frederick Richard. 1974. 'Geological Notes of the Northern Hazaribagh'. *Records of the Geological Survey of India* 7, 23–44.

Marshall, John. 1951. *Taxila*. Cambridge: Cambridge University Press.

Naik, Iqbal Abdul Razzak. 1966. 'The Culture of the Nilgiri Hills with its Catalogue Collection at the British Museum'. Ph.D. dissertation, University of London.

Radhakrishna, B. P., and L. C. Curtis. 1991. *Gold: the Indian Scene.* Bangalore: Geological Society of India.

Rajpitak, Warangkhana, and Nigel Seeley. 1979. 'The Bronze Bowls of Ban Don Ta Phet, Thailand. An Enigma of Prehistoric Metallurgy'. *World Archaeology* 11 (1), 26–31.

Ramaswamy, Vijaya. 2004. 'Vishwakarma Craftsmen in Early Medieval Peninsular India'. *Journal of the Economic and Social History of the Orient* 47 (4), 548–582.

Rea, Alexander. 1915. *Catalogue of the Pre-historic Antiquities from Adichanallur and Perumbai*. Madras: Government Press.

Sewell, Robert. 1882. 'Lists of the Antiquarian Remains in the Presidency of Madras'. *Archaeological Survey of Southern India, Reports, Old Series, Vol. I*. Madras: Government Press.

Srinivasan, Sharada. 1994. 'High-tin Bronze Bowl Making from Kerala, South India, and its Archaeological Implications'. In Asko Parpola and Peter Koskikallio (eds), *South Asian Archaeology 1993*, 695–705. Annales Acadaemia Scientiarum Fennicae, Series B, Vol. 271. Helsinki: Suomalainen Tiedeakatemia.

———. 1997a. 'Present and Past of Southern Indian Crafts for Making Mirrors, Lamps, Bells, Vessels, Cymbals and Gongs: Links with Prehistoric High Tin Bronzes from Mohenjodaro, Taxila, South Indian Megaliths and Later Finds'. *Journal of the Society for South Asian Studies* 13, 209–225.

———. 1997b. 'The Composition of Bronze Slags from Kalyadi in South India, and the Implications for the Problem of Tin in South Indian Antiquity'. In Anthony Sinclair, Elizabeth Slater and John Gowlett (eds), *Archaeological Sciences 1995*, 136–142. Oxford: Oxbow Books.

———. 2010. 'Megalithic High-tin Bronzes and India's Living Prehistory'. In Berenice Bellina, Elizabeth Bacus and Oli Pryce (eds), *50 Years of Archaeology in Southeast Asia: Essays in Honour of Ian Glover*, 260–271. Bangkok: River Books.

———. 2016. 'Tamil Chola Bronzes and Swamimalai Legacy: Metal Sources and Archaeotechnology'. *Journal of Metals* 68 (8), 2207–2221.

Srinivasan, Sharada, and Ian Glover. 1995. 'Wrought and Quenched, and Cast High Tin Bronzes from Kerala State, Southern India. Part I. "Contemporary Manufacture." Part II. "Scientific Investigations." Part III. "Historical Dimension"'. *Journal of Historical Metallurgy* 29 (2), 69–75.

Strabo. 1950–1961. *The Geography of Strabo* [*ca.* 30 BCE], Horace Leonard Jones and J. R. Sitlington Sterrett (trans.). London: W. Heinemann.

Thurston, Edgar, and Kadamki Rangachari. 1909. *Castes and Tribes of Southern India*. Madras: Government Press.

Welter, Jean-Marie, and Roger Guibellini. 2004. 'How was Roman Bronzeware Manufactured?' In Anne Lehoërff (ed.), *L'artisanat métallurgique dans les sociétés anciennes en Méditerranée occidentale. Techniques, lieux et formes de production*, 287–300. Rome: École française de Rome.

Further Reading

'Gold,' 'Megalithic Culture', and 'Prehistoric Plastic Arts'. In *Encyclopædia of the Nilgiri Hills*, Paul Hockings (ed.). New Delhi: Manohar, 2012.

8

Among the Gems from the Nilgiris, the Kota Women Potters

Marie-Claude Mahias

taṭ e·taṭ tïrsxo·ṛ θaṭ / aḍy e·y aḍy kuṟxuly aḍy //
Churning-vessel—which churning-vessel? /
Churning-vessel from the Kota village Tïrsxo·ṛ (Ticga·ḍ). /
Pot—which pot? Pot from the Kota village Kuṟxuly (Kurgo·j).//
Emeneau 1971, song 185, 7

The identification of the Kotas with pottery is inscribed in the language of the Todas, as Kotas are denominated by the term *kwï·f*, cognate with the Tamil *kuyavan* and Malayalam *kuśavan*, meaning 'potter' (Burrow and Emeneau 1984, no. 1762). Kota pottery, attested in their myths of origin and reported by the first Britons to survey the Nilgiris at the dawn of the nineteenth century, has always been recognised here as a women's speciality. It was deeply disrupted over the past two centuries, however, when brass and aluminium vessels became available everywhere and other potters arrived in the regional market too; to such an extent that, when I decided to go to the Nilgiris to ascertain the existence of women potters using the wheel, experts on the region and its inhabitants told me from the outset that Kota pottery belonged to the past. And yet I came across women potters ready to show their work to me, on my very first visit in 1991. This confirmed, first, that techniques cannot be grasped more easily than a myth or a kinship system. More importantly, I was faced at once with the question of the gendered division of activities and their asymmetrical social valuation, which is crucial for understanding any society.

A Unique Case in the World of Ceramics: Bodily Intelligence and Skills

Formerly, Kota women potters made, aside from tobacco pipes and oil lamps, mostly black culinary vessels: pots for cooking vegetables and cereals; dishes and plates for eating off; beakers and cups; jars for carrying or storing water; dairy vessels to keep and curdle milk, to churn yoghurt, to keep butter and buttermilk. Earthenware was widespread, with diverse shapes and sizes intended for specific uses. Vessels were and still are carefully kept (Image 8.1). In all villages, large cooking pots can be found, made three or four generations ago and still stored in the attic, the highest and purest part of the house. The quality of the pots, given their size and solidity, made some women famous and long

Image 8.1: B. K. Madi, proud to show her pots, at Kina·ṛ, 1992
Source: Photo by Marie-Claude Mahias.

remembered by other villagers. Even when the market demand vanished due to economic and social changes, the quality of Kota pottery was never questioned.

The pots still being made today are far fewer and less diverse than they used to be. Everywhere, the women potters say that they do not make vessels as large as they used to, nor the milk vessels with an elongated neck, which required a greater degree of proficiency. The decline in cattle herding and the sale of milk, among both Kotas and Todas, has eliminated the need for most dairy vessels. Only small pots (*tat* and *mu·g*) are still in use today for household milk, for butter and buttermilk processing (Image 8.2).

IMAGE 8.2: Kota-made butter pot on top of a milk pot, carried by a Toda man

Source: Photo by Jacques Millot, 1951; collection of Musée de l'homme, Paris.

Apart from those of the religious leaders, meals are cooked and served in aluminium or steel vessels. On ritual occasions, when larger cooking pots are needed, old ones get reused, something that would not have been allowed earlier. In contrast, inevitable garden pots, vases, and cash boxes have been imposed by development projects in response to a presumed market demand.

In this rainy region, with two annual monsoons, pottery-making has always been seasonal and secondary to agriculture. It involves several operations: extracting and pounding the raw materials on large stone slabs; kneading and moulding lumps of clay; throwing of a preliminary shape (*ébauche*) with the rim, neck, and shoulders completed; after partial drying, enlargement by means of wooden beaters and granite counter-beaters, in order to shape the convex bottom and the rounded belly; burnishing or slipping; thorough drying for several days; then firing in a shallow pit (by open firing), and smoking to blacken the pots (see Images 8.3a-e).

Kota potters shape a preliminary version from a lump of clay centred exactly on the wheel-head by using kinetic energy, in the same way that all other Indian wheel-potters do—a step that assures a true throwing. Unfortunately, this fact has not been widely recognised or has even been denied, this being the exceptional case of a process with the throwing being done entirely by women. Elsewhere in South Asia, women from all potter castes are not allowed to throw on a wheel. The identification of the operation and of the tool has often brought into play ideological arguments because, in the world of caste organisation, the throwing and the wheel are thought to go hand-in-hand with a personal qualification and a social superiority, in terms of both caste and gender. We must therefore briefly clarify both aspects of the question: the way of shaping and the tool, that is, the throwing and the wheel (analysed in detail in Mahias 2002).

The defining criterion of throwing accepted today was formulated over seventy years ago: 'In pottery manufacture the function of the wheel is to supply centrifugal force to a lump of still plastic clay accurately "thrown" on its centre' (Childe 1979 [1954], 195). The energy that shapes the clay does not come mostly from the potter's upper muscles, as in other methods of shaping, but derives from the movement of the tool. Compared with other methods (pressing, scooping, coiling, moulding), throwing constitutes a specific operation, which does not necessarily change the operational processes but entails breakaways situated on several

A: Pounding the clay B: The crucial operation of centring the lump of clay on the wheel-head

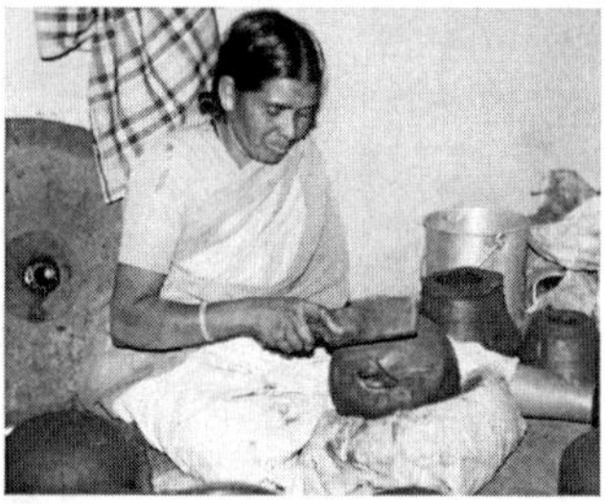

C: Shaping the rim of a cooking pot D: Beating to close the bottom and shape the rounded belly of a cooking pot

E: Beating and burnishing half-dried pots

IMAGES 8.3A–E: The main operations performed by Sintamani and Babiamma (in Ticga·ṛ)

Source: Photos by Marie-Claude Mahias.

levels: in the very principle of functioning, in the psychomotor skills, in the conceptual patterns and cultural representations.

Furthermore, throwing leads us to distinguish between two categories of tools, with a similar function but a different functioning: turntables and wheels. In accordance with the principle that the tool really exists only in the gesture which renders it effective (Leroi-Gourhan 1965, 35), the identification of the wheel relies not upon the morphological features of an object classified on some museum shelf (as has been the case for a long time), but upon the way the object is used. One methodological outcome is that the identification of the operation must come first, and results in the identification of the tool. This position was anticipated by George M. Foster (1959), who clearly distinguished the turntables—rotating devices that do not allow throwing a lump of clay—from the wheels, whether simple or double, that let the potter throw part or the whole of any vessel. Any device used for pottery throwing should therefore be called a wheel, whatever its shape and means of motion.

It is found that four kinds of wheel are used in India: a pivoted spoked-wheel, a pivoted block-wheel, a socketed spoked-wheel, and a socketed block-wheel. All are single wheels, spun by the potter himself with the help of a wooden or bamboo stick, or else by a helper (Saraswati and Behura 1966). Kota potters use a pivoted block-wheel, which varies in shape and installation between villages. In all cases the wheel is spun by an adult, a man or woman. Both hands work together, the left one pulling towards oneself and the right one pushing the movement towards the right, to spin the wheel anticlockwise. A helper (just like an electric motor), giving a continuous impulse, allows for a light, small-diameter wheel, with low inertia (see Images 8.4 and 8.5). This kind of wheel is used by several potters elsewhere, in Tamilnad, Kerala, and Odisha (Behura 1964), but among those groups it is menfolk who shape the clay while a women or man spins the wheel. In those cases, no one calls into question their qualification as wheel-potters; so why deny Kota women the knowledge of throwing and the wheel? How could we fail to see in it an ideological bias, the cultural valorisation of the wheel in the world of castes being incongruent with an operation performed by women, moreover 'tribal' ones?

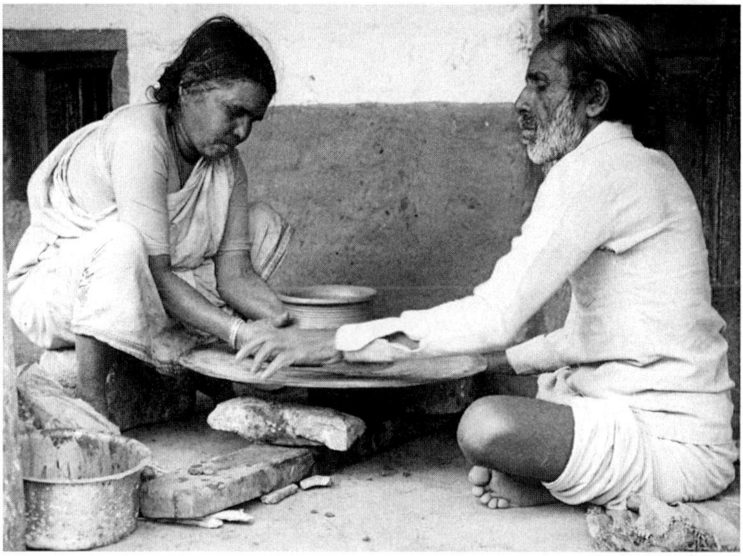

Image 8.4: Janaki Madi and her husband, the blacksmith Mindayan, working together, Ticga·ṛ, 1991

Source: Photo by Marie-Claude Mahias.

In 1993, women potters in Ticga·ṛ village acquired a crank-handled wheel and an electric one, and had no problem in learning how to use them. This proves (were it still necessary to do so) that Kota potters had already developed all the specific skills required for throwing (gestures, postures, and combinations of motor skills). They had embodied both expertise and explicit knowledge. They had generated what cognitive scientists call specialised 'cognitive patterns', which enable one to adjust to any kind of wheel or new situation in an efficient and creative way.

The functioning of the crank-handled wheel rests, like that of all earlier wheels, on the collaboration of two people. It demonstrates that collaboration, far from preventing the evolution, is a feature of a technical line which is, by itself, neither archaic nor static. This modern tool constitutes a true 'innovation',

IMAGE 8.5: Kota potters in Me·na·ṛ, 1992

Source: Photo by Marie-Claude Mahias.

as delineated by sociologists (Akrich, et al. 1988), in that the relation beween the initial project and its implementation is the outcome of a collective action that has enlisted potters, a former schoolteacher-turned-potter, a national planters' association, a development agency, an engineer, a mechanical workshop, and a bank; and yet it remains in the tradition of wheels spun by an assistant. Indeed, this category of wheel is also found in China, in Cambodia with Vietnamese potters, in Burma, and in Mauritius.

Kota pottery has sometimes been judged as being of poor aesthetic quality because it lacks ornamentation. This is to miss the beauty of old, utilitarian pots: the smooth lines of thrown items, the gloss of the black bellies obtained by patient burnishing and by smoking, the solidity achieved by tiresome pounding, long burnishing, and rubbing with castor oil, to make them 'as strong as copper'.

It is time to recognise the great expertise of Kota potters, and to give these 'tribal women', women despised by local administrations but in no way 'backward', their rightful place in the history of ceramics and technology: the place of wheel-potters, a case unique in South Asia and rare in the world, of women who master a whole process with throwing, and whose exceptional achievement forms a challenge to the statistical understanding of human activities and societies. Kota women potters deserve a formal and official award, not to be frozen in an old-fashioned craft to be preserved as such, as if in a museum, but to promote them, to give them the means to advance with their own creativity. Imagine them if in Japan, where no doubt they would already have been honoured as Living National Treasures, preservers of intangible cultural property, and where they would be funded and encouraged to transmit and even enhance their special skills and knowledge. One might dream that had these women been invited there, they could admire other black-coated bowls as experts, discover the *raku* technique, and exchange tips with ceramicists for whom smoking is an art.

Searching for a Market

It is true that Kota potters are not unknown, and have been able to attract the attention of several handicraft organisations: the Khadi Village Industries Board opened a Centre for Red Pottery, which worked in Ticga·ṛ village from 1962 to 1968. This institution believed that a 'modern' training must include glazing with bright colours and firing in a kiln, and that a qualified craftsperson could only be a male. The Office of Rural Development provided a wooden wheel reinforced with iron strips and an iron pivot in Kina·ṛ village, and a wooden wheel with a cast-iron tripod in Me·na·ṛ, which replaced the mud wheels with stone socket and pivot formerly made by the potters themselves. More recently, the Home Science Department of the United Planters' Association of Southern India (UPASI) introduced other kinds of wheel in Ticga·ṛ village: a crank-handled wheel in 1991–1992 and an electric wheel in 1993. Between 1992 and 1996, it also set up several programmes to develop the activity, ensuring potters of a market and the transportation of their products. On the cultural institutions side, a potter from Kurgo·j was invited to visit by the Indira Gandhi Manav Samgrâlaya in Bhopal. The director of the Government Museum took black and red pots as well as small statues from Ticga·ṛ for an exhibition planned in Madras in 1996. Potters have also taken part in exhibitions like the Tea and Tourism Festival and the Craft Mela, which are organised in Ooty every year at the height of the short tourist season.

An NGO (non-government organisation) even published a book on Kota pottery. Not so long ago, three young members of this NGO were interested in beekeeping, and brought in a Danish consultant (Mogens Jensen), a recognised expert on Asian beekeeping. They had for a while been searching for clay to coat the inside of hives in order to maintain a uniform temperature, and to protect the bees against the rains as well as against predators; to no avail. They were therefore convinced that no clay was available in the hills. But great was their astonishment when, in 1996, I lectured at their residence, showing slides and explaining in detail the whole process of pot-making, as well as the unique skills of Kota women, which were then unknown to them. My first article on the subject had already been published in 1994. At that time they nurtured an open hostility towards anthropologists and anthropology, although knowing very little about the subject. My presentation probably aroused their interest, though, as in 2001 the Keystone Foundation published a book pretending to be a 'first time documentation on the Kota black pottery'. They had managed to obtain financing for some research work and this was done by a potter, the only true author of the book. His description is strictly accurate, done by an authentic craftsman and no doubt a knowledgeable and open-minded person. Contrary to most Indian scholars, archaeologists, or curators, he has no hesitation in identifying throwing and the wheel, and also knows how to appreciate the qualities of a pot, the thinness of its walls, lightness, and solidity.

It is interesting that the study could be carried out in Kurgo·j (though unfortunately only its 'administrative' name was used), because the pottery of each Kota village shows distinctive characteristics. Observations confirm that in that village, thought to be the most committed to the old ways, and where relationships with neighbouring Toda hamlets have been maintained for the longest time, younger potters have taken over after the elders died, as had been foreseen (Mahias 2011, 194). These potters are true experts, meticulous, performing the firing in two phases, with careful lay out of the raw pots and fuel, and incisions on the body of the pots, all of which show that nothing has been forgotten or neglected in the technical process. They may have learned this in another village, as I was indeed told by one of them who had learnt with her mother in Me·na·ṛ. This village was already famous for its good potters in 1949, for Mandelbaum was informed that one of them had been invited to Kolme·l village to make pots for a new religious leader there. The book referred to also bears testimony to the celebration of De·rv in Kurgo·j in 1998, whereas it had been suspended for several years due to internal problems in that village.

Unfortunately, the same book ends with the recommendation to modernise the production with the glazing of items. This is exactly what Europeans had already done in the nineteenth century when, paying attention only to decoration, they had rated this pottery as coarse. Actually, glazing was already part of the training imparted to Kotas in the 1960s, as evidenced by several glazed pieces that were kept in the workshop of the trainer. But it is known that glazing needs a high temperature for firing and a special firewood-consuming kiln, which hardly complies with modern technical and ecological requirements. Concerning market access, it was already an aim of the projects run by UPASI in the 1990s, which were meant to ensure a stable income for the women. Despite their good intentions, those programmes had the effect of turning these women into workers, dependent on the market and bank loans, imposing an intensification of the work, and giving priority to quantity over quality. They also brought about a division of tasks, leading to tedious work and a de-skilling of most potters, thus preventing the enhancement of personal skills (Mahias 2011).

Let us now turn our attention to ritual pottery.

To Shape the World: Ground, Women, and Gods

Kota pottery, though deeply disrupted nowadays, has certainly not disappeared. It is still alive, preserved in several calendrical festivals and lifecycle ceremonies that require new vessels. In most cases, it is a matter of cooking food of the past—millet (*Panicum miliare*) and various beans—in earthenware, or of serving special dishes, first offered to gods and then shared between all members of the patriclan eating together from the same plate. Commensality expresses and reinforces the unity and solidarity inside and between lineages, as well as overcoming conflicts.

Two ceremonial occasions require not only the use but also the making of earthenware: De·rv or Kamtra·yn De·rv, the great annual ceremony after the December–January new moon, when gods are invited to reside in the village and are renewed; and the choice of a new religious leader (*mindga·no·n*) who, as the guardian of tradition, may use only earthenware, which his wife must be able to make herself. Although men insist on downplaying pottery as external to the ceremony, the ritual period of De·rv is the great event which women potters enjoy talking about. During that time they have other parts to play, as women, spouses, and daughters, but it is also as potters that they take an active part in De·rv, combined with the emotion of family gatherings, and the excitement of dancing and music late into the night.

Certain ritual activities require new pots, made under very strict conditions of purity, or reserved solely for this occasional use, because some pots get taken within the courtyard of temples or even inside temples, and everything must be renewed and pure during that time: fire, the temple roof, women's hairdo, food. Thus, after an epidemic hit Kolme·l in 1924, the large pots for cooking ceremonial food became a crucial issue in the factional split between those who wanted to stick to old gods and old ways of worship, and other Kotas who advocated accommodating new gods and letting things evolve (Mandelbaum 1941, 234). But no less than vessels, their manufacture is part of the ceremonial activity of this ten-day-long ritual session, and it goes on for six days, each day being more or less devoted to one operation of the process. In no way is it an individual matter: it starts after the cleaning of houses and the ritual lighting by churning of a new fire inside the house of each religious leader, which calls forth gods in the village. Each operation of the process begins with gestures of purification, bearing on persons, materials, tools, and should be done at the right moment and the right place. Extraction of clay, like fetching water or collecting firewood for the collective cooking, leads to long processions preceded, accompanied, then followed by a group of musicians. They are headed by the priests' spouses (*mindga·no·l*), followed by the diviners' spouses, and the spouses of elder ritual specialists, dressed in their white cotton dress (*ki·r* and *muṇḍ*) with their hair wrapped around a bunch of fresh *mandu·* leaves (*Atylosia trinervia*). The pounding of clay compels the participation of all women of the *ke·r*, a territorial unit corresponding ideally to an exogamous patriclan. Pottery operations thus stage the hierarchy of ritual and social functions, the successive generations, the different lineages, and the solidarity required between all women in each patriclan.

Furthermore, the day of 'opening' temples starts with a morning dance by the women (Image 8.6), then the cleansing and purification of the temples by the elders. Later, two women, elders' wives, bring a small lump of clay thrown as if for a bowl, and called 'clay of the nose' (*mu·kman*), to a ritual specialist of their clan or to the religious leader, who takes it into his temple—as happens

IMAGE 8.6: Potters are among the best dancers to honour their gods (Ticga·ṛ 2008)

Source: Photo by Marie-Claude Mahias.

in Ticga·ṛ and Porga·ṛ villages. Two days later, in the morning, the elders light a fire inside these temples. Formerly, when the temple and the smithy were one and the same, they would do some ironwork there. To this end, it was up to the religious leader to shape the 'nose' (*mu·k*), that is, to shape the clay nozzle to the end of the outflow pipes of the bellows. Nowadays he may just put the piece of clay in the temple, which nonetheless reminds people of the time when, as Kotas say, gods dwelt in the smithy.

To sum up: during the whole De·rv ceremony, women potters do their work in the heart of the village, inside the house of the religious leader, and in the higher and purer part of the village too. Only the earthenware may contain the materials of purification (water and cowdung), the component parts of gods' images (clarifed butter, silver coins), and the food cooked by men in the temple courtyards and then shared out among all families. Although ignored by men, pottery work must be added among the most important and beneficial elements that contribute to making the gods, just like people, music, dance, food, and purity (as listed in Wolf 2005, 154). During that time, what is important is not the aesthetic quality of the pottery made, but the consistency between the different elements of its manufacture: the crux being that the right person, socially approved, does what she has to do in the appropriate place and at the prescribed time, and that everything done contributes to honouring the gods. Earthenware and women potters play a crucial role in the course of these ceremonies, which are considered essential to the harmony and continuity of Kota society (see Image 8.6).

Pottery was linked with the learning and embodiment of other social roles. To know pottery was to not only master material processes, but also to become an adult woman with a particular place in a singular society and to know all of its rules. Potting stemmed from a personal inclination, a familial apprenticeship, and a clan membership, thus weaving together individual, familial, and broader social histories.

The Kota social norm is for women to be able to make pots. This ability is a part of feminine identity as it is culturally defined and prescribed, just as the ability of men to be blacksmiths is regarded as natural. Formerly, any man who decided to found a distinct lineage had to be able to build a house and to forge a new spear in the temple of his patriclan. Other crafts also show a gender distribution, but only pottery and ironwork which, according to an origin myth, were taught by the civilising hero Kitu·rpayk (Emeneau 1944), are especially valued, and have (or had) their place amidst the rituals of the annual ceremony of De·rv. These crafts are at the heart of the Kota representation of the relationship between men and women, between human beings and gods, and of themselves as a distinct social entity. However, both activities are not in a symmetrical relation. Once, when the smithy and the temple were one, women were not allowed to enter it, as they should neither see what men do nor where they go, when horns are blown in the middle of the last night of De·rv, a time when the divine presence is felt most intensely. Following the construction of permanent temples, the smithy has been separated, but the entrance to the workshop remains restricted for women, whereas anyone can easily watch potting.

In modern times, the skill of women potters is more crucial to the ceremony than that of the blacksmiths. The ritual activity of ironwork seems to have disappeared, even where good blacksmiths have a workshop. This is at least the case in Kolme·l where 'the memory of the primitive smithy is now represented in each temple by three stones [...]. No activity other than lamp-lighting and praying (briefly) takes place in the temple nowadays' (Wolf 2005, 188). In contrast, pottery remains in the ritual more concretely than ironwork, even if a sham has sometimes been perpetrated. The presentation by the women of the 'clay of the nose', which finds its way into the heart of the temples to activate the fire, is the only gesture that recalls the earlier affinity between temple and smithy. Whereas everything seemed to separate the crafts of each gender—smithy and pottery—this gesture suggests that men and women are complementary when it comes to making gods.

This pattern gives Kotas a unique place in the range of social and imaginary human constructions. Smithy and pottery have indeed been the two great arts of fire, whose result is always uncertain, and for that reason involves mystery and magic. The idea that technical processes and their results play a mediating role between the terrestrial, aquatic, chtonian powers on the one hand and supernatural powers on the other, is widespread. In preindustrial societies worldwide, relations between blacksmith and potter have often been thought of together: as joined or opposed, ranked or on equal terms, but never indifferent (Lévi-Strauss 1985). In this sense, Kotas offer a remarkable variant of this relation, in which both crafts are socially opposed, assigned exclusively to one gender and invisible to the other, but combined to reach and create supernatural powers.

Epilogue

Closely linked with the foundations of Kota society, pottery is also tied in with mutations that have changed the region. But how can we consider reducing it merely to a narrowly commercial activity, taken out of its sociocultural significance and thus devoid of meaning? Kota pottery was valued outside as well as inside the community. Its commodity value has collapsed as the market for utilitarian earthenwares keeps shrinking. Elsewhere in the world, singular artistic creations perpetuate ceramic art. It is inside Kota society that a new valuation of women potters and their work must be looked for. What, in the modern world, may give them joy and prestige, commensurate with their traditional roles? What is the motivation of potters in Mena·ṛ to continue pottery, even though De·rv has not been celebrated there for many years? It is up to the Kotas to decide. No doubt the women will find, in their society and their imaginary, resources and means to maintain and transmit their craft, if freedom to develop their imagination and creativity is ensured.

Acknowledgement

This short account is dedicated to the memory of T. R. Lakshmanan (1940–2005).

References

Akrich, Madeleine, Michel Callon, and Bruno Latour. 1988. 'A quoi tient le succès des innovations. Premier épisode: l'art de l'intéressement'. *Annales des Mines* 11, 4–17.

Behura, Nab Kishore. 1964. 'Social and Cultural Aspects of Pottery in Southern and South Eastern India'. *Bulletin of the Anthropological Survey of India* 13 (1–2), 114–123.

Burrow, Thomas, and Murray B. Emeneau. 1984. *A Dravidian Etymological Dictionary*. Oxford: Clarendon Press, rev. edn.

Childe, V. Gordon. 1979 [1954]. 'Rotary Motion'. In Charles Singer, et al. (eds), *A History of Technology*, Vol 1, *From Early Times to the Fall of Ancient Empires*, 187–215. Oxford: Clarendon Press.

Emeneau, Murray B. 1944. *Kota Texts, Part One.* Berkeley and Los Angeles: University of California Press.

____. 1971. *Toda Songs.* Oxford: Clarendon Press.

Foster, George M. 1959. 'The Potter's Wheel: An Analysis of Idea and Artifact in Invention'. *Southwestern Journal of Anthropology* 15 (2), 99–109.

Keystone Foundation. 2001. *Kota Pottery, a Documentation.* Kotagiri: Keystone Foundation.

Leroi-Gourhan, André. 1965. *Le geste et la parole, II: La mémoire et les rythmes.* Paris: Albin Michel.

Lévi-Strauss, Claude. 1985. *La potière jalouse.* Paris: Plon.

Mahias, Marie-Claude. 1994. 'Façonnage des céramiques en Inde. Un cas de poterie tournée par les femmes'. In *Terre cuite et société. La céramique, document technique, économique, culturel*, 327–41. Juan-les-Pins: Éditions apdca (XIVe Rencontres Internationales d'Archéologie et d'Histoire d'Antibes).

____. 2002. 'Les potières kota. Des femmes qui connaissent plus d'un tour'. In *Le Barattage du monde. Essais d'anthropologie des techniques en Inde*, Ch. 9, 163–196. Paris: Éditions de la Maison des sciences de l'homme (Archéologie expérimentale et ethnographie des techniques).

____. 2004. 'Le tour des potières kota (Inde). Comment une invention moderne permet de comprendre un outil traditionnel'. In *Artisans, Industrie, Nouvelles Révolutions du Moyen-Âge à nos jours*, 297–303. Paris: Société française d'histoire des sciences et des techniques/ENS (Cahiers d'histoire et de philosophie des sciences, no. 52).

____. 2011. 'Les potières kota (Nilgiri). Savoir-faire techniques, distinction des genres et fabrique des dieux'. In Marie-Claude Mahias (ed.), *Construire les savoirs dans l'action. Apprentissages et enjeux sociaux en Asie du Sud*, 159–204. Paris: Éditions de l'EHESS.

Mandelbaum, David G. n.d. *David G. Mandelbaum Papers.* Berkeley: Bancroft Library, 89/129 cz.

____. 1941. 'Social Trends and Personal Pressures: The Growth of a Culture Pattern'. In Leslie Spier, A. Irving Hallowell, and Stanley S. Newman (eds), *Language, Culture, and Personality: Essays in Memory of Edward Sapir*, 219–238. Menasha, Wis.: Sapir Memorial Publication Fund.

Saraswati, Baidyanath, and N. K. Behura. 1966. *Pottery Techniques in Peasant India*. Calcutta: Anthropological Survey of India.
Wolf, Richard K. 2005. *The Black Cow's Footprint: Time, Space, and Music in the Lives of the Kotas of South India*. New Delhi: Permanent Black.

Further Reading

'Pottery'. In *Encyclopædia of the Nilgiri Hills*, Paul Hockings (ed.). New Delhi: Manohar, 2012.

9

Experiencing Music in Tribal South India

On Doing a Recording Project

William Tallotte

As you come from afar to discover my culture,
I myself am getting ready to join another....

—Excerpt from a Toda song
(recorded on 12 January 2005 in Podor)

Making a CD

The publication of ethnographic recordings in commercially issued collections of traditional music is far from insignificant. It poses ethical and legal problems, the most obvious of which is the unauthorised use of musical material and the unfair redistribution of any financial benefits (Guy 2002; Seeger 1996; Zemp 1996). It also raises aesthetic and practical issues related to the conduct of fieldwork, the selection of tracks, and the negotiations with a CD company. With a few exceptions (Aubert 2010, 146; Feld 1995; Seeger 1991), ethnomusicologists have remained very discreet on these latter issues.

The following text retraces my personal involvement in the production of a double-CD set of Irula, Kota, Kur̲umba, and Toda music in a prestigious ethnomusicological recording collection (Tallotte 2012b). It describes some of the stages that made this project possible, from the wanderings during my first travels to the processes of recording, production, and post-production. It discusses in particular the strategies used to select musicians and recordings, and the way in which these strategies, through intercultural dialogue, shared listening experiences and attention to local, emic views on music and musicianship, shaped the making and the aesthetics of this CD.

The Genesis of this Project

When I first visited the Nilgiris in summer 2003, I was doing research in the delta of the Kaveri River on the music of the *periya mēḷam*, an outdoor orchestra of professional musicians playing Karnatak music in Brahmanical temples on the shawm (*nāgasvaram*) and the drum (*tavil*). Despite spending most of my time in this coastal area, I did take regular breaks to travel all around south India and document other folk and tribal shawm traditions. I wanted to learn more and understand, beyond my main fieldwork, the use and function of shawm music in various contrasted socio-religious contexts. In this broader comparative perspective, the Nilgiris were a particularly interesting region: although such a small area, several indigenous groups had their own distinctive ensembles of shawms and drums. Moreover, musical literature was relatively limited: while the instrumental music of the Kotas (Image 9.1) started to be well-documented, thanks to the pioneering work of Richard Wolf (2001), that of other groups remained largely unexplored.

On 6 August 2003, following the advice of Jakka Parthasarathy, then director of the Tribal Research Centre, I went to Kurgo·j (Sōlūr Kōkāl) to meet with D. Udayakumar, a renowned Kota shawm player. He was not there, but I finally ended up, after a few cups of tea, in an overcrowded jeep, accompanying his closest neighbour and some other villagers to a funeral in Porgāṛ (New Kotagiri). Although I was a bit reluctant to show up under such circumstances, one man reassured me, 'You're our guest, so you'll be theirs.' And he was perfectly right: I was warmly welcomed and people encouraged me to record the whole ceremony. The musicians, who were from Ticga·ṛ, kindly asked me to visit them on the following day, which I did; and their village, with its light blue-walled houses clinging to the side of a hill, soon became one of my favourite research spots.

IMAGE 9.1: Kota musicians from Ticga·ṛ performing for a funeral at Porgāṛ, 2003

Source: Photo by William Tallotte.

I did meet Udayakumar two days later in Kurgo·j. He proved to be an excellent musician, one totally devoted to his art. With a warm heart and a great deal of dedication, he opened the doors of his musical world for me, thus helping me understand the intricacies of Kota shawm music. He also introduced me to musicians from other groups, such as S. Madan (second from the left in Image 9.2), an Irula shawm player from the village of Totalinga, to the east of Mudumalai National Park. Thanks to these new connections, I could now work in a more systematic and comparative way, moving from Kota villages on the plateau to Irula and Kuṟumba villages around Masinagudi and Mavanalla. Fascinated by the musical diversity of this region, I soon developed a strong interest in both instrumental and vocal expressions, from Kota and Irula (Kasaba) shawm and drum music to Kota and Beṭṭa-Kuṟumba singing.

IMAGE 9.2: Irula musicians playing for a Hindu festival at Mullikorai, 2003

Source: Photo by William Tallotte.

I came back to the Nilgiris in 2004 and 2005 for another four months. While working with Kotas and other groups I decided, with the help of Nilasin, a Toda lady from Meḷga·s (in Ootacamund), to further explore Toda singing and chanting. The first encounters were impressive: I was completely hypnotised by the sonic quality of the voices and the intertwining and repetitive (somewhat meditative) character of the melodies. Thus I began spending more and more time in Toda hamlets, to the delight of my wife, who was learning Toda embroidery. During this period there came the idea to create a series of CDs, the first of which would be dedicated to Toda singing. In 2008, I proposed a first project to three record companies in France, Switzerland, and the Netherlands; but their answer each time was negative: 'Indian tribal music does not attract enough customers....' Was this argument only commercial? Or did it reflect preconceived ideas about Indian tribal music, and perhaps especially Toda singing (Tallotte 2012a, 618 and 624)? This was not clear. In any event, an opportunity came two years later, while I was working at the Musée du quai Branly in Paris. That new museum had just signed an agreement with the recording label Ocora Radio France to start a new series, with volumes made up of two CDs and extensive liners. I then proposed a project on the music of several indigenous groups, including Irulas (Kasaba and Mele-Nāḍu Irulas), Kotas, Kuṟumbas (both Ālu- and Beṭṭa-Kuṟumbas), and Todas. This project was accepted, and so I came back to the Nilgiris in January 2010 and again in January, March, May, and June 2012 to complete the work and settle the content of the two CDs with performers and some other villagers.

IMAGE 9.3: Beṭṭa-Kuṟumba singers during a recording session at Totalinga, 2003

Source: Photo by William Tallotte.

Selecting Performers: A Game of Strategy and Chance

The music of Irulas, Kotas, Kuṟumbas, and Todas can be incredibly powerful and expressive. It makes people cry during funerals, dance during festivities, and thrill in the presence of deities. Music, as such, is highly valued and people often evaluate how effective musicians and singers are, expressing opinions about their musical competence, their ability to touch listeners, and/or their faculty to bring out the right emotion(s) at the appropriate moment. In view of the importance given to musicianship and musical expressiveness in tribal life, it became clear that the selection of performers was of prime importance: engaging morally with local communities, performers, and future listeners was a precondition to recording performances that would locally be considered legitimate. Hence I initiated discussions with people about the expertise of musicians and the intrinsic qualities of performances. To this end, I organised semi-structured interviews built on short listening sessions and simple, open, straightforward questions: Who are the best musicians or singers in your community, and why? Who is your favourite musician or singer, and why? What is your favourite version of this piece? The answers to such questions varied from person to person, according to his or her community, activity, status, or personal taste. As a general rule, non-musicians based their statements on social criteria like lineage, fame, or ancestry. They could say, for example, that a shawm player was the best in their village because he had been chosen to accompany major ceremonies or had learned the instrument from his father, also a renowned musician. Musicians for their part tended to substantiate their statements with precise comments on sound, music, style, performance, etc. They could agree with non-musicians regarding the merits of the same shawm player, but would typically add something about his music, such as the sonic quality of his performance or the dazzling virtuosity of his fingering technique.

Individual opinions, however, were often influenced by petty rivalries between persons, families, or subgroups; they were not always consistent. As a result, I spent considerable time comparing (*i*) different people's views with each other's; and (*ii*) other people's views with my own perception and appreciation of performances—especially those I had already recorded and could listen to at will. This process was crucial to establishing and developing links with the most appreciated musicians and singers; yet it could not guarantee the realisation of expressive, moving, and technically persuasive recordings. To achieve this, a blend of chance and perseverance was called for. The following episode illustrates this point.

Between 2003 and 2008, I recorded about three hours of Irula shawm (*kwāl*) music during weddings and religious festivals. But this material was hardly usable, due to background noises coming from temple loudspeakers, motor engines, or nearby conversation.[1] In 2010, after several more recent failures, I abandoned the idea of recording Irula shawm music *in situ*… until the unexpected happened. In May 2012, I was told that Ālu-Kurumbas and a few Mele-Nāḍu Irulas would celebrate a festival to honour the mother-goddess Gōpammā in the remote village of Setikkal (in Kotagiri *taluk*). I went there on 28 May, reaching the spot after nightfall. The celebration was going on, and the atmosphere was electric. On the village square, under the starry sky, two Irula shawm players, along with Kuṟumba drummers, were accompanying a scene of possession. A woman was crouched down, huddled, her hair dishevelled. She swayed regularly from right to left, lifting herself up gradually. A group of men encircled her, clapping their hands and vigorously chanting the syllables *ho ho*. The musicians were playing a *dua uga kwāl*, a tune through which a deity (*dua*) is invited to enter and possess (*uga*) a person.[2] I recorded the scene, standing close to the main shawm player. The performance was poignant, and imposed itself as the first track of the second CD: the musicians were outstanding, the piece remarkably expressive, and the music merged seamlessly with the sounds coming from the voices and actions of the participants.

Selecting Recordings: A Web of Criteria

During fieldwork I used to keep up-to-date a selection of outstanding and usable, publishable recordings. This was essential to set up priorities and decide what to do on a regular basis. Selecting, however, was far from simple. It had to be based on technical and aesthetic criteria, as well as on requirements related to editing and research issues. The arrangement of tracks, for example, had to show a sense of balance between groups and, within each group, between genders, repertoires, musical genres, vocal expressions, instruments, and so forth. Likewise, the tracks of each CD had to highlight elements of convergence among groups, so as to connect the project to previous debates on tribal music—at both the scale of the Nilgiris (Wolf 2012) and the subcontinent (Babiracki 1991; Knight 2000/01; Wolf 2000/01). For the sake of precision, I will describe the principal phases of the selection process through an example taken from the CD: the Ālu-Kuṟumba dance tune (*āṭa kōval*) referenced as track 20 in CD 2 [2: 20].[3]

A Recording Opportunity

On 25 May 2012, the night of a name-giving ceremony, I recorded fourteen Ālu-Kuṟumba shawm dance tunes (*āṭa kōval*). The ceremony took place in the village of Chengalpudur (in Coonoor *taluk*). The musicians were S. Arjunal (*kōval* shawm), R. Sasikumar (*gummu* drum), R. Ramesh (*arai* drum), and A. Ashok (*tambaṭai* framed drum).

A First Selection Phase, Based on Technical Criteria

On the same day, I completed the first phase, which involved eliminating pieces that presented sonic defects, whether due to recording errors (for example, a microphone placed too close or too far from the source) or external factors (for example, disturbing sounds, like cell phones, car horns, barking, etc.). In the present case, the problems were minor. The village was far away from roads or other external disturbances. Still, I discarded six out of fourteen tunes for another, unusual reason: two elders regularly interrupted the dances to discuss the connection between shawm tunes and dance steps.

A Second Selection Phase, Based on Personal, Subjective Aesthetic Criteria

In the following days I worked on the subsequent phase, which aimed at familiarising myself with the recordings and reducing the first selection to a few pieces only. To this end, I listened to the remaining eight tunes over and over again in a silent place and through professional headphones. I selected three tunes that I found particularly stimulating.

A Third Selection Phase, Based on Emic Aesthetic Criteria

I came back to Chengalpudur on 1 June 2012 to review my selection with Arjunal and two other musicians, to learn if they agreed with my choices. To begin with, they listened to the three selected tunes and a few other dance tunes; then, they shared their impressions. Their discussion revolved around three key topics: the sound quality, with remarks on intensity, pitch level, and circular breathing; the synchronisation of shawm melodies with drum patterns; and the quality of melodic variations. Finally, they came to the conclusion that one of the three tunes I had selected was better than all the others. According to them, this tune demonstrated Arjunal's inventiveness wonderfully, that is, his ability to vary the basic melodic-rhythmic sequence from which each piece is developed. Their argument convinced me, and I noted this tune as my first choice.

A Fourth Selection Phase, Based on Editing and Research Issues

Interestingly, this tune completed my previous and ongoing selection in terms of representativeness, diversity, and connectedness. It was not only flawless and entertaining, but also met other important requirements. First, it was the perfect contextual counterpart to the Kota and Irula shawm tunes I had already planned to include: it was a dance tune (*āṭa kōval*), while the Kota examples were god [1: 2 and 6] and green funeral tunes [1: 12], and the Irula examples were temple ritual tunes [2: 1 and 10]. Furthermore, it could be compared with two other dance tunes performed on distinct aerophones: one Kota dance tune (*aṭ koḷ*) played on the idioglottal bamboo clarinet (*pulāng*) [1: 10], and one Ālu-Kuṟumba dance tune played on the wooden recorder (*tirili*, Image 9.4) [2: 17]. Second, it was the most appropriate example to illustrate differences of approach in shawm music: the Kurumbas play in solo, repeating and varying in a systematic way a short melodic-rhythmic sequence [2: 20]; the Kotas, in contrast, play in pairs, in unison, and as much as possible with strict repetition [1: 2, 6 and 12]; the Irulas play in pairs too, but the first shawm player allows himself to make minute variations [2: 1 and 10].

Image 9.4: The Ālu-Kuṟumba shawm player S. Arjunal playing the *tirili* recorder at Chengalpudur, 2012

Source: Photo by William Tallotte.

This Ālu-Kuṟumba dance tune conveys ideas about the way in which the tracks of CDs 1 and 2 were first selected. It should be noted, however, that no selection was made or thought about in exactly the same way: fieldwork situations and recording conditions were different each time. Moreover, the gradual accumulation of recordings and first-hand ethnographic information implied a continuous readjustment of previous selections—thus making the latter stages of the selection process increasingly complicated.

Table 9.1: Distribution of vocal and instrumental tracks in CDs 1 and 2

		Kota CD 1: 1-12	Toda CD 1: 13-20	Irula CD 2: 1-10	Beṭṭa-Kuṟumba CD 2: 11-16	Ālu-Kuṟumba CD 2: 17-21
Instrumental tracks (Men only)	Shawm	2, 6, 12		1, 10		20
	Cylinder drum	2, 6, 12		1, 10		20
	Frame drum	2, 6, 12		1, 10		20
	Terracotta drum			10		
	Bamboo clarinet	10				
	Brass trumpet	1				
	Bamboo trumpet			7		
	Recorder					17
Vocal tracks (With instrumental accompaniment)	Solo—woman	7, 9, 11		3, 5, 9		
	Solo—man			4, 6		19
	Duo—women	8	18	2, 8	11, 13	
	Duo—men		16			
	Small group—women		15, 17		12, 14, 15, 16	21
	Small group—men		19			
	Large group—women	3, 4, 5	20			
	Large group—men		13, 14			
	Large group—mixed					18
	With cylinder drum	3, 4, 5, 7, 8, 9				18, 21
	With cymbals	3, 4, 5				
	With bells					18
	With hand-clapping	3, 5, 7, 8, 9	20	2	12, 14, 16	18, 21

Audio Post-Production

In June 2012, I spent three days at Radio France in Paris, with Philippe Malidin (a sound engineer) and Serge Noël-Ranaivo (coordinator of the Ocora collection), to work on audio post-production. I had selected about fifty performances and numbered their likely location in CDs 1 and 2. This selection represented years of work and the culmination of an extensive and passionate dialogue with informants and others. It reflected mutual concerns about musicianship, musicality, local aesthetics, musical diversity, and musical convergence among all four groups. As such, I wanted to preserve it by all means. I knew, however, that post-production had its own priorities: the attention indeed would now shift to the listening comfort and pleasure of future potential listeners or consumers.

The first morning, we agreed on twenty (CD 1) plus another twenty-one pieces (CD 2). This validated my own final selection, with only one exception: the number of Toda songs was reduced (from twelve to eight) because of their repetitive character. I disagreed with this diagnostic but willingly accepted the change, knowing it would not affect the coherence of the project. We agreed then on how best to present and link each track. The initial plan was to fuse the end and beginning of each discrete piece, whether instrumental or vocal, so as to obtain for each CD a continuous soundtrack. In the present case, however, this option was technically too constraining. We therefore chose an intermediary solution: we kept the idea of fusion, but integrated a brief silence between most tracks.

Having taken these decisions, we could now work on a per-song basis for tracks 1 to 20 (for CD 1) and 1 to 21 (for CD 2). This work, realised in the studio with the support of professional audio-editing software, involved minor operations that improved the listening experience but preserved the aesthetics and the subtlety of nuances of initial recordings. Here are three of the most notable (and time-consuming) operations:

- Matching levels to give the feeling that all tracks have the same volume. Since the forty-one selected tracks were recorded over a period of ten years, in various contexts, and with both analog and digital equipment, some were louder than others.
- Adjusting certain frequencies (equalising), so as to improve balance between instruments or voices and/or to attenuate

ambient sounds that might disturb listening. We exploited this possibility, for instance, to lessen the presence of a drum or diminish the rumble of wind noise.

- Working on the beginning and end of tracks in order to provide smooth transitions. To this end we utilised, for example, very subtle fade-ins, fade-outs, and cross-fades—but without reducing the length of pieces or cutting any musical pieces.

The Project and its Enduring Value

Music of the Nilgiri Hills: Kota–Toda–Irula–Kurumba, in its final version, recognises and celebrates the expressive and imaginative world of Indian tribal music. It is both an ethnographic document and a tribute to the artistic genius of instrumentalists and singers whose voice is often ignored, even denied, by the dominant surrounding cultures. It is a specific portrait of Irula, Kota, Kuṟumba, and Toda music that draws attention to traditional aspects of musical practice rather than current, ongoing musical transformations. This choice is neither naive nor romantic, but is carefully thought out. It reflects a facet of Nilgiri tribal music that is still alive, transmitted, performed, listened to, and valued. It does not ignore modern developments, but simply favours aspects of knowledge that become scarcer and scarcer, and that people are still glad to share with others. Although *Music of the Nilgiri Hills* is not a document about musical change, it could be used in the future, along with other audio documents (for example, Wolf 2006, Musical Examples), to assess critically the idea, one often expressed by musicians and community elders, that Nilgiri tribal musical traditions are suffering artistic degradation because of modernisation, new sociocultural norms, and various aspects of acculturation.

It is too early to measure the impact of this CD publication on the academic community or the general public. It is too early as well to determine whether or not this work can benefit local communities. All I know is that musicians and participants who listened to and saw the CD were very pleased. They were honoured to hear themselves, to recognise themselves in photographs, to read their names in the liner notes. Among a long series of touching comments, I recall in particular the words of Nilasin, the Toda lady who composed the song from which the lines opening this chapter are drawn. In the following excerpt she refers to time passing and memory loss, and perhaps more generally to culture loss:

> I have lost the memory of my mother's voice. I cannot envision anymore the timbre of her voice, when speaking or singing. I have forgotten some songs as well. This makes me sad. But these recordings, in a sense, console me. They will help my daughter and my people to recall my voice, my songs.

IMAGE 9.5: Nilasin singing for a Toda bow-giving ceremony at Kwa·ṛθüṇy, 2005

Source: Photo by William Tallotte.

Two centuries after the opening up of the Nilgiris, and over a century after the invention of the first devices for sound-recording and reproduction, ethnographic audio documentation of tribal music is still in its early stages. This project, I hope, will generate (locally) new musical vocations among younger generations and pave the way (more globally) for new audio documentation and research. In the meantime, I hope soon to make accessible the integrality of my 2003–2012 Nilgiri recordings, through a personal website and/or an open-access institutional archive.

Notes

1. My predilection for tracks free of 'non-natural' sounds is not driven by a 'naturalistic aesthetic' (Knopoff 2004, 180), but rather by the desire to produce recordings that can be listened to with pleasure, especially by performers and local communities. In this respect, it is worth recalling that, in everyday life, our auditory system allows us to focus our attention on specific parts of an auditory environment. In other words, we can listen to a musician or a conversation in the middle of the street while tuning out all other kinds of sound present in the surroundings. In experiencing an audio recording, however, our auditory system hardly separates musical sounds from external, more intrusive noises. As such, a car horn on a CD track is likely to cause discomfort and frustration after two or three listenings.

2. Kamil V. Zvelebil (1988, 127) and Richard Wolf (2012, 612) mention the category *dua uga pāṭṭu*, that is, song (*pāṭṭu*) of possession. I have no information on whether or not this tune (*dua uga kwāl*) has been adapted from a song belonging to this category.

3. Indications in square brackets refer to audio tracks in CDs 1 and 2 (Tallotte 2012b). Table 9.1 lists the content of both CDs, thereby allowing the reader to situate each track within a wider context.

Note on Kota Names

All seven Kota villages are better known locally by their Badaga names, which are as follows:

Aggāl, Mēl Kōtagiri: in Kōta, *Porga·ṛ*
Kalagāsa, Gūḍalūru Kōkāl: in Kōta, *Kala·c*
Kīe Kōtagiri, Kīe Nāḍu: in Kōta, *Kina·ṛ*
Kollimale: in Kōta, *Kolme·l*
Tiruccigaḍi: in Kōta, *Ticga·ṛ*

Paḍuguḷu, Sōlūr Kōkāl: in Kōta, *Kurgo·j*
Mēlnāḍu, Kunda Kōtagiri, Kunde Kōkāl: in Kōta, *Me·na·ṛ*

References

Aubert, Laurent. 2010. 'Woodstock en Amazonie et la superstar du ghetto de Kingston. Les droits patrimoniaux et le droit moral face à la réalité du terrain'. *Gradhiva* 12, 140–157.

Babiracki, Carol M. 1991. 'Tribal Music in the Study of Great and Little Traditions of Indian Music'. In Bruno Nettl and Philip V. Bohlman (eds), *Comparative Musicology and Anthropology of Music: Essays on the History of Ethnomusicology*, 69–90. Chicago: University of Chicago Press.

Feld, Steven. 1995. 'From Schizophonia to Schismogenesis: The Discourses and Practices of World Music and World Beat'. In George E. Marcus and Fred R. Myers (eds), *The Traffic in Culture: Refiguring Art and Anthropology*, 96–126. Berkeley and Los Angeles: University of California Press.

Guy, Nancy. 2002. 'Trafficking in Taiwan Aboriginal Voices'. In Sjoerd R. Jaarsma (ed.), *Handle with Care: Ownership and Control of Ethnographic Materials*, 195–209. Pittsburgh: University of Pittsburgh Press.

Knight, Roderic. 2000/01. 'Tribal Music in India: An Introduction'. *Asian Music* 32 (1), 1–4.

Knopoff, Steven. 2004. 'Intrusions and Delusions: Considering the Impact of Recording Technology on the Subject Matter of Ethnomusicological Research'. In Michael Ewans, Rosalind Halton, and John A. Phillips (eds), *Music Research: New Directions for a New Century*, 177–186. London: Cambridge Scholars Press.

Seeger, Anthony. 1991. 'Creating and Confronting Cultures: Issues of Editing and Selection in Records and Videotapes of Musical Performances'. In Max P. Baumann (ed.), *Music in the Dialogue of Cultures: Traditional Music and Cultural Policy*, 290–302. Wilhelmshaven: Florian Noetzel Verlag.

____. 1996. 'Ethnomusicologists, Archives, Professional Organizations, and the Shifting Ethics of Intellectual Property'. *Yearbook for Traditional Music* 28, 87–105.

Tallotte, William. 2012a. 'Toda Music'. In Paul Hockings (ed.), *Encyclopædia of the Nilgiri Hills*, 618–24. New Delhi: Manohar.

Tallotte, William. 2012b. *Music of the Nilgiri Hills: Kota–Toda–Irula–Kurumba.* 2 CD set, Ocora Radio France/Musée du quai Branly, C 560250/51.

Wolf, Richard K. 2000/01. 'Three Perspectives on Music and the Idea of Tribe in India'. *Asian Music* 32 (1), 5–34.

____. 2001. 'Emotional Dimensions of Ritual Music among the Kotas, a South Indian Tribe'. *Ethnomusicology* 45 (3), 379–422.

____. 2006. *The Black Cow's Footprint: Time, Space, and Music in the Lives of the Kotas of South India.* Urbana: University of Illinois Press.

____. 2012. 'Kota and Tribal Music'. In Paul Hockings (ed.), *Encyclopædia of the Nilgiri Hills*, 611–18. New Delhi: Manohar.

Zemp, Hugo. 1996. 'The/An Ethnomusicologist and the Record Business'. *Yearbook for Traditional Music* 28, 36–56.

Zvelebil, Kamil V. 1988. *The Irulas of the Blue Mountains.* New York: Syracuse University.

Part V

Honey & Money

10

'When We Have the Blessings of the Bees, Why Should We Worry?'

Chronicles of a Honeyhunter from the Northeastern Slopes

Pratim Roy and Anita Varghese

Nestled in the valleys of the northeastern Nilgiri slopes are ancestral domains of the Irula and Kurumba tribal communities, who have lived there for countless centuries, growing millet, beans, gourds, and maize on the hillsides, and collecting honey, resin, fruit, and useful materials from the forests. Their villages are mostly situated beside a stream and each one usually has forty to sixty households. Thirty years ago these slopes were less populated, tea plantations ended where moist deciduous and evergreen forests began, tarred roads turned into mud paths which took us to the tribal villages scattered along the slopes. As we started our research work on tribal livelihoods and mountain ecology, we discovered this world of honey-bees, forest dwellers, and honeyhunters.

One such honeyhunter who welcomed us with folded hands was Rāsu, a master magician, priest, farmer, honeyhunter, and respected elder. When we told the honeyhunters that we wanted to make a film about them, they were a bit apprehensive at first; but then so were we, as we only had a general idea and had never done anything like this before. After some discussion the filmmaking went ahead; and as we look back, that would have been an important milestone in our relations with these people. As we were watching, observing, and asking questions, we did not worry about the time. If they asked us to be at a certain place at daybreak, it meant we had to leave home at 3 am to get there. The film was completed and then shown to the honeyhunters, who told us they were happy with it.

In those days, back in the 1990s, the honeyhunters would sit at roadsides with their precious honey in dirty glass bottles, to sell for any price that could be bargained for. In the eyes of the buyer, they were just poor people trying to eke out a living by selling something. Little did the buyers know of the skill and knowledge that lay behind a single bottle of honey! But the film changed all that; more people came to know about the 'Honeyhunters of the Blue Mountains' (also the title of the film). A decade later, when one of our team members was stopped at an estate barricade, the estate manager, upon hearing where she wanted to go, said, 'The village of the honeyhunters! I saw the film on national television. Do you work with them? Please go ahead.' And since then, that barricade has always been open for our team.

When we ask Rāsu what he thinks of the work since then, he ponders awhile and agrees that he is grateful that we started in his village, because otherwise it might have been like other regions, where the honeyhunters have faded away. Rāsu lists the names of over ten young men of his village who are currently honeyhunters, and he is very proud of his two sons having become chief honeyhunters. Up until a few years ago, Rāsu would accompany the group to the cliffs, as helper and guide. He does not think he needs to go any more; besides, his frail health will no longer permit it.

The hills rise very steeply on the northeastern escarpment, and the cliffs that tower over some valleys are the favoured nesting sites for the giant rock bees, *Apis dorsata* (Images 10.1 and 10.2). Come January, they arrive on these cliffs to nest, forage for nectar and pollen, build their hives, nurture the next generation; and then, just before the monsoon, they move back to lower elevations to forage on farm crops. The Kurumbas wait for the bees, a buzz they cannot resist when they learn the honey is ready to harvest. The ancient practice of honey-hunting along the cliffs, using forest vines as ladders, is kept alive through the elders, taught to the young, and gets repeated every year almost as a ritual. Elders like Rāsu have been very conscious of the need to teach the young and, in his

IMAGE 10.1: *Apis dorsata* bees on Nilgiri cliffs

Source: Photo by Vishu-Galidimbham.

IMAGE 10.2: Honeyhunters of the Blue Mountains

Source: Photo by Keystone Foundation.

words, 'We are Kurumbas: we have to take the honey, we have the blessings of the bees to do this. Why should we worry?'

Rāsu remembers how, as a young child, his life was filled with incidents of death and of moving around from one village to another: it was not a happy time, he recalls. His grandfather, Kunna Kāri, and his father Kulan took him into the forest and taught him its ways, and he watched them hunt for honey. His grandfather passed away suddenly and Rāsu's mother wanted the family to move back to her own village in Coonoor town. Kulan followed his wife, and Rāsu was sent to school there. He had two younger sisters, one of whom died at the age of fourteen while the other became blind very early in life; she continued living with him until his recent death. Rāsu's mother also died when he was only twelve years old, so the family moved again to another village in the Kotagiri area. This meant that Rāsu had to stop school and start helping his father with wage work. They lived in this new village with Rāsu's maternal uncle, Nanjan, and his family. However, death seemed to be following them there, too, for Nanjan's wife, mother to his two daughters, died suddenly, as did the second wife he took, after she had given birth to two sons. Nanjan decided he must leave this village, and so they all moved off again to start a new life in yet another village. Nanjan took a third wife but Kulan chose not to remarry: he just worked on the land and took care of his children. One day, while going to work, a local Badaga elder, a centenarian named Rāja, met Kulan and advised him that it was high time Rāsu got married and settled down to family life. He then told Kulan about a young girl called Laxmi, also a Kurumba, orphaned as a child, who would make a good match for him. And so it was that Rāsu agreed to marry, when he was thirty years old. They had a quiet wedding ceremony at the local Vinayagar temple, with only Raja and Kulan present. By then his maternal uncle Nanjan had passed away, followed after a few years by Kulan too. Andi Pā, a Kurumba elder, called Rāsu and asked him to return and assume the responsibility of being the local Kurumba priest. And thus it was that Rāsu moved back into the village of his ancestors.

Box 10.1: Excerpts from a field diary, 4 November 1995—Mathew John

We heard drum beats from the valley as we (Miller, Revd. Mulley, and I) made our way to a late evening meeting at the village. We were told that the Kurumba Andi had died that morning. The news was too direct and sudden for us to absorb, and we kept asking questions, as though people were giving us wrong information. The news was true, and so we took a detour and went straight to Andi's house.

About fifty-odd people were already there, while others had gone to inform close relatives. Andi's body was still inside the house—kept on a mat and covered with a cloth. They just bared the face for us to have a look—a peaceful face, with a coin on his forehead. His trademark, the turban made in just the right way, was placed on his head. There was a little bit of food kept on a banana leaf next to his head—rice, sambar, bread, a glass of coffee. The funeral was planned for the next day, and the body was brought out of the house and laid on the special planks and *guḍikaṭṭu* (an umbrella-like structure). There was much crying and lamenting, while people were coming in to pay their respects with garlands of marigolds. Irula musicians escorted each group of visitors.

Andi had lived about sixty-odd years—a cheerful, smiling figure, he lived long enough to see a number of his grandchildren, one of whom was even married. His jovial manner and paternal presence ensured that the clan lived without too many problems arising between them. He served as a priest for the Badagas. Now, with his demise, the Badagas will leave it to the Kurumbas to choose the next priest (it doesn't necessarily have to be his sons).

On Sunday, in the evening, he had played with children and even given them some money, asking them to call him '*tāta*', as the next day, they would not get a chance to call him so. He met Ramasamy, the village headman, and asked him to have food with him, as tomorrow he might not be able to do so. Ramasamy and Rangasamy, his elder son-in-law, were guarding the tea saplings when he met them. He drank some liquor that night and, in a rare gesture, shared it with Rangasamy.

In the village, after playing with his grandson, he continued drinking a little more and then settled down in the training shed, a favourite place of his. He lit a small fire and continued singing late into the night. Around 3:00 am, he slept. In the morning, when they went to wake him up, they realised that he had left them forever.

Andi Pā lived with his sons Chinna Rāman and Mādan, and his daughters Rāmakka and Sarasu. Rāsu remembers it as a prosperous time, one of peace and growth. Sarasu's husband Rangasāmy was a skilful honeyhunter who had learnt all the necessary techniques from his father-in-law. Chinna Rāman cherished the land and took good care of their crops. Andi Pā lived a good life, but passed away in 1995.

This left a vacuum in the leadership: now was a sad time with a lot of fear about the future. For a while everything seemed all right, until a few years later when Rangasāmy, the chief honeyhunter, Kappai Krishnan, the best maker of the rope ladder, Chinna Rāman, a good farmer, and Kannan (Rāmakka's husband and Andi Pā's son-in-law), a forest wanderer, all passed away, within a span of ten years. Rāsu recalls the names of many more of that generation, people who knew the history of the community, but who had died before reaching old age.

When Rangasāmy was the chief honeyhunter there, Rāsu remembers being a mere helper on each of their expeditions to Suivarai, Pādivarai, Peivarai, and Ūrarai (the names of some honey cliffs). In the early days, he would help Rangasāmy scale down the rope ladder, and the first time they were together, he told him to 'be confident and don't worry about the bees or you might hit your head against the cliff'. He remembers that once, Rangasāmy did hit his head on the cliff, and they had to abandon the hunt. But it was just a temporary setback, as Rangasāmy went back later and managed to get the honey. 'It was a pleasure to be with Kappai Krishnan,' Rāsu reminisces, 'as he would look at the cliff and make an accurate ladder with the right number of steps; he would be able to find the right, mature climber to make the rope, and Kappai's rope was as reliable as he was!' There was no honey cliff that had not been scaled by this team of experts.

The young people, sons of Rangan, Kappai, Velayudhan, Kannan, and Rāsu, would accompany their fathers and uncles on the hunts and assist with some of the tasks. With the sudden passing away of several stalwarts, it seemed for a while that honey-hunting would fade away as a craft. Rāsu was unhappy about this and took it upon himself to train and give confidence to the younger men, and to pass on all the skills and knowledge.

These young people would dismiss that idea at first, and were not interested in taking up the hunt. On one of the honey-hunting trips to Pādivarai, as Rāsu was scaling down the ladder, his middle son was above him and the younger boy was under the cliff, managing the smoke which they create to drive the bees away. It was 8 am and, as he descended the rope, he noticed that the younger boy had started to climb the rope from below and there was the older one above. For Rāsu, it was an unforgettable moment when he guided both his sons on the best ways to take the honey—all three of them hanging on the *māl kodi* (their term for the honey-hunting rope) above the forests, along the steep precipice of Pādivarai. He feels that this spontaneous interest that his sons showed was their initiation into the art of honey-hunting, and that there would be no turning back now.

Today, Kannan's son makes the best rope ladders and is very adept at it. 'When we make the ropes and we throw them down over the cliff, the bees know we have come and they start to inspect the rope and bless it so that it will hold and not give way.' In a way, they are giving permission and 'their blessing to come and take their honey', thinks Rāsu. He goes on to add the story of how the gods had asked the bees for the recipe for making honey. The bees refused to tell them, and so the gods became angry and tried to strangle the bees by tying a cloth around their necks and hips (which is why, even today, bees have a nipped waist); but even then the bees refused to part with the secret. The gods gave up, and the bees told them, 'We will continue to make honey so that the people can eat for their hunger, make medicines with it, and share it with their dear ones.' And Rāsu adds, 'the honey-bees are not to be disregarded: they refused the gods and continue to bless us, the honeyhunters.'

Rāsu was instrumental in keeping the honey-hunting tradition alive in his village and his community. He never gave up on those young people and moves easily amongst them, while being firm, stern, loving, and humble, all at the same time. He has waited patiently for over ten years to see new men take up the work of their forefathers: it has been a long wait but, looking into his eyes, one sees a contented man, one who feels there is hope. When we talk of the future, Rāsu is reserved: he does have his concerns and worries about his people not taking care of the land and too readily agreeing to cut down the trees that were planted by their ancestors. He says:

> The jackfruit trees gave us fruit and so we ate some and took the rest to the market. Today, a vehicle comes down and all the fruit is gathered at one time and sold off, and now they are talking about selling the trees. If the tree that my grandfather planted has to be cut down, then I don't feel like I belong here.

The issues of identity, place, ancestors, sacred groves, and burial sites are integral to the lives of tribal people. Change is inevitable, but how they navigate now while keeping traditions and culture alive depends on many factors. Local leadership is key. Elders like Rāsu have become fewer, many have passed away too early, and many leaders become puppets in the hands of other role players. Tribal ways of life are thus at a crossroads: the young are having to make decisions very fast about what they want to keep and what they are willing to give up. We have seen that the practice of honey-hunting is alive in areas where there are market opportunities for the honey, access to the honey cliffs is not restricted, and elders like Rāsu are around to offer confidence to the young. But for these stalwarts, it would have become a long-forgotten tradition!

Acknowledgements

This chapter is based on a conversation with Pusari Rāsu, a Kurumba honeyhunter. The authors are grateful to all the honeyhunters who have shared their life experiences with us. Rasu Aiyya passed away in August 2021, and we hope this chapter serves to keep his story alive.

The authors would also like to thank Mathew John and Robert Leo, colleagues at Keystone Foundation, for sharing their fieldnotes, and Snehlata Nath for insightful comments on the chapter.

Further Reading

'Honey'. In Paul Hockings (ed.), *Encyclopædia of the Nilgiri Hills*. New Delhi: Manohar, 2012.

11

Cultivating the Money Bush

Tea Production, Socioeconomic Transformation and the Ambivalence of Money

Jens M. Zickgraf

The Nilgiris are a unique place, and much has been reported and is to be admired about their crafts, culture, exchanges, and relationships, both past and present. Yet, even though it provides an omnipresent connection between all such realms, relatively little is known about money and monetary culture in these hills. Here, I take the cultivation of the 'money bush', as the tea plant was called for some time during the twentieth century, as a starting point to address a number of socioeconomic transformations among local Badagas, along with the ambivalent meanings of money in local accounts of life, history, community, worth, and relationships.

The Ambivalence of Money

According to the Marxian paradox, money is fundamentally a social relationship. Yet, in its grown capacity to measure and represent abstract value, money simultaneously acts as a veil for such relations. As Georg Simmel (2005 [1900]) explained this, the mediation of money renders close what was originally distant, and it does so at the cost of rendering distant what was originally close. In light of such 'veiling' and 'distancing', scholars have thus often lamented—quite one-sidedly, indeed—the socially disruptive process of 'monetisation'. However, such perceptions were predominantly born in ideological symbiosis with Western individualism and the model-version (Callon 1998) of a self-regulating, anonymous, and continuously expanding market economy. What more recent theories emphasise is that money itself continues to be made and remade, in the course of history (Graeber 2011; Hart 2001); whenever it is in the possession or reach of actual people (Zelizer 1994; Zickgraf 2017); and wherever it manifests within the boundaries of concrete places and along the trajectories of concrete monetary circuits (Guyer 2004). Money—how it is valued and how it is perceived as both process and medium in society—thus rests far more uneasily between distance and closeness, exchange and identity, calculation and experience. In this chapter, I will exemplify this with regard to the Badagas, the Bought-Leaf (BLF) tea industry which became their collective economic base during the second half of the twentieth century, and the consequent socioeconomic transformations.

The False Coin of Monetisation

'In earlier times we did not know the value of money', and conversely, 'today we are only running after the money', or 'money has spoiled the mind of our people'—such phrases were common among many Badagas I spoke to during 2010–2013. At the time, the local tea industry had suffered from long-term crisis, many Badagas had lost their land, and so, in search of jobs, young Badagas had increasingly left their villages. Moreover, a legal dispute between the heirs of a local tea factory had caused drastic conflicts which mushroomed across many villages. Temporarily, this even led to the excommunication of entire lineages, hamlets, and village sectors, and also threatened the celebration of local festivals for several years.

In the Nilgiris, too, money provides simple explanations for complex historical transformations, contemporary challenges, and omnipresent social tensions and disruptions. However, what puzzled me in the course of the research was how strongly such explanations have a counterpart in local discourse *and* practice: 'No money prospers without relations', 'Without relations there is no money', or even, 'money is like love'.[1] As I will try to show, these two faces of money are intricately entangled in everyday life, as people are indeed 'running after the money' and as local society continues to reproduce itself by way of reproducing monetary relations. In its ambivalence, money thus permeates all aspects of local life—the commercial as much as the ritual sphere, the household, the village, and the most intimate relations, tradition (almost) as much as modernity. However, what really makes the circulation of money meaningful in local accounts of life, history, community, worth, and relationships is how such ambivalence is contextually weighted and negotiated.

Before I turn to the cultivation of the 'money bush' and to the developments that followed upon a period when incomes, expenses, and the velocity of monetary flows had increased significantly, a brief remark on the precolonial situation is pertinent. It seems true that the hill communities (that is, Toda, Badaga, Kota, Irula, and Kurumba) were each specialised in certain economic niches and predominantly practised barter in kind among themselves. However, what deserves scrutiny is the imagery of a once-isolated tribal enclave devoid of money, markets, and the State apparatus, and the way in which it provided contrast and definition to whatever followed upon the advent of Europeans (see Sutton 2009 for a critique of the 'colonizer's gaze' on the Nilgiris). There is ample evidence—from archaeology and the remnants of ancient hill forts (Hockings 2013, 51–67), to oral (and later written) mythology (for example, Balasubramaniam 2009, 86–89; Rivers 1906; Zagarell 1994, 196–198), up to at least the early colonial reports (for example, Ward 1880 [1821]), and not forgetting a whole range of still vivid traditions (see below)—to show that money (that is, coinage) must have played a significant role locally. As I argue elsewhere (Zickgraf 2018, 83–106), money may or may not have predominantly defined commodity prices on the plateau itself. Its circulation, however, was highly relevant in the fields of ritual, marital, and political alliance and gift-giving. This involved political relations with chieftains in the plains, which required revenue payments and temple endowments in coin as well as regular trade of some hill produce for money. Overall it seems that Badagas—after they had settled on the plateau as the major agriculturalists and as the politically dominant group there—assumed in many respects (that is, regarding economic, ritual, and political or territorial integration) an intermediary position between highland and lowland society and, with it, between mutually entangled socioeconomic relations, or indeed 'spheres of exchange' (Bohannan 1955; *cf.* Guyer 2004, 27 ff.), that were each characterised and differentiated through the non-use, ancillary use, or explicit use of coinage.

Why is this important? As I shall show, such traditions may still inform the different emphases which may be laid on money as a social relation *vs.* money as a neutral measure of abstract value, and how this involves cooperation, solidarity, as well as profit-seeking in contemporary networks of business, finance, ritual, and community. Yet, likewise, it urges us to scrutinise a misleading colonialist narrative which correctly reports that European presence and investments set in motion a number of significant transformations, but falsely tends to break this influence down to the impact of money as such. British rule and presence thus introduced to the Nilgiri plateau a whole range of new marketing facilities, new crops, new technologies, new property rights and revenue systems, as well as new forms of wage labour and, importantly, schools and education. All of these innovations intensified the scope and velocity of local monetary flows, while British investments in particular placed emphasis on the different functions and meanings of money. Yet ideally this should never have prevented asking the more anthropologically relevant questions about how local people make sense—and continue to make sense—of 'their' money, how monetisation includes people's active participation rather than passive compulsion in systemic developments imposed from the outside, and thus to emphasise how we can, in a monetised world, take monetary cultures, past or present, in their own right. To exemplify this, I now turn to the Badagas, how they started cultivating the 'money bush', and how they cultivate money in ongoing processes of economic transformation and social reproduction.

Cultivating the Money Bush

> Just as, for the first time on this planet, humans were moving from agriculture to industry and from a country-based to city-based civilisation, tea was emerging as one of the world's favourite drinks. Thus, tea was able to set the patterns and trends that many other commodities would follow.
>
> (Macfarlane and Macfarlane 2003, 96)

> In these days, when tea has become almost a necessity of life in England and her widespread colonies, [….] to the natives of India themselves the production of this article would be of the greatest value. […] If part of these lands produced tea, he [the native farmer] would then have […] a commodity that would be of great value in the markets.
>
> (Fortune 1852, 394–395)

Contrary to money—and although due credit should revert to China—the tea plant was among the more genuine innovations that the British left to the Nilgiris. British tea production in India was a prestigious and capital-intense endeavour. Pushed forward by the East India Company (at that time the world's largest capitalist corporation), it took the form of the plantation estate, which the Macfarlanes hauntingly describe as 'outdoor factories' almost militarily planned,

> to 'industrialize' every stage of the production as far as possible […] to apply science and management skills […] from the clearing of land, through planting and picking, all the way to the finished product […] combin[ing] the capitalist financing, labour organization and mechanization as used in industrial production in a normal factory. (2003, 189–190)

As such, the tea business in India remained by and large reserved for white colonial elites.

In principle, this was true for the Nilgiris as well, although it should be noted that the tea business fully took root here only late in the nineteenth century and was perhaps less rigidly organised. Remarkably, however, it was still within the colonial period that local Badagas successfully entered the stage as pioneers of an alternative small-grower model. What henceforth emerged, in marked contrast to the plantation estate, with its inclusive factories, workforce, housing, rigorous planning, and massive economies of scale, was the so-called 'Bought-Leaf' (BLF) sector, which operates through independent tea factories that procure a daily supply of green leaf from a multitude of (in principle) equally independent leaf agents and small growers.

Under British rule, Badagas all over the plateau had first shifted to the production of various European vegetables and fruits to sell in local markets. In the vicinity of plantation estates, wage labour had become an additional and increasingly important source of income. However, at the beginning of the twentieth century some Badagas, particularly in the Aravēṇu area near Kotagiri town, had found a niche in cultivating tea bushes on their small plots of land and selling the daily harvest of green leaf to the nearby plantation estates.[2] It did not take long for some well-connected indigenous entrepreneurs to take charge of organising the collection and transport of leaf from the scattered fields to the plantation factories, as well as handle the supply of pesticides and fertilisers. In this function, they became the first independent 'leaf agents'. Moreover, in the 1930s there were already a few simple indigenous tea manufactures established, where green leaf was processed manually for local sale and consumption. Yet, starting just a few years before Independence, what truly marked the beginning of a new era on the hills was when a group of eighteen shareholders from several villages in the area pooled their money, expertise, and institutional contacts in order to obtain a license and construct (to my knowledge) the first fully mechanised and indigenously owned tea factory, Cross Hill factory (which was opened in 1945 and still exists). That factory could henceforth process green leaf from a rising number of local small growers and could officially sell the processed tea through international auction centres in Coonoor and Coimbatore. In the decades to come, Badagas set up more than twenty factories in and around Aruvēṇu alone, while the model of the BLF sector quickly spread to much of the Nilgiri plateau.

For Badagas, who, according to Hockings (2013, 211–246), had gone through a long period of stress, disorientation, and internal conflict under British rule—which had arguably prompted doubts in many Badagas about the very survival of their community and culture—the tea industry became yet another essential part of what Gudeman (2001) terms a community's 'base' or 'foundation' (that is, the sum of a community's shared material, intellectual, social, and symbolic resources). Among other aspects, such as mythology, kinship, village origins, and settlement structure (see Chapter 6, this volume), being a Badaga soon meant for many being a tea cultivator. Yet cultivating the 'money bush'—their name for the tea plant through times of economic prosperity—also meant to become dependent on the market value of a single cash crop, while the actual flow and distribution of money resonated with ever more dynamic changes in the local structures of power and accumulation. Within scarcely one generation many Badagas were able to significantly increase living standards, to employ (immigrant) day labourers to work in the fields, and to send their children to school and college instead. Yet, not all were that fortunate. Economic success or failures became omnipresent, and were quickly seen as factors of social differentiation.

The core of the BLF sector—the cultivation of tea, the collection and transport of green leaf, and its processing in the local factories—was almost exclusively borne by the Badagas. As Heidemann (2006) observed in the 1980s, these developments involved an inherent tension between cooperation, communal solidarity, and competition, which characterised relations between factory owners, leaf agents, and small growers. However, such tension and ambivalence did not only apply to the tea business alone. Rather, their dynamics involved and reflected the constitution of the entire community—including politics and ritual, kinship and the ancestral structure of settlements, as well as ongoing contradictions between 'traditional' norms and everyday practices (ibid.).

The founding of the first factories, for example, started as cooperative shareholder projects whose composition reflected, above all, the need for capital and professional expertise. As both were rare to start with, shareholders often joined hands across the traditional boundaries of the ten phratries, many lineages, and hundreds of patrilocal settlements. Later, however, such shareholder projects often fell apart, recruited supporters, and constructed competing factories, or reproduced various narratives of success, fraud, commitment, and failure exactly along these lines (Zickgraf 2018, 123–136). Not unlike the foundation of the first houses and first temples in villages, and not unlike the separation of brothers, the establishing and ownership of factories thus became another brick in the structure, recognition, and hierarchy of ancestral settlements and councils (see Chapter 6, this volume). In retrospect, the ascent of the early factory founders, how they accumulated wealth, how they spent it, and how they not uncommonly lost it too, became legendary tales—providing the foundational myths and the morals of a new era when control over ancestral territory was significantly, but never totally, replaced by control over money, and which were often interpreted differently by various fractions of the community.

In their capacity to control and channel huge amounts of money, individual factory owners emerged as powerful leaders and reformers among the Badagas. This was often paired with more modern attitudes and the aspiration of several factory owners to enter modern party politics. Such new leadership did not straightforwardly replace traditional moral values or hereditary forms of political and ritual authority. Rather, they legitimised, contradicted, and augmented each other, in constant interaction. Factory owners and other aspiring members of the community came into power because they were able to accumulate money and sideline competitors. With money in hand, however, they could simultaneously establish themselves as particularly committed members of their communities. Thus, factory owners often made highly visible contributions to the common good. Some built, renovated, or enlarged village temples. Others constructed wells, hospitals, roads, community halls, and schools. In the Aruvēṇu area, several factory owners were able to repurchase (and resell among Badagas) ancestral land from a previously British-owned estate; one of them also became the founder of the first cooperative agricultural bank. Virtually all factory owners made considerable donations to their village temples or took care of annual feasts during ritual processions and gatherings. They likewise helped members of their villages and kin with various kinds of credit, jobs, and contacts. In the traditional councils, of course, such generous spending helped them to recruit supporters and to pursue their interests. Up to the present day there have been repeated instances where factory owners took personal feuds or business matters into the realm of essential community affairs—sometimes with the consequence of triggering conflict among vast segments of Badaga society. Indeed, factory owners were often blamed for 'unnecessarily' recreating and reinforcing factionalism and tensions in Badaga society. Importantly, however, the success, wealth, and influence of factory owners and the way in which they used to share these did strongly underline the recognition, solidarity, and internal 'strength' of 'their' particular settlements, houses, families, lineages, or phratries—each being perceived as an elastic concept and indispensable to both the notion and feeling of local community and the wellbeing, power, and prosperity of Badaga society at large.

Indeed, this kind of recognition and the way it involves competition and yet necessitates cooperation seem essential. Hence, if Badagas are to be called a community, and insofar as one wishes to describe the tea business or even the ambiguity of money as part of their collectively shared base, it is important to see that while the very idea of community calls for widespread internal solidarity, it is (and probably always was) competition and tensions among its various and interdigitating (!) units—from individual to family, lineage, clan, and phratry, and from house to *kēri* (a row of houses, part of each village), *haṭṭi* (a hamlet), *ūru* (a first-founded head village with satellite hamlets), *nāḍu* or *sīme* (four basic indigenous territorial divisions), up to the entire community—that keep their shared identity as Badagas and the idea of communal solidarity alive. Inevitably, though, the cultivation of the money bush, and with it the actual flows and distribution of money, became a domain through which internal relations as well as the state, quality, or prosperity of the community at large could be experienced, negotiated, and—in part—remade.

This generally involved a growing range of financial networks and instruments among villagers, family members, friends, and business partners, which in turn reflected rising expenses for the maintenance of tea gardens, the employment of day labourers, consumption, education, and the more ostentatious celebrations of village festivals and family functions. A general norm was applied equally to internal finance and spending (see below): particularly in the realm of social reproduction, no one should bear any significant expense alone. Overall debt, highly variable loan conditions, and redemption reflected on the perceived quality, hierarchy, and structural degree of relations which they could both enforce and undermine.

Regarding the tea business as such, 'interest-free' advance payments were among the major financial instruments. Advance payments were channelled 'top down', from factories to leaf agents and small growers. Advances helped to get a business started, to plant or prune tea bushes, to pay for manure and fertiliser, to put up sheds for the collection of leaf, or to purchase vehicles for its transport, as well as to overcome shortages during lean seasons or price depressions. Given on trust and explicitly without charging interest (at least not directly), such payments could generally be expected and valued in recognition of communal ties, in anticipation of long-term relations, and as expressions of goodwill, confidence, cooperation, solidarity, and mutual interdependence. Yet, of course, advance payments had other dimensions too: factory owners sought to avoid open price competition by fixing the weekly rate for green leaf, whereas actual competition was carried out far less transparently on behalf of the individual advances given to leaf agents or (in order to avoid the bargaining power of the latter) directly to small growers. In a similar vein, leaf agents used advance payments to secure the loyalty of suppliers and to sideline competitors. Moreover, in areas where there was a sufficient number of tea factories, small growers and leaf agents took advantage by taking advance payments from multiple sources and from diverting their supplies accordingly. Advance payments were thus subject to continued interpretation and re-interpretation.

The fact that they were given doubtless contributed to the rise and success of the BLF sector. Yet up and down the local value chain, advance payments created a lack of transparency around the actual prices paid for green leaf, which resulted in various kinds of more or less hidden deceit, dependency, and exploitation (on 'confidence swindles', see Zickgraf 2018, 328ff.). The same lack of transparency, however, allowed people to reformulate or blur these facts in terms of cooperation or solidarity, to value personal relations and internal hierarchies rather than valuing the market, while it also provided a degree of protection against the involvement of outsiders (ibid.).

What added further dynamics were the booms and subsequent crises that were triggered by the rise and fall in the international demand for tea. During long-term boom periods, and in expectation of stable or even rising tea prices, money was more readily and cheaply available. Along with other forms of credit, advance payments were extended not only to facilitate investments in tea, but also to the realm of social reproduction. Marriages, festival expenses, medical emergencies, and education fees were all good reasons for which advances might be expected, and for which they were given. More than business, such events (and their expense) spoke directly to the core values and relations of community. They continue to involve extended and intergenerational family and village ties, and therefore necessitate the demonstration of widespread cooperation and solidarity (see below). Meanwhile, the financial expectations which well-to-do members of the community generally faced and the kind of hidden competition which advance payments facilitated among factories repeatedly led to situations where factory owners found themselves running into crushing debt. In turn, when price depressions led to the breakdown of liquidity, this would test the stability of relations. Inevitably perhaps, these were situations when 'markets cascaded into the realm of community' (Gudeman 2008, 59–61), and when financially sound factories or new investors could easily opt in.

Hence, what characterised the cultivation of the money bush during the twentieth century, of which advance payments formed an integral part, was the frequent up-and-down of international tea prices and the corresponding fact that Badagas were increasingly caught within mutual circuits of expenses, debt, and expectations that arose during boom periods, which were based on an ideal of internal cooperation and which frequently led to bankruptcy, to factory or land sales, or to successive changes in local structures of ownership, power, and accumulation. In the current century, however, the situation has changed considerably: since the turn of the century, tea prices have broken down, this time drastically and for long (Kullan 2006). In recent years, a growing number of factories had gone bankrupt, but they later re-emerged as parts of larger factory-groupings. These groups—still largely in the hands of Badagas—assume today greater market power, develop their own brands and marketing structures, employ dependent leaf agents, and have in part abandoned the practice of paying advances other than for manure and, for goodwill, a yearly 'festival advance'. The tea business appears less cooperative today. This, however, also seems to reflect further factors. In the wake of crisis, official regulations have been imposed concerning the weekly fixing of green leaf prices. Meanwhile, many Badagas sell land (in part because of accumulated debt, but also because land prices have sharply increased due to a real-estate boom). Many 'pawn' their lands in temporary lease agreements with Tamil settlers, who used to be their major workforce in earlier decades but who now often cultivate tea gardens on their own account (for the land, they pay a sum of money in advance that must be returned at the end of the lease contract). Alongside land sales and higher education, less coherent commercial activities, and in particular, labour migration and modern urban jobs have gained much greater relevance among younger people. Although it is true that many Badagas still depend on tea, for many others tea production is becoming a somewhat remote tradition practised by fathers or forefathers during what seems in retrospect to have been the golden age of their money bush. In this light, tea cultivation remains esteemed, and landed property is still maintained as far as possible. But tea is commonly not the only—and perhaps no longer—the major source of income for Badagas.

Therefore, going beyond the tea industry, it is essential to see another aspect that has been further 'cultivated' along with the money bush: 'social expenses'—how they continue to reflect basic structures in the community, and how they contribute to the perception that 'no money prospers without relations'.

As was briefly indicated above, making, characterising, and expressing social relationships have been among the predominant historic uses of money on the plateau. Indeed, if one was willing to judge from relevant 'traditions' among contemporary Badagas, one might have to ask whether there ever really was any essential aspect of their internal structure and foundations that did not require, or originate from, some sort of payment. Hence, whether it is the demarcation of territory, political authority, ritual responsibility, and clan or village membership; or whether it is basic marital alliance, the worship of gods, the remembrance of foundation myths and the deeds of ancestors, the blessing of elders, deaths and funerals, or collective agreements and the subordination of individuals under the verdict of traditional councils—each official event or activity following the essential lines of the social structure tends to involve the performance of a monetary transaction. This being said, 'social expenses' nevertheless articulate much differently today, particularly as money has become a nearly universal means of exchange, while the community at large increasingly lacks, in economic terms, a collectively shared base *other than* corporate finance, internal monetary flows, and collective funds. These, however, are regarded and managed with particular attention. In light of this, it is useful to distinguish between expenses that are *formally required* in the remembrance and continuation of deep, hereditary social structures, and *more informal* ones that are perhaps even more productive socially but far more subject to personal styles, capacities, prestige, and negotiable expectations. Again, their relation is dynamic as one informs, contradicts, or elevates the other.

Once upon a time, expenses that I choose here to term *formally required* may have been a costly factor of life and privilege. Today, however, their value is symbolic and must be bearable for all. For example, the payment of a bridewealth (*honnu*) is still regarded as the only 'true' economic requirement of a marriage, but with just Rs 100 or 200 involved it is financially a negligible transaction. Likewise, if marital alliance is both the beginning and the continuation of all kinship and all territorial integration, for each Badaga house it is mandatory to jointly pay with annual routines (as well as during more specific occasions) various kinds of *kāṇike* (small monetary offerings) to certain ancestor stones, temples, traditional councils, or family elders. Such payments are invaluable precisely because they are made in remembrance and/or in confirmation of ties, relationships, and hierarchies that indisputably exist. They are out of the realm of economic comparison and so take the form of the smallest available denominations. By extension, membership in villages involves the annual duty to pay house taxes (*vari*) to the funds of various units and subunits of a particular settlement or settlement cluster (respectively, a council legitimised through a first-founded Great House and a temple). These may at times involve more substantial sums of money, but what characterises them is that they are authoritatively levied in equal amounts upon each member of a territorial unit, and that they should remain bearable. All of these transactions are performed—and sometimes outright 'staged'—under particular (collective) attention in rituals and processions, and all of them reflect upon the basic structures and values of society. Indeed, in this regard there is a quite literal sense of 'paying attention'. Hence, what lends such payments 'high' value is not, or not predominantly, the expense as such, but collective memory and the repeated act of payment itself.

In contrast, expenses that I have just termed as the *more informal* ones involve today a whole range of comparatively new social standards, financial networks, and consumption patterns. They make social life dear and they form part of a societal dynamic that values communal ties and solidarity *along with* individual economic success, commitment, and personal reputation. Hence, while families, houses, and villages are ultimately just knots in a continuously developing chain of relations, it is their desire for *more* recognition (see above), no less than the desire to express true personal love and affection, which may continuously require much more. Standards are set by the rich and then trickle down to the middle class and the poor. In many respects, however, such expenses appear along the same lines as the formal ones to which they add value, definition, and redefinition.

Hence, to stick here only with the examples I just mentioned: what the symbolic expense of a bridewealth just initiates are (in some respect 'unnecessary') gifts in gold, dowry (although, as a rule, dowry should not be demanded among Badagas), attractive celebrations in modern wedding halls or hotels, and the reception of as many guests as possible—not to speak of what follows as a consequence of marriage: house construction, car purchase, childbirth, lifecycle rites, education for grandchildren, medical treatment of in-laws, hosting in-laws during festivals, making donations to the in-laws' temples, etc. And yet such expenses commonly require and gain financial support from the entire family. Why? Because the responsibility, the prestige, and the ensuing relationships can be shared as a base for future alliances.

The dimensions, however, become clearer once the payment of *kāṇike* is reconsidered. Members of certain groups jointly pay *kāṇike* to certain places, ancestors, or other authorities. The practice can be described as an act of commemorating collective origins and of acknowledging in this way the existence of mutual ties. Yet what gets added in everyday life to the commemorative payment of a *kāṇike* are the expenses which actual networks of kin and territory imply *in their continuation*: the norm that no one, no single house or village, in the network should ever bear any significant expense alone (even if s/he can). And indeed, this is firmly institutionalised. Whether it be the construction or renovation of a village temple, the erection of a community hall, the celebration of weddings, childbirth, or funerals, medical treatment in a hospital or the opening of a shop or other business, or the establishment of a new community fund—in principle always the same rule applies: those who stand in relationship (which may include close and distant family, neighbours, friends, and all well-wishers or, in territorial terms, houses, village parts, hamlets, head villages, neighbouring settlements, affinal villages, etc.) should 'show their presence' and make a contribution.

In other words, showing one's presence in society and perceiving the presence of others literally involves the mutual obligation to 'pay' a visit. As one female villager explained: 'With 50 rupees you can go for a funeral, with 100 rupees you can go for a marriage, and you need at least 200 rupees to visit somebody in the hospital.'[3] What she referred to were minimum rates she considered appropriate in the instances mentioned, and with regard to an extensively institutionalised system of mutual support (locally known as *tellāṭi*). Such payments are generally expected, but not compulsory (contrary to *kāṇike* and *vari*). Rather, they are voluntary investments in reciprocal relations wherein the given amounts may vary according to both the structural and the perceived closeness of a social tie, and according to personal status and individual financial capacity. Depending on both the structural reach and personal maintenance of such networks, these are expenses that may occur almost weekly. Yet they will also come back—often with an increment in money and (once continued over time and generations) with an increment in the quality of the relationship (sometimes up to a future marital alliance), and ideally also leading to an even larger sum of money that might be spent for a future social event at one's own house.

Finally, to return to 'village taxes' (*vari*): their collection lies at the core of contemporary village festivals and of the collective funds that villages or village sectors maintain. They are equal in amount for each house and are levied so as to meet the basic expenses for whatever the responsible council regards as necessary for the common good (the conduct of rituals and assemblies, the maintenance of temples and of relations with other villages, the hosting of guests during festivals, construction of wells, improvement of roads, even charity, the foundation of cooperative businesses or the provision of cheap loan facilities for emergencies and village members). But what adds to taxes, what makes it possible to celebrate greater festivals, to host more guests, and to significantly grow the village funds are *donations* that come along.

Donations are attracted by the very fact that a tax is collected. They are given as an extra commitment in the name of individual houses (and factories and subordinate or associated hamlets) as well as by guests who visit a festival. Crucially, however, since paying a tax means accepting political subordination, whereas individual donations are a way to emphasise a particular presence or standing in society, it is here that internal tensions of the community, among its various social, political, and historically developed units as well as between rich and casual members, most frequently and most publicly articulate. In extreme cases, conflicts among various factions of a village or small territory lead to embarrassing situations where a festival cannot be celebrated, where donations are not accepted, and where it is not possible to collect a tax. Yet the consequence of this, namely that all members of a village or entire settlement cluster would have to share the bad reputation that ensues, commonly works well enough to resolve such conflicts (at least temporarily). In turn—and this appears to me as the essence of why people often voice the sentiment that 'no money prospers without relations'—*if* the basic monetary circuits (in this latter example, the collection of a tax) succeed, returns (in this example, donations) will abundantly follow: funds, networks, and alliances will prosper along with the expense. Ancestors' origins, deeds, and obligations will be remembered—if not always in the exact knowledge of the community's oral memories, then at least in the actual account books of villages and houses. And because there is competition between the various units or fractions of a community, good examples (and good entries) will motivate others to follow suit.

Conclusion

What was said in the previous section is subject to much further dynamics and has implications for a broad range of community-based financial instruments, funding trusts and institutions which are today of growing relevance and which l could not treat here (*cf.* Zickgraf 2018). However, the general logic I wanted to articulate is the (re)productive tension between competition and solidarity, how it applies ubiquitously to the house and the market, how it leads from the past into the future, how it keeps the notion of community alive, and how it involves the ambivalence of money. In fact, what seems to characterise the perception and evaluation of money among Badagas—and perhaps even more generally in India—is its moral, long-term inseparability from the internal—from the person, the house, the family, and the community; and from the closest, most intimate, most essential, and most emotional relations a person can inherit and (re-)create in the course of a lifetime, in the chain of ancestry, and from one generation to the next. Provocatively speaking, these relations cannot be monetised because they already are, because they were, and because no money prospers without relations.

Badagas, like everyone else, are 'running after the money'. However, this is exactly one of those aspects of local monetary culture which in my view are prone to be misunderstood once Western categories are applied as if they were either/or—in particular, once cooperation and competition, community and market, wealth in people and wealth in money are treated non-dialectically; and when pure individualism or worse, 'the' economy (imagined as the impersonal mechanisms of price and universal comparison) becomes the major lens through which monetary relations are perceived. From any viewpoint (the house, the village, the nation, the globe), money bears a dialectic potential for both integration and disruption, yet its ambivalence has also been cultivated locally from ancient times through the colonial era and the golden age of the money bush, up to the present day. In this process, economy and society have been subject to continuous transformation.

Today, new houses are built far beyond the confines of ancestral territory. For many Badagas, village life is certainly no longer the dominant mode of existence, and some may have lost their roots entirely. In economic terms, agriculture, and subsequently tea production, have lost their former relevance as a collectively shared base. For many Badagas, this means facing an uncertain, non-agrarian future. Yet what seems to remain so far and what even seems to have intensified over time is the emphasis that Badagas lay on money as a way to make and remember social ties. As the editor of this volume once observed with regard to the difficulty of defining what kinship means to Badagas: 'The family that pays together stays together' (Hockings 1982, 874). As true as this is and as far as this principle can be extended from house to society, we cannot know what exactly this means for the future of Badagas as a community. Not least, however, money itself has changed. Along with the labour out-migration of the community's educated youth, transnational remittances, new communication technologies, and quick digital transactions enter the stage today, allowing members of the community to pay and to show their presence without visiting—that is, to make 'absent presences' (Kusimba, et al. 2013), thereby feeding a great deal of funds which are still managed locally in ancestral (or parental) houses and councils as well as in more modern trusts and associations. To conclude: money remains fundamentally a social relationship. Meanwhile, the question which applies equally to Badagas as well as to humanity at large, and to which people may develop different responses, is the way in which we can perceive and emphasise the ambiguities of money in the making and remaking of society—how we actually perform in turning monetary relations into relations of account and worth.

Notes

1. In 2012–2013, I conducted a socioeconomic survey among 117 households in the Badaga village of Jakkanāri. In this survey I also asked people to voice their personal opinions about money. The quotes here and above represent some of the more prominent answers. Males tended to be a bit more negative about money's transformative effects, while females more frequently emphasised the role of money in creating or representing social relationships. (In this chapter, I am, however, not further elaborating on the gendered dimensions of money; but see Zickgraf 2018).

2. At the time, some of the first fully mechanised tea factories were established at nearby plantations. This created temporarily an

over-capacity, so that the plantations were more than ready to purchase additional green leaf from small growers.

3. Interview with B. Slojana, Jakkanāri Kīlkēri, 18 February 2012.

References

Balasubramaniam, Bellan. 2009. *Paamé: The History and Culture of the Badagas of the Nilgiris*. Bangalore: Elkon.

Bohannan, Paul. 1955. 'Some Principles of Exchange and Investment among the Tiv'. *American Anthropologist* 57 (1), 60–70.

Callon, Michel (ed.). 1998. *The Laws of the Markets*. Oxford: Blackwell.

Fortune, Robert. 1852. *A Journey to the Tea Countries of China; Including Sung-lo and the Bohea Hills; With a Short Notice of the East India Company's Tea Plantations in the Himalaya Mountains*. London: John Murray.

Graeber, David. 2011. *Debt: The First 5000 Years*. New York: Melville House Publishing.

Gudeman, Stephen. 2001. *The Anthropology of Economy*. Malden: Blackwell.

——. 2008. *Economy's Tension: The Dialectics of Community and Market*. New York: Berghahn.

Guyer, Jane. 2004. *Marginal Gains: Monetary Transactions in Atlantic Africa*. Chicago: University of Chicago Press.

Hart, Keith. 2001. *Money in an Unequal World*. New York: Texere.

Heidemann, Frank. 2006. *Akka Bakka: Religion, Politik und duale Souveränität der Badaga in den Nilgiri Süd-Indiens*. Berlin: LIT-Verlag.

Hockings, Paul. 1982. 'Badaga Kinship Rules in Their Socio-Economic Context'. *Anthropos* 77 (5/6), 851–874.

——. 2013. *So Long a Saga: Four Centuries of Badaga Social History*. New Delhi: Manohar.

Kullan, T. M. 2006. *Toxic Tea Market in the Nilgiris, Nilgiris Profusely Bleeds, Save Nilgiris' Classic Tea*. Coimbatore: Hill Tea Prints.

Kusimba, Sibel, Harpieth Chaggar, Elizabeth Gross, and Gabriel Kunyu. 2013. 'Social Networks of Mobile Money in Kenya'. IMTFI (Institute for Money, Technology and Financial Inclusion): Working Paper 2013 (1). Available at https://www.imtfi.uci.edu/files/2013-1_kusimba_1.pdf (accessed February 2023).

Macfarlane, Alan, and Iris Macfarlane. 2003. *Green Gold: The Empire of Tea; a Remarkable History of the Plant that Took Over the World*. London: Ebury.

Rivers, William H. R. 1906. *The Todas*. London: Macmillan.
Simmel, Georg. 2005 [1900]. *The Philosophy of Money*. London: Routledge, 3rd edn.
Sutton, Deborah. 2009. *Other Landscapes: Colonialism and the Predicament of Authority in Nineteenth-Century South India*. Copenhagen: NIAS.
Ward, Benjamin S. 1880 [1821]. 'Geographical and Statistical Memoir of a Survey of the Neelgherry Mountains in the Province of Coimbatore Made in 1821 under the Superintendence of Captain B. S. Ward, Deputy Surveyor-General'. In H. B. Grigg (ed.), *A Manual of the Nílagiri District in the Madras Presidency*, lxxxviii. Madras: Government Press.
Zagarell, Allen. 1994. 'State and Community in the Nilgiri Mountains'. *Michigan Academician* 26 (1), 183–204.
Zelizer, Viviana A. 1994. *The Social Meaning of Money*. New York: Basic Books.
Zickgraf, Jens M. 2017. 'Becoming like Money: Proximity and the Social Aesthetics of "moneyness"'. *Hau: Journal of Ethnographic Theory* 7 (1), 303–326.
——. 2018. *Rupien in der Dollar-Zone: Geld als Prozess und Medium gesellschaftlicher Teilhabe. Eine Ethnographie (Badaga, Nilgiris District, Indien)*. Münster: LIT (Reihe Indus).

Further Reading

'Banking', 'Barter', 'Coinage', 'Co-operation', 'Hydroelectric Systems', 'Markets', 'Plantations', 'Tea', 'Tourism', and 'UPASI'. In *Encyclopædia of the Nilgiri Hills*, Paul Hockings (ed.). New Delhi: Manohar, 2012.

Part VI

Personalities

12

Twenty-first Century Toda Recollections of the British Raj

TARUN CHHABRA

John Sullivan

Although many Todas are aware that John Sullivan—or Salvïn-ars, as he is known to them—was the first Englishman to settle in the Nilgiris, their recollections about the event after two centuries are really quite dim. Not a single song composed in his honour can be recalled. My friend Kwaṯo·ṛ-kwïṭṇ began his journey to Amuno·ṛ, the Toda afterworld, last July, and with his passing it has become impossible to learn whether any such oral compositions were known to elders of his or earlier generations. Since the corpus of old Toda songs that I audio-recorded does not have any songs directly relating to Sullivan, and neither does Emeneau's corpus (1971), I suspect that he had been relegated to the back-burner in the collective Toda memory even as early as a century ago.

Elders like Pōḷkö·ṟ recall hearing from earlier generations that when Sullivan reached the upper Nilgiri plateau in 1819 and decided three years later to set up base around present-day Ootacamund, he first asked the Badagas how they dealt with the Toda people (see Plate 8, this volume). It was explained to him that besides many other forms of patriclan and family-based interaction, they gave the closest principal Toda hamlet a share of freshly harvested grain known as *ku·ṛ* (actually a bamboo basket), and a large measure known as *kwa·x* indicated the quantity to be given. This was done in acknowledgement of the Todas as 'sons of the soil', as well as to invoke the blessings of Toda deities to ensure a bountiful Badaga harvest. In return, the Todas would give them ghee, honey, umbrellas, walking sticks, milk-churning sticks, bamboo vessels and shoots, along with embroidered cloaks.

It is reported that Sullivan heard them out and went on to offer the Todas of the Ka·s̲ and Meḷga·s̲ patriclans compensation for an amount of land equal to that of a goatskin, to which they acquiesced. The story goes on to describe how he had someone bring a goatskin before the Toda elders, then cleverly proceeded to place sections of this hide across different areas of what is now Ootacamund (or Ooty), and thereby laid claim to this land.[1] The government later compensated the Todas for the loss of lands associated with ten of their hamlets situated in the vicinity of Ootacamund, in return for their agreement to accept a sum of Rs 150 per annum in perpetuity (Price 2012 [1908]: 469). It has now been several decades since the Todas went to claim this paltry sum. Nonetheless, from the time that Sullivan learned this concept from the Badagas, any governmental lease agreement with the Todas has been known as *ku·ṛvo·y poṇm*.

Todas recall that the first hamlet to be alienated to the British was the Ka·s̲ clan's male funeral site of Patmod̲. This was where Sullivan built his residence, 'Stonehouse', and the entire locality is known by this epithet even today. Todas know this building as '*kal bogïḷm*', which is a Toda-ised form of the Tamil *kal bangala* (stone bungalow). This is unexpected, as the literal Toda translation of 'Stonehouse' should be *kas̲kwa·ṭ*.

There is a belief among some elders that Sullivan later arranged to have some tree saplings brought to the Nilgiris and had them planted in five small experimental plots in the Toda heartland. A single sapling of *Eucalyptus globulus* from Australia was apparently planted on Pïnba·n Hill, on the Wenlock Downs (located below Omga·s̲ hamlet; see Chhabra 2015, 315). This was known as 'One Tree Hill' during British days, and possibly it was so named to honour the tree that Sullivan had planted. That hill now houses a forest of exotic trees. The next batch of a few *Acacia melanoxylon* saplings was planted at a place known as Kwï·θö·ks̲ in the 'Windy Saddle' area on Wenlock Downs. Since *tö·ks̲* means a buffalo sacrificial stone, this site is likely to have been in the vicinity of one of Te·fax clan's funeral sites (ibid., 115). Another set of the same species was planted near Meso̲θy hamlet in the Governor's Shola area, on a hillock known as Pïṇθïṭ. This is the only site where Todas claim that some of Sullivan's trees survive into this century. A few saplings of the same species were said to have been planted around the hill known as Kud̲θïṭ or Kud̲o·s̲ in the vicinity of Iṣa·r̲o·ṛ hamlet. The final site where the same species was planted is believed to have been above what is now the Toda Christian settlement of Kwï·kōl(n)kwar̲ (better known as Pu·mod̲) in the Governor's Shola area, and the hillock is known as Kwïjme·ṇθïṭ.

John Sullivan is also credited with appointing a Toda as a *monegar* (*monyxo·r̲n* in Toda), who was a representative dealing with the government on behalf of the community (as the Todas did not have a traditional headman; see Chapter 4, this volume). The first Toda *monyxo·r̲n* was Te·ty of the Kï·wïṛ patriclan, and his family continued to hold this office until Sinva·t̲wï·, the last appointee (Image 12.1). The post was abolished for all communities by the Tamil Nadu state government several decades ago, and replaced

Image 12.1: Sinva·t̲wï·, the last Toda *monegar*, undergoing priestly ordination rites at Kï·wïṛ hamlet

Source: Tarun Chhabra.

by a Village Administrative Officer (VAO) position.[2] Although this male lineage of the Kï·wïṛ patriclan (Tö·fiḷy division) held this post for so long, it is reported that a man belonging to the To·ṟθaṣ division occasionally functioned as an assistant *monyxo·ṟn*, or as a member of the tribal council, like Sirya·ṟ of the To·ṟo·ṛ patriclan.

Just a few decades after Sullivan's experiment, Todas recall that the British went on to plant *E. globulus* on a large scale in the following Toda areas: the first was in the vicinity of the Ka·ṣ clan female funeral site, Ki·ḷmoḏ, in the Governor's Shola area; this, along with the adjacent shola, is known as Kalishola today. The second plot was at a place called Peme·ṇbaḷ, which can still be seen above Kï·wïṛ hamlet. The third plantation in those early days was at Karypoṯy, located close to the Ooty–Gudalur road, near the 'ninth-mile' junction. The final plot was at Na·ṣyu·rox in the Kö·fdaṟ (Korakunda) area. Later, in the 1860s, a blue-gum plantation came up at Aramby (Aṟanboḷy in Toda) near Ka·ṣ hamlet. One of its trees is now reported to be the tallest in India.

James W. Breeks

James W. Breeks (see Plate 6, this volume) was the first administrative head (the Commissioner) of the newly-formed Nilgiris district, and he is recalled by senior Todas through various events related to his short tenure. One incident still in the collective memory of many elders is of Breeks—or Pirkic-ars in Toda—visiting To·ṟo·ṛ hamlet and exhorting them to end the practice of buffalo sacrifice at their funerals. This resulted in a heated altercation, at the end of which Nö·ṟnïṣ and Tirsi·Θy reportedly took hold of the reins of Breeks's horse, and demanded that he allow this age-old practice to continue. According to the Todas, Breeks relented.

Nö·ṟnïs composed a song (*nö·w*) about this event, and many elders remember its lilting tune and sing it. When I audio-recorded a variety of Toda songs many years ago, this was a prominent contribution. The song covers some of the important features related to To·ṟo·ṛ hamlet and clan, by posing a question in a three-syllabic word of the first sentence in a couplet (in case a word is shorter, it is stretched by adding a vowel); the answer comes in the second three-syllabic unit of the same sentence. The second sentence of the paired couplet follows similarly. The tune that makes this song so enchanting is added after each three-syllabic chant. The text goes like this:

> *I-no·ṛ-e·θ, Ko·xe·s̠y / I-pōh-e·θ, Mu·θvōh //*
> Which sacred place is this? Ko·xe·s̠y / Which very sacred dairy-temple is this? Mu·θvōh //
> *I-pōh-e·θ, Tï·pïs̠vōh / I-twï·-e·θ, Twï·te·pax //*
> Which sacred temple is this? Tï·pïs̠vōh / Which sacred buffalo pen is this? Twï·te·pax //
> *I-öṛn-e·θ, Kö·kis̠ykud̠θ / I-kö·ṟ-e·θ, Tï·ki·s̠ykö·ṟ //*
> Which sacred place is this? The buffalo track Kö·kis̠ykud̠θ / Which sacred pool is this? Tï·ki·s̠ykö·ṟ //
> *I-öṛn-e·θ, I·švaḷ / I-kas̠-e·θ, Pi·štykas̠ //*
> Which sacred place (slope) is this? I·švaḷ / Which sacred stone is this? Pi·štykas̠ //
> *I-to·ṟ-e·θ, Pïlkwï·ṛθo·ṟ / I-to·ṟ-e·θ, Pe·θo·ṟ //*
> Which patriclan is this? Pïlkwï·ṛθo·ṟ / Which patriclan is this? Pe·θo·ṟ //
> *I-öṛn-e·θ, Piḷyvïnbaḷ / I-ïr-e·θ, Ïviḷymo·s̠ //*
> Which sacred area (valley) is this? Piḷypïnbaḷ / Which sacred buffalo is this? Piḷymo·s̠ //
> *I-poḷy-e·θ, Poḷyki·s̠yaḷf / I-twï·-e·θ, Twï·tüḷcwï· //*
> Which temple is this? Poḷyki·s̠yaḷf / Which buffalo pen [at the male funeral place] is this? Twï·tüḷcwï· //
> *I-twa·s̠-e·θ, Twa·s̠mïne·s / I-ïr-e·θ, Ïrpuki·s̠y //*
> Which sacred shola thicket is this? Mïne·s / Which sacred buffalo is this? Puki·s̠y //
> *I-tïṭ-e·θ, Kwï·ṛme·ngwï·ṛ / I-öṛn-e·θ, Kwï·ṛme·ngwïṭy //*
> Which hill is this? Me·ngwï·ṛ / Which hill slope is this? Me·ngwïṭy //
> *I-tïṭ-e·θ, Kö·ṟtüḷykö·ṟ / I-tïṭ-e·θ, Pïłtüḷpïł //*
> Which sacred hill is this? Tüḷykö·ṟ / Which mountain is this? Tüḷpïł // [3]
> *I-twa·s̠-e·θ, Ïṇe·ṟpašt / I-ïr-e·θ, Ïnö·ṟo·f //*
> Which sacred shola is this? Ïṇe·ṟpašt / Which sacred buffalo is this? Nö·ṟo·f //

I-twa·s̠-e·θ, Twa·s̠kuṣoṭy / I-ïr-e·θ, Ïpu·ṣum //
Which sacred thicket is this? Kuṣoṭy / Which sacred buffalo is this? Pu·ṣum //
I-pōh-e·θ, PōhTe·lgwï·ṛ / I-no·ṛ-e·θ, Tö·Pöḷkoṭy //
Which most sacred dairy-temple is this? Pōhte·lgwï·ṛ / Which sacred place is this? Tö·pöḷkoṭy //

Senior Todas recall that a Ker̠ïr clansman, Nö·r̠otKwïṭṇ (named after a sacred stony pit and stream where a god is believed to have tied down the sun's rays; Chhabra 2015, 30) and his wife, Sarkōr (from: Sarkar = government), had a daughter whom they named Pirki·ʐ, after J. W. Breeks. This is interesting as it represents an unusual example of a man's name being feminised in Toda by adding that most common suffix 'i·ʐ'.

King George VI

A much more distant British administrator who is still remembered—once again through a song and story—is King George VI. The story relates how, a little less than a century ago, a man of the Ïṇkity clan, Parkwï·ṛ, had a wife, Simïl (a Ker̠ïr *ku·x*), who developed a friendship with a Muslim trader who had a shop near the Badaga village of Naḍuhaṭṭi. This merchant would visit her every now and then and tip some Ïṇkity clansmen to look the other way. Reportedly, even Parkwï·ṛ got wind of this relationship later.

When Simïl became pregnant, the trader had the audacity to tell Parkwï·ṛ that he would perform the paternity rites (*pïsiṭt*), as she was carrying his child! Parkwï·ṛ calmly replied that this was impossible: only a Toda husband could do so. Enraged, the haughty shopkeeper disdainfully spat on the Toda, resulting in the men coming to blows. Other Ïṇkity clansmen soon joined in the melee and gave the man a sound thrashing, causing grievous injury. Following a complaint, two Todas were jailed in Coimbatore.

Some months later, the coronation of King George VI took place and an amnesty was granted to many prisoners. With this twist of fate, those Todas were released and were on their way back to Ïṇkity at night. They had just reached the nearby male funeral place, Twï·vem, when both men started to compose a song (*nö·w*) describing in a haunting melancholic tune some of their traumatic experiences. Their clansmen, who did not know of their release, heard the song from a distance and were terrified, believing that their spirits were returning to the hamlet!

Meanwhile, Simïl lost that baby and was sent back to her natal Ker̲ïr patriclan. After purificatory rituals at the low-lying Siriyūr temple (which is Hindu, not Toda), a No·ṣ clansman Tö·vah (a well-known oracle of his time, named after the Parson's Valley river) married her and they had a son, Moṇyxe·ṇ. This story was told to me by Kwat̲o·ṛ-kwïṭṇ many years ago, but very recently Nilavaty, of the To·r̲o·ṛ clan, recalled the song and began humming it.

Hunting for Sport

Toda elders also recall from the Imperial days that the British often engaged Toda males as assistants when they were out hunting game (*shikar*), and quite a few suffered serious consequences. For example, there is a funeral song composed about a Toda boy tracker who was inadvertently shot dead by a British hunter, one that is still remembered.

The To·r̲o·ṛ people recollect stories associated with Mr Minchin (Mincin-ars in Toda), who had a plantation in the Glenmorgan area, and can point out his now somewhat run-down bungalow. One such anecdote was narrated to me by Kwat̲o·ṛ-kwïṭṇ a long time ago when we were both camping in the area around Mount Kar̲o·ṛ. He showed me an imposing rock at the edge of the plateau (Image 12.2), on which a confrontation between an enormous male gaur (the largest wild bovine) and a hungry tiger unfolded. The sounds attracted a small crowd of Todas who called in Minchin, who nonchalantly shot both animals.

Another very well-known incident relates to a time when Minchin was hunting Nilgiri tahr (or *ibex*, as the British erroneously called them) in the Glenmorgan area (Image 12.3), accompanied by his young Toda tracker. By the time they reached the cliffs

IMAGE 12.2: The view from the *öθkwïḷykas* ('the rock with a lovely view') near Pašta·ṟ

Source: Tarun Chhabra.

(Image 12.4), a thick blanket of fog (*oṭmoẕ* in Toda) had risen and engulfed the landscape; when a tahr saddleback suddenly came crashing out of a shola thicket known to Todas as Kwaṛkaṣtwa·ṣ. Minchin quickly fired at it and as the buck disappeared into the

IMAGE 12.3: Pašta·r̲ hamlet in Glenmorgan, 2019; this area was a favourite hunting ground for the British

Source: Tarun Chhabra.

IMAGE 12.4: The cliff face—a freefall—over which Tüḷyoȥkwï·ṛ was trying to retrieve a wounded tahr shot by Mr Minchin

Source: Tarun Chhabra.

mist, he ordered his Toda helper, Tüḷyoẓkwï·ṛ, to retrieve the wounded animal. The adept Toda lad went after the wild mountain goat in a flash. Minchin waited patiently for the tracker to return with his quarry, but when neither showed up, he was aghast to realise that his assistant might have gone over the cliff (Image 12.4).

After searching in vain, he returned home shaken and finally sent word about the unfortunate turn of events to the boy's family, who began to mourn. Later that day, some menfolk walked over to this sacred cliff—where the Toda deity Ko·ḷvoy is believed to reside (see Image 12.5)—in search of this boy, fearing the worst. By this time the fog had lifted and as the search party scanned the escarpment from the opposite flank, they were pleasantly surprised to see the figure of Tüḷyoẓkwï·ṛ precariously perched on a tree that was jutting out from the cliff face. Indeed, a true cliff-hanger in every sense!

Minchin was informed, and shortly after that they fabricated a wooden box suspended from the cliff top with strong ropes (some

IMAGE 12.5: The cliff seen in Image 12.4 is also very sacred to the Todas, being the abode of one of their major deities, Ko·ḷvoy; its door-like entrance is seen here

Source: Tarun Chhabra.

maintain that metal chains were used). As soon as this reached the level where the youth had held onto a protruding tree after a freefall, he slowly crawled into the box and was pulled up. Much celebration followed.

There were hunting expeditions that had effects on Toda culture as well. The Nïṛy clansmen are reminded of this every day when the dairyman-priest sprinkles freshly-drawn sacred milk on the *po·s̱oṭytkas̱* (the 'milk-pouring stone') that has the sacred chant-word (or *kwas̱m*) *ïmuṛykas̱*. The story goes that a British manager of the nearby Parkside Tea Estate had been pursuing a tiger for over three days when the animal hid in a thicket near Nïṛy hamlet, closely followed by the hunter on horseback. As he lifted his gun to fire, his horse jerked quite violently, resulting in the bullet going off-tangent and hitting the sacred *ïmuṛykas̱* stone, which was slightly chipped as a consequence. The hunter was injured and somewhat shaken as he fell to the ground. On Toda advice, he later offered a buffalo for the *ïrnaṛtyt* ceremony to atone for his improper action.

Generally, the elders are aware that British hunters were quick to respond to requests from their ancestors regarding predators that attacked their buffaloes regularly. There are a number of set words—paired units in three syllables—that are added to couplets in Toda songs which mention British hunters, more generally as well. For example:

> *O·ṭpüḷymox / Kwï·ṭpïḷteṣ //*
> The son of a tiger at the shola entrance / The gun on the shola pathway //
> *Kaṯeṣe·t / Karymaθkufy //*
> Taking up the black gun / Packing in the black gunpowder //
> *Swa·leve·ṭ / Arseve·ṭ //*
> Hunting in the jungle / The Westerner out hunting //
> *Kwï·ṭïṣars / No·ṭïṣto·ṟ //*
> British in the courts / Toda clans in the sacred places //
> *Arsaṯmu·ntïrgmo· / A·naṯmu·ntïrg-mo· //*
> May the Westerner move away [without troubling us] / May the elephant [that is, all wild animals] move away //

Todas say that such incantations as this were used by them to ward off any malevolent activity from the British.

> *Arsevaṛ(k) / A·neku·ḍt(k) //*
> The crowd of Westerners / The assembly of elephants //
> *A·nemöṭ / Arsenaṛ //*
> The steps of an elephant / The walk of a Westerner //
> *Kwï·ṭïṣars / To·ṭïṣθo·ṟ //*
> The British men in the courts / The men in the plantation //
> *Arswïṛmo·t / Pö·ṛwïṛke·ḷv //*
> The speech of British people / The words of the outsiders //

Toda elders recall that British hunters would arrive on horseback at their hamlets in search of woodcock each winter; these were the favourite of marksmen as the birds fly in a zigzag manner when flushed, and so are very difficult to shoot down. I have been shown cobbled bridle paths used by the British around Toda hamlets, which are partially intact even today.

Missionaries

Among both the orthodox and Christian Toda community, the only British missionary whose name is readily recalled is Catharine F. Ling, better known to the former as Li(n)g-missy and to the latter as Lingamma. Miss Ling was the first missionary to launch the quest (which others, like J. Friedrich Metz, had already attempted; however, she was the first to make inroads) to convert these people to Christianity. Orthodox Toda elders recall that she and her Church of England Zenana Missionary Society gradually set up six small schools for Toda children, most of them located in Toda settings.

The first, in 1890, was reportedly at A·s̱moḏ hamlet, belonging to the Kï·wïṛ clan and located in the Governor's Shola area. This might explain why the first convert, Kišker̠, came from this patriclan, albeit much later. It is likely that he first received instruction here before moving on to the Pykara school that had a boarding facility. The second school, opened in 1893, was at Pïs̱vaḷ, located where the present-day Pykara Forest Colony now stands. Then came a school situated in the heart of the Wenlock Downs (Ma_so·ṛ), just off the Ooty–Gudalur road 'ninth-mile' post, at a place known in Toda as Kiskotyvïḷ. This was followed by another instruction site at Kwaṛo·ḷvïḷ (in fact, the place is even today referred to as the 'school slope' in common Toda speech; otherwise, it was known as Sussigundi), located not far from Arto·ḷ hamlet in the Glenmorgan area. Yet another school came up between Wellington and Kotagiri towns, presumably at one of the erstwhile hamlets belonging to the Ïṇkity clan, to cater to the Toda hamlets closer to eastern parts of the plateau. There are no recollections of this school at all. A sixth centre of learning was initially established in the Kandal area of Ooty, before shifting to 'Dunmere' in the Fern Hill locality later on. This is now well-known as the Gell Memorial School, although some Toda elders continue to refer to it as *ars maḏtykwa·ṭ*, that is, 'the Western woman's [Ling-missy's] bungalow'.

As mentioned, the first Toda convert was Kiške_r, who was baptised in 1904. Some Todas claim that his actual name was Kiškyvïn, and Kiške_r became the commonly-used sobriquet only later. This fits in better with its origin—from the name of his clan's sacred buffaloes—*ki·škyveṭ*. Interestingly, some elders remember why Kiške_r was driven towards the missionaries and finally became the first convert—his antipathy towards his influential cousin Kwï·_syaḷf, with whom there was reportedly much in-fighting. Both the orthodox and Christian Todas know that he went on to become a catechist. It is also in the memory of senior people that two girls from the To·_ro·ṛ clan—Sodamut and Sindavïḷ—joined Kiške_r a few years later. Pōḷkö·_r recalls that the first convert from his Mö·ṛ clan who joined Ling-missy's fold was Tö·muṣkuḷṇ (named after the hill from where the Toda deity Ö·n rules their afterworld). The reason given for this radical move was that he did not get along with his elder brother O·ḍwïn (named after another sacred hill, and whom incidentally I knew well).

Some Toda elders know that Kwaṛo·n, from the Pïrgo·ṛ clan, an early convert, was groomed by Ling-missy to become the first graduate among the entire community—way back in 1925.

Such memories are especially clear in the minds of senior Toda Christians. For instance, N. Y. Sunder, whose ancestors were from the Nïṛy clan, recalls that his father Öwgwï·ṛ was groomed by Lingmissy and baptised as Nathaniel at the tender age of fourteen. According to Sunder, at least two of the early converts—Kwaṛo·n (later, Revd. Kodan) and Tï·ṛkuḍ (later Gideon, from the Ka·s̠ clan)—named a daughter Catharine after Miss Ling. However, even senior Toda Christians are unable to recall the names of any other missionary, although there were several. Unlike the orthodox community, where only senior members are familiar with Lingmissy, almost every Toda Christian knows her as a mentor. This is partly due to the influence of the Catharine Ling Toda Mission (CLTM), which was established in 1933 and continues to exert considerable influence on this Christian community even today.

A perusal of the handwritten minute book of the very first CLTM Committee shows that this was formed to continue Miss Ling's Toda work after she retired to England, and that she continued to be its member and attended their meetings until October 1933 (and thus, contrary to general belief, only retired perhaps in 1934). This notebook also mentions the aims of the CLTM, and the meeting held to frame these objectives states that: 'the following plan was proposed for carrying on the work [of the Toda Mission] when Miss Ling proceeds on furlough prior to retirement.' The fact that Miss Ling continued to be actively in charge is demonstrated not only by the fact that she attended these meetings until October 1933, but also by the mention in this book that 'this committee [CLTM] would come immediately into being and take over charge from Miss Ling as soon as it was convenient to her to hand over'. A glance through this book also gives us the names of the other members of the first CLTM Committee, for they were the ones who continued Miss Ling's work from the end of 1933, and who apparently caused so much distress to the first Toda converts that Miss Ling was forced to come out from retirement in England and return to the Nilgiris in 1938 for a couple more years.

The Ooty Hunt

The most awaited event in the Nilgiris during the British Raj was the annual Ooty Hunt season for jackals (since foxes are not found here); it was conducted on horseback across the Wenlock Downs. Since it involved the crossing of many Toda settlements and occurred throughout their heartland, this activity is recalled by many elders. Todas were not only engaged to assist the British 'gentry', but a side feature of this event also occurred exclusively for them. This was a cross-country race for Toda menfolk that took place along various routes on the Wenlock Downs, for example, across what is now known as the 'Windy Saddle' area in the vicinity of the Government Sheep-Breeding Centre.

One of the first British-related stories that I heard from Todas was told by Kwaṯo·ṛ-kwïṭṇ, relating how, as a lad, he had won the rolling trophy at this race, apparently by invigorating himself through the regular consumption of the tubers of a terrestrial orchid known as *öštkwï·ṛ* (*Satyrium nepalense*; see Chhabra 2015, 416). Some accounts claim that the first prize given by the British was as much as Rs 50, a colossal sum in those days, while the second and third prizes on offer were Rs 25 and Rs 15, respectively; even a few consolation prizes at Rs 2 each were reportedly handed out. The man who won the first prize on three occasions was awarded the rolling trophy at a special function held alongside the other main prize-giving ceremony of the Ooty Hunt. Along with Kwaṯo·ṛ-kwïṭṇ, another name mentioned among the trophy winners was Koṛof-kwïṭṇ of the Meḷga·s patriclan.

According to Pōḷkö·ṟ, a 'buffalo show' also featured on the sidelines of the Ooty Hunt, where Todas were asked to present their finest buffaloes, prizes being given for the best-looking specimens.

Conflicts

The British are still remembered with nostalgia, as they are said to have shown great admiration for traditional Toda culture; besides, they did try to insulate these people from outside influences. One refrain that I constantly heard from elders was that the community became morose once India gained its independence.

Nonetheless, there were many areas of conflict with the colonials, too, especially due to the early acquisition of Toda territory to establish several major townships. Ka·s̱ hamlet, for instance, cannot forget that a large portion of their sacred land, including a major part of Kandalmund shola, was acquired for a mere Rs 400 to later become the property of the Ootacamund Club. Although the government did later restore some of the alienated land to the Todas (Price 2012 [1908], 263), mental scars remain. The Ïṇkity patriclan also lost their major settlements when the military cantonment of Wellington was established in the 1850s, and were given meagre compensation in exchange.

Elders recall that developmental projects even during British days had their impact on Toda culture. It is pointed out that the Pykara Dam caused the flooding of the sacred crossing-points along the course of the sacred Ko·ḷyki·n River, besides submerging several migratory buffalo paths (Chhabra 2015, 326–333). In turn, this led to the abandonment of associated dry-season hamlets, and so contributed to the termination of the most sacred *ti·*-dairy institution. It is also remembered that the dam across the Kateri waterfall (Kupïn was̱y in Toda) in 1905 was the first hydroelectric project in the Nilgiris, and indeed in all of India.

Even the marvellous narrow-gauge Nilgiri Mountain Railway (now a UNESCO-designated heritage feature) had its after-effects for the Todas. This is because, just before the train reaches its final destination of Ootacamund, it passes along a hillside located directly above the dairy-temple at Küšu hamlet. Since Toda females are not permitted to enter the hallowed area above this temple, the location of the railway tracks presented the community with a predicament, one that they finally resolved by declaring that henceforth, no Toda females were to ride on the train over this stretch of track. Therefore Toda women travelling to the plains by train must get on at Lovedale station, not Ooty; and those coming from the lowlands must disembark there and travel into Ooty by other means. This regulation is still enforced (although most locals now find it more convenient to journey to and from the plains by road, anyway).

Linguistic Influence

In the Nilgiris of the twenty-first century, the *lingua franca* is very much Tamil, and its influence on the languages of the indigenous groups is quite a significant one, and continues to grow. Interestingly, however, there are a large number of English-derived words that have entered the Toda lexicon after undergoing suitable 'Toda-isation'. Some examples: *kaḷko·ṛ* (Collector/administrative head of district); *to·ko·ṛ* (doctor); *boṭlu·r* (butler); *mōnïzer* (manager); *sirkiẓ* (circus); *egi·rmuṭ* (agreement); *pōrkuc* (barracks); *kwï·ṭ* (court), etc. There are also words like *si·poy* (sepoy) that have entered English from other Indian languages, especially Badaga, and then found their way into Toda.

* * *

To sum up, from the early days after the arrival of a few Britons in 1819, an enduring romantic fascination for the Todas with their seemingly quaint culture, striking countenance, and magically beautiful landscapes, began to unfold for their newfound 'colonial masters'. Moreover, these men had met their match in an aboriginal group that showed absolutely no sense of subservience at all. Indeed, the Todas appeared to look upon Western culture with distinct condescension. John Sullivan himself notes that:

> It was [only] for the second time that they saw white men, but I was perplexed by their majestically calm attitude; it resembled so little the slavish manners of the natives in India whom we were accustomed to see. They seemed to await our arrival. (Blavatsky 1930, 79)

The Toda elders then explained that their oracles had prophesied that a race of men would one day come from beyond the seas and settle near them. When Sullivan conversed with the Todas over the ensuing years, he was astonished to note that they understood the British well and were not afraid to state this. He writes in his memoirs: 'Spontaneously and very justly, [they] understood our national character and our faults' (ibid., 105). Sullivan found himself quickly 'conquered' by the Toda people and he was to remain their friend and protector for nearly thirty years. To a large extent, the Todas also built up an emotional bond with those erstwhile colonial 'masters'.

Notes

1. Emeneau gives a different version of this story (1994, 406–407), mentioning a sheepskin (see Chapter 4, this volume). It is also highly improbable that Todas would have encountered Sullivan while descending the Nilgiri slopes, and that he would have asked them to carry him up! It is well-known that Sullivan first established his residence at Kannērimukku (near Dimbaṭṭi) on the eastern edge of the plateau, and moved to Ooty only in 1822. Therefore, if he was already established in the Nilgiris, he would hardly have been coming up unaided. This account also mentions that the Todas were going down to a place known as Pe·ṭ (which Emeneau thinks might be Meṭṭupāḷayam) to get salt, rice, etc. But it is also well-known to Todas that Pe·ṭ actually referred to a place located beyond Mānārekāḍu in Kerala, which could be reached by going beyond the Kurumba hamlet Po·ny or Bāni, on the southwest Nilgiri slopes (see Chhabra 2015, 32–33, on how this has been visited since ancient times). This story has been quoted (Hockings 2012, 883) with the disqualifier that it is likely to be fictional as sheep were not found anywhere in the Nilgiris. However, I was emphatically told that it was goatskin (not sheepskin), and that goats have been reared by some Irulas and Kurumbas for centuries. In Tamil, the same word (*āḍu*) is often used for both goat and sheep, but Todas have a distinct term for sheep, that is, *kuṟy*. It is unlikely that the story was invented by Todas later. Rather, it appears that Sullivan might have adapted the story from one he was already familiar with, as it had been mentioned by Virgil concerning Queen Dido's acquisition of the site of Carthage (with the exception of the change to a goatskin).

2. Although no Toda has become a VAO as yet, at the Sholur village panchayat (the local-level elected body), which has been designated as reserved for Scheduled Tribes, Todas (including one woman) have served as Panchayat President.

3. See Chhabra (2015, 319) for details of these hills.

References

Blavatsky, Helena P. 1930. *The People of the Blue Mountains*. Wheaton, IL.: Theosophical Press.

Chhabra, Tarun. 2015. *The Toda Landscape: Explorations in Cultural Ecology*. Harvard Oriental Series, Vol. 79. Cambridge, MA, and New Delhi: Harvard University Press, and Orient BlackSwan.

Emeneau, Murray B. 1971. *Toda Songs*. Oxford: Clarendon Press.

_____. 1994. *Dravidian Studies: Selected Papers*. New Delhi: Motilal Banarsidass.

Hockings, Paul (ed.). 2012. *Encyclopædia of the Nilgiri Hills*. New Delhi: Manohar.

Price, J. Frederick. 2012 [1908]. *Ootacamund. A History*. New Delhi: Rupa.

Further Reading

'Breeks', 'British', 'Christian Todas', 'Hunting Literature', 'Ling', and 'Sullivan'. In *Encyclopædia of the Nilgiri Hills*, Paul Hockings (ed.). New Delhi: Manohar, 2012.

13

The Sadist Who Sired a South Indian Scholar-Administrator

Paul Hockings

Sir Frederick Price's History

Anyone who has taken a serious interest in the history of the Nilgiri region has certainly come across a most elegant-looking book on the local history: *Ootacamund, a History*, by Sir Frederick Price (1908, and fortunately republished in 2002). Its original publisher, the Government of Madras, had commissioned this five years beforehand, and clearly spared no expense in the book's production. It is beautifully bound in half-leather, with pages of 30 x 38 cms, and has sixteen large photographs by A. T. W. Penn, a local photographer (see Chapter 14, this volume), as well as nine maps, plans, and drawings. The print is large, so that elderly readers can happily use the book. It runs to 281 pages, and is blessed with a 21-page index and several Appendices, including one that lists all of the *European* homes in the hill station of Ootacamund in 1858 and 1905, along with names of the original owners. (A specialist can usefully compare this particular list with lists of Ooty's houses and who was renting them during The Season, lists that were published every few weeks in issues of the local newspaper, *The South of India Observer*, for over half a century.)

Price's history, which hardly mentions the existence of indigenous inhabitants, starts with a detailed account of European visits to the Nilgiris prior to 1818, and includes an intriguing facsimile of B. S. Ward's Nilgiri map of 1822. Then Price outlines the expeditions of John Sullivan in 1819, which initiated the modernisation of the area. Misleadingly, it was as if 'history began in the second decade of the nineteenth century with the arrival of Europeans intent on settlement and was consolidated and augmented thereafter by a series of arrivals and introductions' (Sutton 2009, 2).

The next chapter of the book is devoted to the first British house built in Ooty, Sullivan's quite substantial 'Stonehouse', and includes a plan of it. This is followed by further information on John Sullivan's many pioneering activities, along with his photograph. It is the only chapter that has much to say about the indigenous Todas and Badagas of the area, for otherwise this *History* is essentially a record of European endeavour.

Next we have an account of the artificial Ooty Lake's early years, and its several physical disasters. Now that the town was recognised as a hill station—the first in south India—various governors made their visits, each of which is recounted in detail here. This is followed by the story of how Government House came to be built; and then accounts of further visits by governors-general and viceroys. T. B. Macaulay's stay merits a whole chapter, as he was here long enough to draft the Indian Penal Code while his sister looked after him at the Ooty Club.

These chapters are followed by a thorough account of the building of Ooty's several churches, both Protestant and Catholic, a section that runs to many pages, pride of place of course going to St. Stephen's, the main Anglican church. Some persons buried in its graveyard get detailed documentation here too.

This church section is followed by several quite short chapters: on schools, public buildings, early hospitals and dispensaries, libraries and museums. A chapter on horticulture and the botanical garden is valuable for its explanation of the great variety of species imported experimentally from England, Australia, and elsewhere.

A central institution for Europeans from a very early time has been the Ooty Club, where Macaulay stayed. A plan helps us understand how the Club was modified from a private home, quite a grand one, into the clubhouse that many readers are familiar with. Other short chapters are presented on the Masonic Lodge (another important social institution in the nineteenth century), and the Armory built for the Nilgiri Volunteers.

Then comes a long section devoted to 'old and otherwise noteworthy houses', dealt with in alphabetical order. After this, Price goes back to the early years of the British occupance of this town site to discuss the history of its use as a military establishment, mainly for recuperating soldiers and veterans. He then talks about how Ooty became a municipality in 1866, and the improvements in civic infrastructure that followed—water, street lights, drainage, the expanded market, etc.

The local sojourners were ever looking for amusements, especially British ones, so next we get an account of the famed Ooty Hunt, racing, polo, cricket, and golf, *inter alia.* Some discussion of drives and walks in the nearby area suggests that British residents could manage to lead quite an active life here if they wished.

There follows a section covering all sorts of urban topics: theatricals, brewing, the observatory, etc. But it is noticeable that neither here nor elsewhere in the book does Price make any mention of musical performances or of Ooty's popular music hall (see Chapter 14, this volume); yet during at least the last quarter of the nineteenth century there had been an Ooty Musical Association that gave concerts, and the music hall lasted for many years, too, thanks to a devoted corps of touring performers. (It eventually became housing for the poor.)

Finally there is a valuable closing chapter, 'Ootacamund Past and Present', which includes several plans of the town at different stages in its development. Throughout the whole book, a great deal of local history and details about particular British people make for a dense picture of this Queen of Hill Stations; indeed, perhaps more detail than most readers can digest.

But we need to look more closely at one short chapter, a really strange one because of *what it leaves out.* I refer to Price's coverage of local schools, all of which were run in the nineteenth century either as small private enterprises or were affiliated with particular Christian church organisations. Price describes several quite minor institutions, 'Old Dame's schools' run by one or two spinsters, most of which collapsed rapidly once the teachers married, moved elsewhere, or passed away. Yet what was and is regarded as a major school in Madras Presidency, the Lawrence Memorial School (formerly Lawrence Asylum), receives *absolutely no mention* in this chapter. This large building project, the biggest school in the town, designed by Robert Fellowes Chisholm (in 1865–1869), used an Italianate style reminiscent of Queen Victoria's favourite residence, Osborne House, with a tall campanile added. Price's book index *does* have references to the initial buying of Sullivan's old home, 'Stonehouse', for the Asylum; the previous use of 'Lower Norwood' for this school; the lake near the school, also the road there, Madras Sappers working there, its press, its Volunteer Rifle Corps, the police station and copses there, even the school organ—but nothing about the building itself, even though it was one of the major Italianate buildings in all of south India and certainly a jewel in Ooty's crown! Price's book also has a whole chapter on Government House (now known as Raj Bhavan), even going into great details about its cost. But although he refers twice to the 'Consulting Architect to Government', he does not mention that it was actually R. F. Chisholm who designed that building too! Nor that Chisholm designed Ootacamund's library (apparently his very first assignment) and the post office, both in a Gothic Revival style. In contrast, a recent British writer has described Chisholm as 'the leading Victorian architect to practise in Madras', and 'one of the most versatile architects to work in British India' (see Michell 1998). Eventually Chisholm was to complete the design for the Lakshmi Vilas (1880–1890), a colossal palace for the Gaekwar of Baroda that has been touted as the most expensive private building ever to be erected by any one individual *anywhere* during the entire nineteenth century—very likely too, for the structure is enormous.

Why Frederick Price should have so completely cold-shouldered an outstanding architect in this manner is difficult to fathom; and not even mentioning the Lawrence Memorial School in a chapter on Ooty's schools is even stranger. Was it because Price was a purist who could not stomach Chisholm's interest in fusing Western and Oriental features in his buildings, at least from 1871 onwards, which are in an Indo-Saracenic style? Or was it that Price bore some grudge against the Lawrence Asylum, which had originated as a school for military orphans? Or had Price been heartily offended by some aspect of Chisholm's personal manners or 'artistic temperament' or his ability to work alongside Indian craftsmen? The two men surely knew each other, for Chisholm was the Consulting Architect to the Madras Government (1872–1886) when Price became the Chief Secretary, and there were many years when both men were in Madras or both in Ooty, sometimes even in the same room, so encounters between them would have been unavoidable. Did they have some personal altercation, possibly because Chisholm found out about Price's ghastly parentage, and might even have taunted him over it? Can there ever be an answer?

Price's treatment of this distinguished architect, ignoring him altogether in this large and otherwise detailed book, was churlish, to say the least. His failure to mention public musical performances or the Ooty music hall only compounds Price's apparent dismissal of the finer arts *in toto*. In vivid contrast, he has slightly more to say, at *twelve* different places in the book, about the two local jails, for Europeans and 'Natives'.

Which leads us directly to the question of who exactly was this usually meticulous local historian, what indeed was his background, and how did he end up in the Nilgiris at the turn of the twentieth century?

The Horrific Father

Frederick Price was in all probability the first Australian ever to pass the exams for the Indian Civil Service. He was a son of John Giles Price, who was born in England in 1808. The young John Price, fourth among the fourteen legitimate children of Sir Rose Price, had studied at Charterhouse School and then Brasenose College, Oxford, leaving there in 1829 without taking a degree. In those days, lots of young men did this: coming from a remote area like Cornwall, they just wanted to live in Oxford for awhile, not for the education but to acquire a bit of social polish, find some fancy friends, and have a good time.

John Price's prospects were quite uncertain, for the 1833 Emancipation Act that had put an end to slavery had also put an end to his family's fortunes, which depended on Worthy Park, an old sugar plantation run by slave labour in Jamaica (Craton and Walvin 1970). As the sugar business was rapidly declining for the Prices, eventually their large estate in Cornwall had to be sold in 1867.

Meanwhile, John had to move on. Arriving in Tasmania early in 1836, he soon married Mary Franklin, a niece of Sir John Franklin, the famed Arctic explorer, who was for some years the lieutenant-governor of Van Diemen's Land (as Tasmania was then called). She had come from a military family in Bengal. In Hobart town, people looked up to John Price then because he was minor aristocracy, the son of a Cornish Baronet, as well as a local magistrate; so Mary had made what was deemed a good marriage, albeit in a bad place. She produced eight children in Australia, six of whom survived to adulthood; John Frederick was the oldest, born on 3 October 1839.

He was only six when his father, after doing a bit of farming on a land grant, was appointed as Commandant of the penal establishment on Norfolk Island, a tiny, utterly remote place in the middle of the Pacific, 640 km north of New Zealand and 1,400 km east of Brisbane. It was a prison from which nobody ever escaped, basically intended to hold and punish a couple of thousand convicts who, after penal transportation from Britain, had committed further crimes while in Australia. John Price stayed there for six years (1846–1853), and throughout that time was accompanied by his wife and their several children.

This is not the place to recount the well-known details of Price's reign of terror (Hughes 1987, 543–551). That a human being could inflict such brutality on convicts is scarcely believable: days of solitary unlit confinement for walking too slowly; long bouts of flogging for possessing a trace of tobacco, indeed, flogging for just about any infraction, such as forgetting one's shoelaces or having a pet bird. Price even found reason to have a blind man flogged. Price's poor wife Mary was facing 'surroundings whose unexcelled natural beauty were tainted by the viciousness of the gaoled and the gaolers, linked with a husband of marked peculiarities of temperament' (Barry 1964, 24)—and John Price was evidently the most vicious person on that island. He ordered floggings of convicts nearly every day, ghastly events that could last an hour or more, by which time the victim would be standing in a pool of his own blood and would probably be in a state of hypovolemic shock. Some men lost so much flesh that their backbones were revealed, and of course some died. Occasionally those who had done something particularly evil in Price's view were hanged on the spot, although according to law they should first have been sent for trial in Sydney. How female convicts were treated one shudders to think—for there was a large contingent of women on Norfolk Island too. At least one Commandant was so brutal that from time to time he ordered a woman to be flogged. She was then stripped naked and paraded before the male convicts, who were ordered to stand around watching her torture as the hapless victim screamed and bled like an animal while tied to a sort of pillory.

Whether John Price's children witnessed these floggings and hangings is unknown, but they certainly must have heard the groans and cries of their father's victims: that would have been an almost daily experience for Frederick from the age of six to thirteen, and they could always talk to convicts too. Furthermore, since the island was described by mainland officials as a 'veritable Sodom', with sundry pædophiles and 200 feral 'bastard children' (from female convicts) running around freely on its fertile 13 square miles, one can only wonder what else the boy witnessed during those years. There was nobody but his mother to protect Frederick, and we do not know how well she managed. He and his siblings were youngsters who must have suffered from complex trauma marked by multiple and chronic stressors, the cumulative influence of which would have led to immediate and long-term behavioural, functional, and mental health outcomes about which we can only guess. Such complexly traumatised children would have to focus on their survival, and evidently did not direct their energies towards any formal schooling while on Norfolk Island (Kinniburgh, et al. 2005).

John Price had an uncanny command of the argot of the criminal underworld, which made such a deep impression on convicts that some thought he must have actually been imprisoned himself. It is not impossible—we do not know what he was doing between 1829 and 1835, but there is no record in Britain's National Archives of his incarceration anywhere. It is just possible that he spent those years at the family's sugar plantation, Worthy Park, in Jamaica, which had long been 'mismanaged and heavily indebted after a century of operations' (Gosse 2012, 65); and one might speculate that he had spent time there abusing the family's slaves (which included a gang of twenty-seven children aged 6–7), but there is actually no evidence that John was ever in Jamaica. However, he had definitely been closeted with criminals for several months during that long voyage to Australia. He seemed to understand the way a criminal's mind worked, which, coupled with his merciless administering of 'the law', was to give him total power over every convict.

But why would Price's aristocratic English family ever have taken the strange step of sending their Oxford-educated son off to Australia in 1835, armed with some letters of introduction, knowing they were unlikely to see him again, and when that country was still arguably one of the most barbarous places on earth? (The total European population of the entire continent when Price arrived there was about 123,310.) By this time his father was dead; but one possible explanation for the son's sudden departure was that the late father, Sir Rose Price (who had himself managed the family's Jamaican estate, Worthy Park, back in 1792–1795, during which years he had sired a flock of known half-caste and quadroon children; Craton and Walvin 1970, 182, n53), had become exasperated by his son's weak performance—if indeed John was ever the manager of their sugar plantation—or else his weak personality. Sugar production was in serious decline at the time. No matter who was actually the manager of the family's property in 1830, it was then using 420 African slaves, while four years later, in 1834, their number, now as wage labourers, was down to 295, largely because of a much-increased mortality rate (ibid., 199; also Gosse 2012, 67, 74). But this is empty speculation about John, as there is no mention whatever of his presence in Jamaica in the very detailed study we have of the Prices' slave-estate during that period (Craton and Walvin 1970).

The Capital Crime of Sodomy

Another, more likely explanation for his departure from England, however, is that John Price, who later had a very close relationship with a particular convict overseer, was a sodomite—a capital offence until 1861—and had gained his cachet and flashy dress sense from moving around in the illicit gay rough-trade scene back in England. Although we know nothing definite about John's predilections, there is solid evidence that his elder brother, Charles Dutton Price, was of this secret fraternity; for when their father, Sir Rose Price, died in 1834, his will

> cut off his eldest surviving son, literally, with a shilling, 'which is more than his base and unnatural conduct towards me and my family deserves but I will and I hope that though for a time he may persist in the career of vice and infamy which now mark his conduct he may die a penitent sinner in the strict sense of our Blessed Saviour.' (Craton and Walvin 1970, 203)

Two events must have traumatised many secret homosexuals in those days. On 21 August 1834, the 57-year-old William Hocking (no relation to the author) went to the gallows in Bodmin Jail for sodomy. This was very close to the Price family estate in Cornwall, and that execution occurred just one month before the death of Sir Rose Price and, as it happened, one month after the Emancipation Act had come into force, economically dooming all Jamaican slave-owners like Sir Rose. The following year the last male couple ever to be executed in Britain for this crime died outside Newgate Prison, on 27 November 1835. Hensleigh Wedgwood, the magistrate who had sent that last unfortunate pair for trial, wrote to the Home Secretary that this is 'the only capital crime that is committed by rich men but owing to the circumstances I have mentioned [that is, their access to total privacy] they are never convicted'. After that there were no more hangings: imprisonment or transportation to Australia was the punishment. (During that decade, however, only 2 per cent of judicial hangings in Britain were for the offence of sodomy.) Surely John Price decided to flee at that very moment because he was too afraid of being found out, for he left Britain for good within several weeks of this ghastly public spectacle in London (which he may well have witnessed; see Image 13.1)—and most probably on the very next ship bound for Australia. He reached Hobart in May 1836 (the voyage usually taking four to five months, via Rio de Janeiro, where there could be a long layover). The ship might have been either the 'Surrey' or the 'Thomas Harrison', both of which sailed from Cork at the end of 1835, bound for Sydney (and Cork was easily accessible by sea from John Price's birthplace at Penzance, Cornwall, where he had most probably gone to say farewell to his remaining relatives).

IMAGE 13.1: The last public hanging of sodomites outside Newgate Prison, London, 27 November 1835

Source: From an old print, courtesy of Richard Clark. The picture is typical of a Newgate hanging at this time. Note the man on the left with his large wand: he would be the City Marshall, and the man next to him was probably the Ordinary, an officer of Newgate. Note too how the ropes are tied to ensure a minimal drop. The nooses were attached in the Press Yard at the same time as the men's wrists were bound, and then James Pratt and John Smith were led out of the Debtor's Door and ascended the ten steps to the platform. The ropes were then thrown over the beam and tied as shown.

The impetus for John Price's extreme cruelty later on, while Commandant, possibly harks back to a pamphlet that his father Rose had published in 1832 ('ludicrous if it were not faintly horrific';

Craton and Walvin 1970, 191). This included grim details about the merciless flogging of African slaves in Jamaica, and its necessity. The 'theory' behind John Price's behaviour on Norfolk Island was that potential criminals in Britain and Australia should be so frightened by what was rumoured about the penal establishment that they would never risk being convicted of any crime, lest they end up in such a prison. But, as Sir John Barry, a former justice of the Supreme Court of Victoria, pointed out, 'Unless there is a law specifically authorizing the infliction of a punishment in addition to imprisonment, such as flogging, solitary confinement or fetters, neither the judge nor the gaoler has power to impose it' (Barry 1964, 25–26). As for hanging, it could only be ordered by a court of law in Sydney, following a trial. Not that this constrained John Price in his remote Oceanic eyrie, where he supervised almost daily floggings and quite a few hangings.

Eventually, though, he was relieved of his post, as the authorities in Hobart—advised by several horrified churchmen—had realised that his unstinting use of the lash indicated some sort of mental illness, for which reason they had terminated his appointment. This was in 1853. Two years later the penal settlement on Norfolk Island was abandoned anyway, as the transportation of convicts was no longer being practised. And yet, soon afterwards, John Price was provisionally appointed Inspector-General of Penal Establishments for the new colony of Victoria; and moving his family to Melbourne, he took up that post.

By this time John Price was said, understandably, to be 'the most hated man in Australia'. In his new position, he was overseeing large gangs of convicts who were housed offshore in wrecked ships, the 'hulks', but then brought ashore each day to labour in heavy construction projects. On 26 March 1857 Price came amongst a group of eighty-two men working in a quarry, confident as always in his power over the life of others—'he was a man of commanding presence, of great physical strength, and absolutely without fear' (Barry 1964, 39)—and he always carried a brace of pistols; but these convicts had been making plans. That afternoon, it was reported,

> the men attacked, trying to drag him to a tent made of bits of dismantled ship. There they had prepared a noose with which to hang him.... He managed to break away from them and run. However, there were a hundred men around that quarry. As he tried to avoid the different gangs, someone managed to hit him with a heavy stone, knocking him over. After that, he was finished. The convicts hit him with anything they had in their hands at the time—hammers, stones, crowbars. There wasn't much left of him by the time they were finished, but he survived for another day before finally dying. (Gibb 1895)

Image 13.2: The murder of John Price near Melbourne, 26 March 1857

Source: An artist's impression, from Gibb 1895; note the hulk in the upper right of the sketch.

The seven officers protecting Price had already fled. Those convicts must have been well aware that they could be hanged for what they did; and seven of them were. However, as nearly half of Australia's population (just under one million by then) consisted of convicts and ex-convicts, there was universal rejoicing in the towns and in the hulks. The venerable Melbourne newspaper, *The Age*, was only voicing popular opinion when it wrote:

> But, if the truth be told, there can be no doubt whatever that Mr. Price was guilty of the cruelty attributed to him, and that

> his untimely and unfortunate end is the melancholy result of the vindictive feeling which his own conduct and policy has fostered in the minds of the convicts under his charge. The whole affair lies in a nutshell. He was a cruel man, and his cruelty came back to him. (Quoted in Barry 1964, 110)

St Paul put it much more succinctly: 'Whatsoever a man soweth that shall he also reap.'

John Price Immortalised

Some years later, the Australian writer Marcus Clarke was to use John Price as the precise model for Maurice Frere, the villain in his famed novel, *For the Term of his Natural Life* (1874). Clarke had migrated to Melbourne only six years after Price's death, and as he did a lot of research there and in Hobart into the convict system, he was very well informed before writing his novel. This perhaps suggests an answer to the anomaly indicated earlier, as to why Frederick Price could never bring himself to write about the architect, Robert Chisholm. Clarke's novel was so successful that it was published in Britain, Australia, and America during its first few years, and reviews appeared in *The Spectator* as well as in Australian newspapers like the *Sydney Morning Herald* and *The Australasian*. It needs little stretch of the imagination to presume that Chisholm must have read at least one of these reviews in some Madras reading-room, probably one in *The Spectator*, and then heard from someone there or from a review that the infamous Maurice Frere was based on the real-life John Price. Did Chisholm taunt Frederick Price with this knowledge? Or did he perhaps even dare to show Price our Image 13.2?

At the time of the murder Frederick was 17½ and in his second year at the recently opened University of Melbourne; he was only the eighteenth student ever to be enrolled there. He studied Latin, Greek, Geometry, Algebra, Geology, Zoology, and Logic; but after passing in his second year he left the University, nine months after his father's death. He had begun to realise that the name of Price was no longer an entrée to colonial society and higher office; moreover, his mother and several younger siblings had meagre prospects. Eventually Frederick took the ICS exams in 1861 and headed for Madras, where in all likelihood nobody knew anything about his father—especially as, at the very moment of his death, all British eyes had been trained on the outbreak of mutiny in northern India. Soon after reaching Madras, Frederick married his wife, Alice.

If indeed Frederick Price knew that his father was homosexual—and it is only a supposition, though a likely one—he would have been conflicted throughout his entire adult life by the irony that his own parent, although a magistrate and agent of government, had secretly been committing sodomy, in those days considered a terrible crime; whereas ultimately it was the convicts, by definition criminals, who had rendered justice against this unconvicted monster after he had been practising a capital offence for decades. John was the quintessence of evil, a truly Shakespearean villain. Since the word doubtless spread around about his penchant for young men, a heinous crime in those days, people would have felt even more fiercely resentful at the thought that they had themselves been transported for seven or fourteen years for such trivial offences as stealing a tool or some food, whereas John Price was their brutal and never-convicted taskmaster and tormentor.

Over his career during the next thirty-five years, the son, J. Frederick Price, advanced through several Madras Civil Service positions, the first Australian to do so. Seemingly he was a model bureaucrat, fluent in Latin, Tamil, and of course English, and capable of handling a wide range of administrative tasks. His wife bore six children, two of whom would become brigadiers-general. During 1878–1887, her husband was Collector of Chingleput (Chengalpattu), near Madras (Chennai), a position that John Sullivan had held some sixty years before. Sadly, in 1878 he learnt that his brother, James Franklin Price, had been slaughtered by natives on Mulgrave (now Badu) Island in the Torres Straits. Then, for nine years, Price was a Member of the Legislative Council and served several Madras Governors as their Chief Secretary, the highest career office there. It is noticeable that when he retired in

1898 and was awarded the KCSI, he opted not to be called Sir John Price, but rather, Sir Frederick Price.

After retirement, he produced two remarkable books which demonstrated that he was truly a scholar-administrator, a Cicero for southern India, if you will. One was *Ootacamund, a History* (1908), as described, and the other was his translation of the huge private *Diary of Ananda Ranga Piḷḷai* (1904–1924), written during 1736–1761 by the Dubash of the Governor of Pondicherry (Puducherry). This latter book confirmed beyond all doubt that Price was a master of the Tamil language, often called 'the Latin of the East' (whereas at university, he had failed Greek). Price completed this vast project in collaboration with Kadamki Rangachariyar, BA, a brilliant Tamil Brahmin who was also assisting Edgar Thurston in compiling *Castes and Tribes of Southern India* (1909).

While working on these literary 'labours of love', as they would appear to have been, Price had been living in Ootacamund for a dozen or more years with his wife, when it was a town of around 18,600 population. (Of those people, a couple of thousand were Europeans, and there were also several hundred Eurasians.) But eventually the couple retired to Exmouth, in Devon, to 'Trengwainton', a house named after his grandfather's former estate, which lay not far to the west. It was here that, exactly seventy years after his father's dramatic if predictable end, Frederick too died on 12 June 1927, at the age of eighty-seven. In another four days he became the last family member to be interred in the Price mausoleum near Penzance. And over ninety years later, he is still remembered with respect by all those who have studied the history of the Nilgiri area.

The psychological contrasts between father and son raise some unanswered questions. The first is whether the evident personality characteristics of John Price as both a closeted homosexual and a sadist are functionally linked in some way, or whether these were two separable episodes: was it the oft-reported experiences in a nineteenth-century English public school and doubtless with his elder brother too that had led him to homosexual behaviour in his youth, whereas it was finding himself in supreme authority over hundreds of miserable men and women that tempted him into sadism later on? Did some years quietly spent on his family's slave-run estate in Jamaica possibly play any part in his psycho-sexual development? Another question is whether awareness on the part of Frederick Price of his father's criminal and psychological weakness fostered a counter-reaction in the son's behaviour, marked by a much more typical Victorian family life and a successful career of exemplary, law-abiding service to the state for which he worked?

There lingers a more general question about the overseas contacts of south Indian officials. Given that Madras Presidency and the Australian colonies in the later nineteenth century formed important parts of the British Empire, were officials in that Presidency as ignorant of Australian affairs as this chapter has implied? After all, useful plants were being imported from Australia to the Nilgiris and elsewhere in some quantity, and some miners had worked in both the Wainad and Australia, which had its gold rush in 1851. Mangoes from India reached the Queensland colony in the mid-nineteenth century. Was there nobody else in the district who might informally confirm or spread the scandalous word about Frederick Price's family?

Indeed there was, and it was a young woman: none other, in fact, than the Leading Lady of Ooty Society (such as it was around 1870). She was Susan Maria Breeks, wife of the Commissioner of the Nilgiris, Jim Breeks (1830–1872). She had been born in London in 1841, but at the age of five found herself settled in Hobart Town, since her father, Sir William Denison, had just become the Governor of Van Diemen's Land, in the footsteps of Sir John Franklin (Blackett-Ord 2015).

It is inconceivable that Susan Breeks did not spend time and share confidences with Frederick Price whenever he was in Ooty, as she was only two years younger than he, and both had spent part of their childhoods in Hobart Town, his birthplace—a city then not much larger than Ootacamund. However, they could not have met as children, because by the time the Denisons arrived in Hobart, Frederick was already living with his family on Norfolk Island. The Denison family had remained in Hobart until 1855, when Sir William was appointed Governor of New South Wales. The *Sydney Morning Herald* was already a quarter-century old, and was not the only newspaper there; and so, when John Price was murdered two years after Denison's arrival, that dramatic news was immediately known to all and sundry.

A competent and fairly progressive administrator, Sir William spent six years in Sydney before becoming Governor of Madras Presidency. Although based in Madras, he soon got the chance to lease Bishopsdown, a large house in Ooty. Susan soon found herself living alone with her father in Government House, as the rest of the family had moved back to England. The two usually spent the hot months in Ootacamund. Susan was now nearing twenty. At that time the Private Secretary to the Governor was James Wilkinson Breeks, who was thirty-two when appointed to this coveted position—which Frederick Price was soon to assume. Then Jim Breeks and Susan got married in Madras, in 1863. By that time Robert Chisholm was on the cusp of a brilliant career, designing public buildings in Madras and Ootacamund. He was only four years older than Susan, and was completing work on the Nilgiri Library in 1869. Inevitably, the two must have had plenty of social contact in the small town. It can safely be assumed that Chisholm knew something of Price's sordid family background from Susan Breeks, in addition to what he probably heard in other government circles or read in the papers. Nothing could have halted the ready circulation of salacious gossip, or 'gup' as they used to call it there. As some wit observed long ago, *Sic transit gloria Ootacamundi*!

Acknowledgements

My sincere thanks to Peter Biella, Richard Clark, Gaurav Datta, David MacDougall, Amar Ojha, Christopher Penn, and the archivists of Brasenose College, Trengwainton Gardens, and the University of Melbourne.

References

Barry, John V. 1964. *The Life and Death of John Price, a Study of the Exercise of Naked Power.* Melbourne: Melbourne University Press; London and New York: Cambridge University Press.

Blackett-Ord, Rosemary. 2015. *Susan Breeks of Helbeck: Victorian Ladies in Australia, India and Westmorland*. Kirkby Stephen, Cumbria: Hayloft Publishing Ltd.

Clarke, Marcus Andrew Hislop. 1874. *For the Term of his Natural Life*. Melbourne: W. Fairfax & Co. [frequently reprinted].

Reviews of Clarke, *His Natural Life*:

1874. *The Australasian*, 16 May.

1874. *Sydney Morning Herald*, 21 May.

1875. 'An Australian Novelist'. *The Spectator* 48 (2472), 1426–1428.

Craton, Michael, and James Walvin. 1970. *A Jamaican Plantation: The History of Worthy Park, 1670–1970*. London: W. H. Allen.

Gibb, Eric. 1895. *Thrilling Incidents of the Convict System in Australia: How it Grew and was Nourished and How it Declined, and What Evils and What Good Have Arisen from it*. London: Hammond and Green.

Gosse, Dave St Aubyn. 2012. 'Worthy Park: Example of Management for Survival'. In his *Abolition and Plantation Management in Jamaica 1807–1838*, 63–91. Kingston, Jamaica: University of the West Indies Press.

Hughes, Robert. 1987. *The Fatal Shore, the Epic of Australia's Founding*. New York: Alfred A. Knopf.

Kinniburgh, Kristine Jentoft, Margaret Blaustein, Joseph Spinazzola, and Bessel A. van der Kolk. 2005. 'Attachment, Self-Regulation, and Competency: A Comprehensive Intervention Framework for Children with Complex Trauma'. *Psychiatric Annals* 35 (5), 424–430.

Michell, George. 1998., *Blue Guide Southern India*. London: Blue Guides Publication.

Price, J. Frederick. 1904–1924. *The Private Diary of Ananda Ranga Pillai, Dubash to Joseph François Dupleix, Governor of Pondichery, from 1736 to 1761*, J. Frederick Price and Kadamki Rangachariyar (eds and trans.). Madras: Superintendent, Government Press, 12 vols (reprinted 1927, 1985, 2006, 2016).

——. 1908. *Ootacamund. A History*. Compiled for Government. Madras: Superintendent, Government Press (reprint, Calcutta: Rupa and Company, 2012, 2 vols).

Price, Rose. 1832. *Pledges in Colonial Slavery, to Candidates for Seats in Parliament, Rightly Considered*. Penzance: privately printed (by Sir Rose Price).

South of India Observer. 1864–1959. *The South of India Observer*. Ootacamund: South of India Observer Press (newspaper files; title varies; many issues now in the British Library; microfilm at the Memorial Library, University of Wisconsin, Madison).

Sutton, Deborah. 2009. *Other Landscapes: Colonialism and the Predicament of Authority in Nineteenth-Century South India.* Hyderabad: Orient BlackSwan.

Thurston, Edgar, and Kadamki Rangachari. 1909. *Castes and Tribes of Southern India.* Madras: Superintendent, Government Press, 7 vols.

Further Reading

Hughes, Robert. 1987. *The Fatal Shore, the Epic of Australia's Founding.* New York: Alfred A. Knopf.

'Chisholm'. In *Encyclopædia of the Nilgiri Hills,* Paul Hockings (ed.). New Delhi: Manohar, 2012.

14

A Nineteenth-Century Photographer of the Nilgiris and its People

CHRISTOPHER PENN

In the section on 'Local news' that appeared in the Ootacamund newspaper *The South of India Observer* of 29 April 1911 (p. 12), there was an article captioned 'Farewell to Mr. A. T. W. Penn':

> We have once again to chronicle another farewell gathering to one of the oldest residents on these Hills.... The Chaplains and the choir of St. Stephen's Church met at Misquith's rooms in the evening of last Wednesday to say good bye to Mr. Penn, the oldest member of the choir, and to his family, who are now leaving India for good.
>
> Mr. Penn, as the readers of this paper know, arrived in Ootacamund as far back as the year 1865 as a young man, and now goes back to his place of birth, a man full of years. Soon after Mr. Penn's arrival in Ootacamund, he enlisted himself as a member of St. Stephen's Church Choir and has been a staunch and regular member of it up to now, i.e. he has been a chorister for nearly 45 years, a record seldom reached. The Organist at that time was Mr. Charles Misquith,[1] the eldest brother of our present Organist, and both choir and organ were placed on the present gallery of the church. Mr. Penn being of a very musical turn of mind and the possessor of a very fine tenor voice, was the organiser of many musical treats....
>
> The veteran chorister appeared much moved as he returned thanks for all the good things said about him. St. Stephen's, he said, was endeared to him for it was here he was married and at this font all his children, with only one exception, were baptized. He was proud to say this and he would often think of the dear old church in his retirement

> at Home. Mr. Penn and family sail from Colombo on the 4th proximo by an Orient Liner.

Mr A. T. W. Penn was born in Street, Somerset, in 1849. He left his West Country home before he was twelve years old, trained in London as a photographer, and in 1864 sailed out to Madras. He was employed there by Nicholas Brothers, a photographic company with studios in Madras and Ooty. In 1865, now aged sixteen, Penn was sent to run the Ooty studio. It was there (Plates 1–3) that he was married in 1870, raised his family, and then worked for almost half-a-century.

Ooty, Coonoor, and Kotagiri were valued by the European population primarily as 'hill stations'. Ooty, where the Governor of Madras and Council were in residence every April to September, was the political and religious centre of the Nilgiris; but Coonoor was the business centre, where the United Planters' Association of Southern India (UPASI), formed in 1893, had its headquarters.

The market for a photographer there was for portraits of clients taken in the studio, and landscapes and photographs of the Nilgiri people that were sold to tourists as mementos of their visit. Early in the twentieth century, picture-postcards and stereoscopic views were also a big item among souvenir hunters.

A prominent feature of Ooty was the lake, which had been formed by John Sullivan in 1824 by damming the water flowing down mountain streams into the Ooty valley. An embankment, known as 'the Bund', ran across the middle of the lake (Plate 3). In the 1890s, the lower part of the lake had become unsanitary and so was drained to create a racecourse, thus halving the size of the lake.

In 1867, two years after Penn had reached Ooty, James Wilkinson Breeks was appointed as the first Commissioner (subsequently termed the Collector) of the Nilgiris. On 1 August 1867, he took charge of the new district: it had previously been administered as a *taluk* of Coimbatore District. Breeks had served as private secretary to the Governor of Madras, Sir William Denison, whose daughter he had married. He was a polymath, interested in a wide range of subjects, including archaeology and ethnology. Thus he was ideally suited to fulfil a request from the

Hon. Secretary for Trustees of the India Museum, Calcutta, to the Secretary to Government, Fort St George, dated 27 May 1871,

> to obtain ... all objects that are the products of the ... manufacturing skill [of the aboriginal and other jungle races in India] and that will serve to illustrate the habits and modes of life of those indigenous races that have remained but little affected by foreign civilisation....

With the help of the missionary-scholar J. Friedrich Metz, of the Basel Mission in nearby Ketti, Breeks set to work immediately to make a record of five 'tribes' of the Nilgiris—the Irulas, Badagas, Todas, Kotas, and Kurumbas—of their habits and customs, utensils and ornaments (Plate 4).

The two men placed equal importance on making a record of the prehistoric remains of archaeological interest (Plate 5), naming them (mostly in Gaelic!) in accordance with parallel features found in prehistoric Britain: the cairns (circular enclosures formed either by a rough stone wall, or heap, or by single stones), barrows (burial mounds), kistvaens (vaults of large stone slabs, closed in on every side), and cromlechs (similar enclosures, open on one side).

Almost all the necessary information had been obtained, and the greater part of the rough draft of a book written, before Breeks died of liver disease on 6 June 1872. His work, *An Account of the Primitive Tribes and Monuments of the Nīlagiris*, was edited by his widow and published in London for the India Museum (by W. H. Allen and Co.) in 1873.

Breeks had in a short period left his mark on the District, in particular by launching the Agri-Horticultural Society there. Following his death, the people of Ootacamund decided to found a school in his name, the Breeks' Memorial School. Penn, who, as mentioned at the farewell gathering, had a good tenor voice, took part in a number of concerts to raise funds for this school, which opened in 1874 and was situated not far from the Collector's office, where the lawcourts now stand. Penn donated a photographic portrait of Breeks (Plate 6) to the school, where it now hangs.

The population of Ooty, frequently praised as 'the Queen of Hill Stations', increased dramatically in the summer months, as sojourners, including the entire governing establishment of Madras, retreated from the heat and the unhealthy conditions of the plains to the pleasant cool of the hills. This was the time, from April to September each year, when Penn would have been most busy, taking portraits in his studio, which was strategically located between the Collector's office and the Nilgiri Library. In the winter months, from 1865 to 1875 when he was working for the Nicholas company, he travelled elsewhere in south India, building up his stock of photos of historic sites, such as the temple on the rock in Trichinopoly. Apart from portrait photographs taken in the studio, such as that of the Nizam of Hyderabad (Plate 7), and local events, including the annual Ooty Hunt breakfast photos, of which there is a series by Penn covering quite a few years, his primary market was for tourists, visitors who sought mementos such as photos of historic sites, landscapes, or the people of India. Penn became well-known for his ethnographic photographs, especially those of Toda people (Plate 8), often considered the lords of the Nilgiri plateau, to whom the other tribes were said to pay homage.

Furthermore, photographers in India in the nineteenth century were concerned about making a record of local skills and practices, such as basket or rattan mat manufacture, as shown in Penn's photograph bearing the simple caption, 'A wayside scene' (Plate 9).

In 1870, Penn had married Elizabeth (Zillie) Eagan (Plate 10) in St. Stephen's church. Her father was an Irishman who had set up a successful boot and shoe manufacturing company in Bangalore after serving with the British army in the Crimea. Zillie was a most attractive young girl, doubtless owing her looks to her Eurasian mother. In 1871 their eldest son Albert Edgar was born, and their second, Walter Oswald, a year later, followed by Cuthbert James in 1873 and Harold Dunstan, grandfather of this author, in 1875. Four daughters, Lillian, Muriel, Gwendoline, and Emmerline, were born during the six years 1878–1884, and their last child, a son, Christian Eric, came along in 1888.

Walter Oswald died within a year of being born, and Cuthbert James also, the latter in tragic circumstances, having been poisoned by eating chemicals from his father's studio. His distraught mother,

Zillie, blamed Cuthbert James's nanny and, without a shred of evidence, the poor girl was found guilty by the local court; but the sentence was overturned on appeal to the High Court in Madras—an appeal paid for by the citizens of Ooty, to whom it was clear that a great injustice had been done. A. T. W. Penn sent a memorial photograph (Plate 11) of the dead child to all his friends and relations.

When Penn started off in the profession of photography, it was looked on as a form of alchemy. Immense skill and patience were required, both to take and to develop the image on a wet collodion-coated glass plate and then to print it onto albumen-coated paper. But in the late 1880s, the introduction of the Kodak camera opened the process up to amateurs. The professional photographic business was hit in a manner not unlike that resulting from the introduction of digital photography in our own day, and many of the businesses failed. Penn too suffered: in 1899, unable to service his debts, he was forced to sell his house, studio, and all its contents, except for the photographic equipment.

Without a studio he could no longer practice as a photographer, and so he reinvented himself as an auctioneer, property dealer, and general trader. But then, in the early years of the twentieth century, the introduction of picture-postcards (a huge market worldwide) and photogravure printing for book illustrations allowed him to work as a photographer once more. In 1907–1908 he travelled down to the southernmost part of the subcontinent to take photographs of Amy Wilson-Carmichael's mission for her book *Lotus buds* (published in London in 1910). In the introduction, Amy writes:

> The photographs … were taken by Mr Penn, of Ootacamund, whose work is known to all who care to possess good photographs of the south Indian hills. The babies were a new experience to him, and something of a trial, I fear, after the mountains, which can be trusted to sit still.

The review in *The Westminster Gazette* in London ran:

> The feature of the book is fifty photogravure illustrations from photographs specially taken of the children. Many of

> these—indeed all of them—are very charming. Some of them are mere babies, others of larger growth, but in each case the photographer, Mr Penn, of Ootacamund, has succeeded in presenting pictures, which will elicit high admiration. The laughing faces, curly hair, and fine physical development of the little Indians make photographs exceedingly attractive. Indeed, we have never seen a more 'taking' series of children of the Orient. (see Plate 12)

But it had become time for Penn to retire, and so in 1912 he returned to England with his wife and three unmarried daughters; but 'home', he was soon to discover, was not in England but in south India where his heart lay, and after World War I ended, he returned with Zillie to live in Coonoor. There he died in 1924, and was buried in the nearby Tiger Hill cemetery (Plate 13).

Note

1. Charles Misquith was the owner of Misquith & Co. of Madras (founded in 1842), a shop that sold musical instruments, and still operates in Chennai as 'Musee Musical'.

Reference

Wilson-Carmichael, Amy. 1910. *Lotus Buds*. With fifty photogravure illustrations from photos specially taken for this work. London: Morgan and Scott.

Further Reading

'Penn' and 'Photography'. In *Encyclopædia of the Nilgiri Hills*, Paul Hockings (ed.). New Delhi: Manohar, 2012.

Plate 1: St. Stephen's church, Ootacamund, *ca* 1880

Source: Penn archive 01.13.005.

Plate 2: A. T. W. Penn and Charles Misquith making music, *ca* 1870

Source: Penn archive 01.17.004.

Plate 3: Ooty lake, with the Bund, *ca* 1880

Source: Penn archive 01.78.006.

Plate 4: The five tribes of the Nilgiri Hills, *ca* 1872

Source: Breeks 1873: Plate 1.

PLATE 5: Cromlechs, the Dodduru group, *ca* 1872

Source: Penn archive 12.115.056.

PLATE 6: James W. Breeks, *ca* 1871

Source: Breeks Memorial School.

Plate 7: The Nizam of Hyderabad

Source: Penn archive 01.85.001.

put poison in his food. This was a form of *seyvinai*. Nilakanth had gathered certain herbs from the forest to treat him. After spinning the *vibhuti* and praying, he placed a camphor cube in the middle of the powder. He lit this with a match and watched it burn, after which he spun the powder again. After a short pause, he lit another camphor cube, this time placing it into the steel cup of water. It floated and continued to burn, and after a few seconds the camphor cube moved to the edge of the cup. He then explained that this was a very bad sign, and that it meant that the case was potentially fatal ('near the end'). But he could still save the person with treatment. He then lit another camphor fragment and uttered *mantirams*. This time the camphor stayed closer to the middle: this was a better diagnosis.

At this point, Nilakanth placed another burning camphor cube in the water. It moved around rapidly and strangely, bobbing from edge to edge of the cup, as compared to the first two cubes. He said this was indicative of the young man's diagnosis of 'bad magic'. The young man, Nilakanth explained, could be cured with the forest medicines mixed with coconut oil. This would cause purging and release the toxin from his body. But the cure also depended upon the saying of *mantirams* in order to exorcise the evil presence in his stomach. We asked if he could tell who had caused the bad magic. He said he could, but would only inform the patient indirectly. This was so that it would not lead to more conflict within the community.

The conversation turned towards '*mana noi*' (mental illnesses). He said he could treat this. We asked about 'tension', the English word that is used ubiquitously in India for stress. He said nowadays, '*kavilai jasti*' (there is too much worry or stress). But many people were victims of 'bad wind' caused by an *Odi*. The *Odi* comes to you when walking in the forest. It comes as a wind, but is felt particularly on the back, neck, and arms. One becomes immobilised.

To ward off the *Odi*, ancestral offerings are necessary, but increasingly neglected—a ubiquitous theme and cause of moral and existential anxiety within local communities, as we will see. But one can chase away the *Odi* also through *mantirams*. Nilakanth said he sometimes sings songs that cannot be sung at any other time except in the healing ritual. We could see drums of various sizes hanging on the front porch. *Seyvinai* was a big problem, he said, and for this one needed a healer, not a hospital. When asked what the causes of *seyvinai* were, he mentioned 'outside knowledge' coming into the community. He elaborated on this by speaking of wealth, and the jealousy it creates in the formerly egalitarian ethos of tribal life. But I also wondered if he was blaming *seyvinai* on cultural influences from the outside, such as the wider Tamilian culture, where this concept has much currency.

We asked about the kinds of cases he was seeing frequently now, and he said that there were also new diseases that he could not treat, which required 'hospital' treatment. These were things like blood pressure, heart disease, and cancer. But he did have a remedy for gangrene, a co-morbid condition with diabetes, and people could come, he said, to the village for a more sustained treatment.

This healer vignette captures commonly heard themes within Irula and Ālu Kurumba communities in recent times. In sum, a gap has opened up between socioeconomic transformations within the cash economy and the belief systems that used to integrate a more egalitarian social order. As anthropologists have long noted all over the world, sorcery accusations are pervasive in times of rapidly growing inequality, as a result of socioeconomic changes (see, for example, Bailey 1994; Demmer 2016; Epstein 1959; Vitebsky 2017).

The economic marginality faced by some Adivasi communities within the Nilgiri Biosphere Reserve often leads to outmigration to urban areas. Many also work in the extensive tea plantation economy as wage labourers. Over the past few years of intermittent research, I have often heard that social problems, particularly depression, alcoholism, and violence, were reaching alarming levels as a result of cultural decline and stress within communities. Biomedical and psychiatric care was largely inaccessible to most Adivasis, despite concerted efforts by NGOs to partner with local hospitals in order to provide referrals to Bangalore or Coimbatore.[3]

Adivasi communities in the Nilgiris face several interrelated challenges impacting upon their well-being. First, reduced access to land, due to a combination of factors including circumscription by the Forestry Department, encroaching dangerous wildlife due to habitat loss (elephants, leopards, bison, tigers), and expanded commercial land acquisition for plantation and urban uses, as well as the public food delivery system,[4] has undermined the cultivation of millet, their traditional dietary and ritual staple. As many local residents put it, 'food was medicine', and 'now we are sick'. Others say, 'everything now is poison', pointing to pesticides, human waste, sugar, and processed foods. Second, many have left their respective village-based communities and migrated to distant cities for employment. One consequence of this shift in livelihood and residence has been the neglect of community-based ritual life centred upon ancestral 'sacred groves' (*dēva sholla*). The ritual life surrounding sacred groves and their connection to cultivation practices being disrupted has produced consequential shifts in diet and access to traditional medicines. Asthma, epilepsy, gangrene, and sickle-cell anaemia are said by local healers to be on the rise. The biomedical infrastructure as well as traditional healing practices have proven inadequate. Significantly, there has been a rise in various 'new illnesses' (*pudu noi/sangata vantata*), many possibly of psychogenic origin. Community healers speak of escalating community violence and illness due to fears or suspicions of sorcery (*seyvinai*), as well as generalised anxiety (*bayum*) which grips local residents. Healers say that this anxiety arises from the neglect of ancestral traditions, and the cosmic protections afforded by the ancestors when properly honoured. Alcohol abuse is said to be on the rise due to stress, and local healers speak of an escalation of mental illness. In order to capture some texture to these problems, I turn again to select voices from Irula and Ālu Kurumba communities, noting that these are characteristic of wider sentiments.

Voices from the Village

Rajkumar, an articulate young man from the Ālu Kurumba community, spoke of *prani*—small 'spirit beings' that can affect health. These, he explained, are believed to cause bad things to happen. *Prani* can cause pain in the body or 'wounds', he explained, adding that there is greater fear of these malevolent agents nowadays as a result of the loss of the traditional means for community protection. He explained further that the fear of malevolent beings is manifested in a fear of being alone in the forest. This is increasing, he explained, because the ancestor spirits have not been looked after properly with the loss of sacred groves, or more specifically, of their neglect by the young who are busy pursuing individual economic needs over and above the community. Out of this abandonment of tradition, a sense of haunting persists and is worsening, he (and others) told us.

There is also, he said, an increasing fear of sorcery. *Chara* (more commonly called *seyvinai* by locals) is transmitted through food and spells and is a 'specialty of the Kurumba', the traditional healers and sorcerers of the hills (Kapp and Hockings 1989). In previous times, the Kurumba had been contracted by other tribes to provide sorcery and even counter-sorcery protection against foes. In recent times, the accusations *within* the Kurumba community seem to be escalating as the targets are now undetermined. But since Kurumbas are still believed to control this secret knowledge, there is anxiety about where these forces are now being directed, given that their target no longer bears a name and is thus less contained.

Rajkumar did mention, however, that the efficacy of local healing and sorcery is not so great now as before; and this was due to the decline in *marundukaran*s (healers, literally, 'medicine people'). Increasingly, healers have failed to transmit their knowledge to an uninterested or fearful next generation. And with a loss of faith also occurring within the community, the authority of the healer has been largely supplanted by biomedicine. He thus implied that the question of efficacy is directly correlated to the faith of the community, as Lévi-Strauss (1963) famously argued. Biomedical care, whatever its merits, has failed to strengthen community ties as traditional healing had. Rajkumar said mental health problems are significantly worse now with the loss of faith in traditional healing and ways of life. There was increasing depression, fighting, and alcohol abuse within the Ālu Kurumba community. With the community shrinking to less than 1,700 members nowadays, it had begun to implode with these problems, resulting in less social cohesion. He described a vicious cycle where violence and depression drove the community apart, which ultimately weakened the very social and cultural institutions that mitigated these problems.

Several local healers also discussed health challenges within the Irula and Ālu Kurumba communities. They described new diseases (*pudu noi vantanta*) and the coming of biomedicine. Locals were increasingly going to a hospital for various illnesses. Now, 'there is a loss of faith (*ippe namibikai illai*)' in the local healing traditions. 'Medicines in the hospitals do not soothe and diseases often worsen in the hospital. These medicines don't work at home because we are forest people,' one healer explained. With dietary changes, 'epilepsy has tripled', one healer claimed. In this context, it is really not clear whether the word *epilepsy* was simply doubling for 'fits', as it often does in South Asia.[5]

Healers often described a dilemma that is impacting the community profoundly. Most communities had abandoned agriculture, depending on wage labour and government handouts for rice and oil, as well as state guarantees for work (on various infrastructural projects).[6] Without active cultivation, wild animals came closer to hamlets as the forests expanded. On the other hand, cultivation itself has become increasingly dangerous, with elephants coming into gardens. Thus, the pernicious cycle of abandonment of cultivation is motivated by concerns for safety, as well as other employment options. The practice of cultivation used to be protected by rituals conducted within the sacred groves (*deva sholla*), I was told. These are increasingly being abandoned, however, leading to danger from elephants, leopards, tigers, gaur (bison), etc. Related to this observation is a sense that as social taboos are increasingly transgressed—for example, relaxed rules about intermarriage between communities—new dangers are affecting the community. It is even said that tigers, leopards, and elephants attack people in their communities because of transgressions against tradition. This form of self-blame for hardship was common, but also pernicious in two senses: first, it exacerbated the existential anxiety felt by marginalised communities; and second, it tended to occlude the structural forces of agro-capitalism that created precariousness for vulnerable communities such as the Irula or Ālu Kurumba.

Indeed, healers argued that medicines are harder to get because of the expansion of tea and coffee estates: nowadays healers had to go much further into the forest to collect medicinal plants. After the installation of camera traps, the locals were accused, I was told, of poaching by forestry department officials, even upon ancestral lands that have been used for generations of their community in a similar way.

As Rajkumar had mentioned, healers said that violence within the community is increasing. In these cases of intra-community violence, 'local healing practices worked best,' he said. The future of traditional knowledge was, however, uncertain. If it were forgotten or abandoned, the healers predicted a rise in substance abuse, bad nutrition, and bad parenting (which the children will inherit). In seeking relief from physical and mental disease, patients would seek 'quick' treatment in a hospital. This 'hospital' kind of medicine, however dramatic its short-term effects, is 'harmful to the body and spirit'. The general lament was expressed by many that the traditional healing knowledge would not continue. 'The children don't have interest,' it was argued. They 'are no longer in the village', and '*nambikai illai*' (faith is lost).[7]

Healers often spoke of the difficulties in transmitting their knowledge. First, only some people have the 'power' to heal. It is a calling, albeit one that can be taught to some extent. But some healers, despite having learnt traditional medicine, do not have the 'power' to heal. The status of healer is not disconnected from spiritual potency. Second, to learn of the medicinal plants that are effective means to watch and learn. The name of the plant cannot be spoken if it is to remain effective. Thus, to apprentice with a healer means that one must simply shadow him over time.

The healers said that the first step in addressing these problems would be to grow millet in the forest again. Cultivation would generate a commitment to the land, and by extension the community, which would have residual effects on cultural knowledge, healing, and other integrative aspects of the culture. Lingarajan (a pseudonym), a senior Ālu Kurumba healer, explained that many did in fact go to the hospital for biomedical care. With new 'diet patterns', around half of all illnesses were now treated in hospitals and clinics, he suggested. He spoke about a herbal smoke produced by a ritual fire that used to be quite a common cure. Now, in these times of reduced floral diversity, this healing practice was dying off. He said, 'we were together' in those days, but became separate and now 'buy our own food'. In earlier times, millet cultivation was not just a food source, but a form of ritualised social bonding as well. With the advent of a cash economy, or its acceleration, people were incentivised to become more individualistic, seeking out the earnings they needed to purchase food and other items. Moreover, with the provisioning of rice, the incentive for growing millets was substantially lessened, given the increased risks of elephant raids.

Not only were the numbers of able workers much lower in the village due to outmigration and dispersal, but growing traditional crops also required 'social health and unity'. Again, repeating the central motif in the Kurumba and Irula hills, 'Unity was there before—people would obey leadership.' But now there were three main causes of disunity: food from the public delivery system by the government schemes had offered disincentives for the hard and risky labour of cultivation. As a result of all this, people had become lazy. This led to the abandonment of many ritual traditions and the sense of unity and cosmic protection that they afforded.

Third, leadership was gradually weakened at the local level. Priests and headmen no longer exercised much authority, thus hastening the decline of social institutions, including being the catalyst for this decline, the incentive to grow millet for ancestral offerings.

I met several times with the aforementioned Lingarajan in his remote jungle hamlet. He served clients from numerous villages and tribes in the region, and was respected for his healing knowledge and spiritual power. Our conversation often turned to the problem of '*bayum*' that afflicts people increasingly as they enter the forest. This is caused, he explained, by the neglect of the old ways and by increasing individualism. But treating it required a special concoction made of some mixture of ash and a liquid to form a kind of paste. Lingarajan prepared some of the paste in front of me and mentioned that he had to prepare it for a young woman who was suffering *bayum*. He emphasised the abandonment of sacred traditions which, among other things, included the cultivation of millet for ritual offerings. This dilemma was not lost on most older Kurumbas who, I found, also felt the anxiety related to the neglect of sacred groves. In this sense livelihood, religion, and spatial practices—their tight integration within a single behavioural and symbolic ideology—were underscored and unified through the symptom of *bayum*. His remedy now prepared, Lingarajan had to test it. To divine whether it was effective or not—that is, if it would cure the patient—one had to throw it against the wall of the house: if it would stick, the medicine would work. In this case, he threw a handful of the ash paste against the house and it did indeed stick.

The problem of succession came up in our conversation. Young people had little or no incentive to sacrifice the time needed to learn the craft of healing. As it involved patient observation over a long period, one would need to materially support individuals who wanted to learn healing for a livelihood. Thus, with the young more interested in earning money, not an unreasonable goal given their marginality, to create a *gurukal* (traditional school) one would need some financial incentives, which were non-existent. But even then, it was explained that learning the correct remedies and medicines from the forest was only half the issue. Lingarajan's sisters and wife were healers in their own right too; but a key difference was that they only understood which plants would cure which ailment. They did not possess the power of divination, and with it, the visionary and healing capacity to treat sorcery.

On the other hand, as we have seen, if the diseases are 'new', resulting from changes in diet or other stressors on the body associated with modernity, then 'we must send them to the hospital'. In a sense, it was very simple: traditional illnesses shaped by local beliefs were best treated by local practices and beliefs; but if the illnesses were inexplicable or unrecognisable, then biomedicine was called for. The existential problem, then, was caused by a disjuncture between a rapidly changing socioeconomic structure and a somewhat resilient set of cultural and spiritual beliefs.

Bridging Healing Paradigms

While I have briefly described the fear that is plaguing some local communities, it must be underscored that the healers I met with have proposed solutions for this and other specific problems that afflict their communities. The healers, along with other community members I have spoken to, suggest that the solutions must occur at three levels: the government, the community, and the local NGOs, which must coordinate efforts between them. NGO work had in fact helped some healers connect these dots in a coherent manner. But whereas urban-based academics and clinicians often see the problem as being one of expanded biomedical access, the local healers see the crises within their communities as local problems that require local solutions. Here, a doorway has been opened for community-based care that might serve as a bridge between the new diseases and the need for biomedicine, as well as a revival of traditional practices to mitigate more culture-specific forms of illness. This is an area for more discussion—both theoretical and pragmatic—but which cannot be taken up in this brief sketch of illness narratives within the Irula and Ālu Kurumba communities.

But to underscore the dilemma, there seems to be an inevitable decline in traditional medicine due to an inability to transmit the healing tradition, coupled with a growing lack of faith among younger people, who turn increasingly to biomedical care. Moreover, that care is needed due to the 'new diseases' that present themselves as impervious to traditional treatments. Finally, a care gap has opened up between the decline of traditional medicine (despite an apparent spike in sorcery accusations) on the one hand, and the lack of access, on the other, to specialist biomedical care, particularly with regard to psychiatry and neurology.[8] Increasingly, the typologies and categories of psychiatric diagnosis are arriving in rural India, including in areas where many Adivasis are experiencing both a sense of deep psychological and social crisis, as hinted at in this short chapter, and a decline in traditional care. The need for cultural bridges across healing paradigms is thus acute and urgent.

Notes

1. N. Selvi, from the Keystone Foundation, was my research partner for this and many other encounters with healers and community members. Nilakanth's age was hard to guess, but was perhaps in the late fifties or early sixties.

2. The *Muḍuga Odi*, he had explained on an earlier visit, would kill their victim after paralysing them, then resurrect their bodies as zombies who would return to their communities as the 'living dead'. *Muḍuga Odi*s came from the Kerala side of the Nilgiri mountains, he explained, but could no longer be found in his area.

3. The Keystone Foundation has partnered with The Banyan, Ashwini Hospital, and advisors from NIMHANS to create a community wellbeing programme at Keystone, aimed at providing community-based counselling and basic medical triage to communities facing various types of psychosocial stress, particularly Adivasi communities. I have participated in this collaboration as an anthropologist-consultant.

4. Rice and oil are distributed to low-income communities in Tamil Nadu in an effort to combat malnutrition. One unintended consequence of this well-intentioned policy has been to further erode the cultivation of traditional staples such as millets.

5. This would be misdiagnosed as epilepsy, from a biomedical standpoint, and would be called non-epileptic 'pseudo seizures', or conversion disorders. In India, 'fits' is a term that often conflates non-epileptic and epileptic seizures.

6. The Mahatma Gandhi National Rural Employment Guarantee Act (MGNREGA) guarantees 100 days of paid labour per annum for those underemployed and meeting certain financial criteria. In Tamil Nadu, and perhaps elsewhere, this has led to work in infrastructure, such as laying down of roads and cables; but it has also encouraged cultivation, even on collective tribal lands. Often, that cultivation is for cash crops, however, and not to revive ancestral millet cultivation.

7. One common form of counselling involves asking the couple to sit quietly before god (in a shrine), and then, I was told, the problem simply leaves (*kavalai podratu*). This treatment, however, becomes harder to accomplish without access to sacred groves and the necessary faith.

8. Although I could not address urban psychiatric care within this short chapter, my project also encompasses the expansion of biomedical psychiatry within urban populaces. Moreover, I am investigating the extent to which referrals to urban hospitals do occur, and to what effect.

Acknowledgements

I wish to thank the Keystone Foundation for their support and guidance, and in particular N. Selvi, Snehlata Nath, Revd. Philip Mulley, and Archana Sivaramakrishnan; as well as the Cornell and Keystone students who have participated in the Nilgiris Field Learning Centre, and from whom I have also learned much.

References

Bailey, Frederick G. 1994. *The Witch Hunt, or the Triumph of Morality*. Ithaca, NY: Cornell University Press.

Demmer, Ulrich. 2016. *Towards Another Reason: Identity Politics and Ethical Worlds in South India*. New Delhi: Oxford University Press.

Epstein, Scarlett. 1959. 'A Sociological Analysis of Witch Beliefs in a Mysore Village'. *Eastern Anthropologist* 12 (4), 234–251.

Kapp, Dieter B., and Paul Hockings. 1989. 'The Kurumba Tribes'. In Paul Hockings (ed.), *Blue Mountains: The Ethnography and Biogeography of a South Indian Region*, 232–248. Delhi: Oxford University Press.

Lévi-Strauss, Claude. 1963. 'The Sorcerer and His Magic'. In his *Structural Anthropology*, 167–185. New York: Basic Books.

Vitebsky, Piers. 2017. *Living Without the Dead: Loss and Redemption in a Jungle Cosmos*. Chicago: University of Chicago Press.

Further Reading

'Ethnobotany', 'Hospitals', 'Medicine', 'Nilgiri Adivasi Welfare Association', 'Public Health', and 'Sorcery'. In *Encyclopædia of the Nilgiri Hills*, Paul Hockings (ed.). New Delhi: Manohar, 2012.

16

The German Nilgiri Family

Team Members of the Indo-German Nilgiris Development Project

Peter Neunhäuser

The potato, together with the British, came to India a couple of centuries ago and soon settled on the Nilgiri hills. But after about 140 years of continuous cultivation, potato diseases appeared there, with the result that the yields dropped off: it was an enormous challenge for many well-to-do and influential Badaga farmers! While looking around for some way to save the potato economy, they soon realised that their best bet lay with the Germans. After all, one of the worst threats to the health of potatoes, the Golden Nematode, was not scientifically named after a noted German university for nothing: this was *Heterodera ROSTOCKIENSIS.*

And so it was that in 1967 India's Minister of Finance, Thiru C. Subramaniam, and the German Minister of Agriculture, Hermann Höcherl, signed a contract creating the Indo-German Nilgiris Development Project (INDP). Shortly thereafter, alongside the Project Leader, a dozen German experts were sent to the Nilgiri Hills to man this project: a general agronomist, a potato agronomist, three horticulturists, a plant pathologist, a soil scientist, a water engineer, a land-use planner, a workshop manager, and one economist for marketing and one for farm economy.

In order to improve the quality of potato seed and also to conduct trials of other vegetables, farm managers from Germany were posted at each of the seven State Seed Farms. A mechanical workshop was necessary to service the project vehicles and agricultural machinery, to train local drivers and mechanics, and do the repairs. In total, twenty-two experts from Germany worked for the INDP—which was at the time one of the biggest of all German overseas projects.

The strategy they adopted was clear enough:

Step 1: Reduce the infestation of potatoes with the Golden Nematode by using the Bayer chemical pesticide Dasanit, since manual eradication of cyst nematodes is impossible.

Step 2: Find crops for rotation which have a similar market value to the potato, while at the same time improving the quality of potato seed. These alternative crops, other than potato, would not just sell locally; more distant markets had to be found to guarantee a good and stable income. The most successful crops here proved to be cabbage, carrots, and cauliflower, which were marketed as far away as Mysore, Bangalore, and Bombay.

IMAGE 16.1: The young German team in 1969 in Ooty (when they first met with this book's editor)

Source: Peter Neunhäuser.

Most of the experts on this project were young Germans with families. They brought along with them their small children, and then more children were born during the years of their stay, 1967–1978. I remember that once a year, the Protestant German pastor used to come up to Ooty from Madras to baptise last year's crop of newborns. In spite of all the heavy work in the project, it was a happy group of young families.

But what has happened to all of them since they left India? Where are they now, half-a-century later? Actually, the ties formed back in those days were and are still strong. The group still meets at regular intervals, along with their spouses or, alas, the widows, in one or another of the members' places throughout Germany, although these events have declined in frequency in more recent years (Images 16.2 and 16.3). But as our numbers are slowly thinning, we now meet at shorter intervals, at present just once a year.

IMAGE 16.2: Our recent team meeting in 2018, at the Lüneburger Heide, a German nature preserve

Source: Peter Neunhäuser.

Since 2004, we have met ten times at many different places—the Island of Rügen in the Baltic Sea, the Lüneburger Heide, Hannover, Berlin, Bacharach in the Rhein Valley, Weinsberg in Würtemberg. The most recent meeting was in August 2018, again in the Lüneburger Heide, a beautiful nature preserve, with a dozen people attending. In 2019, the meeting was to be held at the town of Stade, near Hamburg.

IMAGE 16.3: The Vijayanagaram farm in Ooty (now changed to a public rose garden); visited in 2005

Source: Peter Neunhäuser.

The social interplay among the German group and also with the Indian colleagues, neighbours, friends, and other people we met in everyday life, has brought us all together, promoting plenty of mutual understanding and some lasting friendships. In India, we used to go on excursions on long weekends in the immediate region, to the game sanctuary near Masinagudi or to the Dasara festival in Mysore, or just took a train ride on Sunday morning on the Nilgiri mountain train, or went on a short outing to watch the sunset from Doddabetta peak. Holidays were otherwise spent in Goa, on the backwaters near Cochin, at Mahabalipuram; and other trips were organised to Cape Comorin, called, in Tamil, Kanya Kumari (my second daughter, who was born in Vellore, is named Kumari). All such activities helped give the German team the stamina and strength to face the demanding project work in such a sensitive ecological environment as these steep mountains.

Some of the consultants were keen to find out what had happened to their work of decades before; and so in 2005 a small group went back to south India and up into the mountains, just to revisit their old haunts.

They found that one of the state seed farms, Vijayanagaram, in the centre of Ooty, which had originally been set up to grow seed potatoes, had since been converted into a rose garden. But nearby, in the valleys of the plateau, vegetables and potatoes are still being grown under irrigation. The need to rotate the cultivation of potatoes with other vegetables has taken firm root in the minds of local farmers.

As recently as 2013, when I revisited the project area, I found that the cultivation of other vegetables surpassed that of potatoes. Cultivation practices have developed, sprinkler irrigation has been introduced—instead of sprinkling water over the field with a bucket—and new varieties are being grown. I met a farmer who also deals in vegetable seed, and who visits Holland twice a year to import seeds of new vegetable varieties.

IMAGE 16.4: The Nilgiri Project revisited: here, a proud vegetable farmer shows the author his irrigated field, with carrot and garlic

Source: Peter Neunhäuser.

Moreover, other types of vegetable are being grown, like garlic, for example. It was good to see how commercial vegetable farming has taken firm root in the area and is now developing under its own steam.

And the German team members? Whenever they meet, they talk about the old days when they were young, and reminisce over those many experiences and adventures. They chat about the lives of the children born in Ooty, Vellore, or Kotagiri. How many grandchildren have you got now? How are they doing? So, as you can see, happy family chatter still goes on about the German Nilgiris project!

Further Reading

'Indo-German Nilgiris Development Project' and 'Potato'. In *Encyclopædia of the Nilgiri Hills*, Paul Hockings (ed.). New Delhi: Manohar, 2012.

Part VII

Coda

17

The Symbiosis in the Nilgiris

Indu K. Mallah

Is there a meeting point between legend and history? Is there a meeting point between conservation and development? And is there indeed a meeting point between exploitation and expiation? Where does myth end, and metaphor begin? Where does idealism end, and pragmatism begin? And where indeed does rhetoric end, and reality begin?

These are some of the questions that come to one's mind while reflecting on the symbiotic spirit of the Nilgiris. The Nilgiris, or the Blue Mountains as the British called them because of the shimmering blue haze surrounding them when viewed from a distance, are part of the larger mountain chain of the Western Ghats in south India. The Nilgiris and its inhabitants have attracted attention because of certain unusual characteristics which have survived from precolonial times, through the colonial period and India's Independence, to current times.

The history of the Nilgiris dates back to the eleventh and twelfth centuries. It was part of the kingdoms ruled by most of the rulers of south India—the Cheras, the Cholas, the Pandyas, the Rashtrakutas, the Gangas, the Pallavas, the Kadambas, and the Hoysalas. The Hoysala king, Vishnuvardhana, conquered the Nilgiris in the twelfth century.

The oldest inscription which mentions the district belongs, in the opinion of Lewis Rice, as stated in his work *Epigraphia Carnatica*, to *ca* AD 930 and shows that the Wynad was then part of the well-known Ganga Dynasty of Mysore. Between the close of the tenth century AD, and the beginning of the twelfth century, the Gangas were ousted from Wynad by the Kadambas. King Vishnuvardhana, who ruled from 1104–1141, is said to have captured Wynad, as well as the Nilgiri Plateau. There is mention of King Kala of Kukal, which is a Badaga village still in existence in Kotagiri, in the Nilgiris.

It is interesting to note that the Nilgiri Hills were considered 'holy hills'. The Abbe Dubois says that even a sight of their summits was considered sufficient to remove sin.

In 1310, the Hoysala line was overthrown by the rulers of the Delhi Sultanate.

In the early part of the sixteenth century, both Wynad and the Nilgiris fell under the famous Hindu kings of Vijayanagar, who established their capital at Hampi and the present-day Bellary district.

In 1565, the Vijayanagar dynasty was overthrown by the kings of the Deccan, in the memorable battle of Talaikota. In 1610, King Raja Wodeyar of Mysore drove the Vijayanagar general out of Srirangapatna and two years later, he was granted Srirangapatna and the Ummatur country around it by the then nominal king of Vijayanagar. Thenceforth, the kings of Mysore became the rulers of the Wynad and titular possessors of the Nilgiri Hills, which were under the immediate rule of their dependents, called the Udaiyars or Rajas of Ummatur.

According to many earlier chroniclers, the present-day Gudalur in the Nilgiris was part of the Kadamba and Ganga territories of Wynad, until the tenth century CE. The Hoysala control of the Nilgiris is amply proved by several inscriptions highlighting their capture of these hills. Muslim invasion under Malik Kafur ended the Hoysala suzerainty. Shortly afterwards, a minor dynasty based at Ummatur (about 50 km north of the River Moyar) emerged as the rulers (Arasus) of the Nilgiris. These Ummatur rulers were fierce rivals of the Vijayanagar Empire. It took all the might of Krishnadevaraya to subdue them by the year 1512. A short interregnum of the Vijayanagar vassals followed, before the NIlgiri Hills were annexed by the Mysore ruler, Chikkadevaraya Wodeyar, in 1677.

Between then and the British occupation of the Nilgiris in 1799, no record survives, but the Jesuit priest Ferriera (or Finicio) records that the Todas and the Badagas (two leading groups of tribal/indigenous people) were already settled there at this time. (The Nilgiri Hills were, and still are, home to a number of tribals and other indigenous peoples.)

The main groups of tribal and indigenous peoples living in the Nilgiris are the Todas, the Badagas, the Kotas, the Kurumbas, the Irulas, and the Paniyas. The broad umbrella of the Kurumbas include the Mullu Kurumbas, Alu Kurumbas, Jenu Kurumbas, and Betta Kurumbas, Although the Badagas are not, strictly speaking, tribals, notwithstanding the strong lobby amongst them to be granted tribal status, they are the largest indigenous group living in the Nilgiris, and though there has been a lot of conjecture about their so-called migration from Mysore, given the fact that the Nilgiris was part of Wynad, which was part of the Mysore domains (now Karnataka), which again was part of the Vijayanagar Empire, the question of migration does not arise. During British rule, Ootacamund, the capital of the Nilgiris, was the summer capital of the then Madras Presidency; after Independence, in 1956, during the linguistic division of the states, the Nilgiris came to be included in the state of Tamil Nadu.

The Badagas (originally known as the Gowdas) were the original agriculturists of the Nilgiris.. The Todas were, and still are to a large extent, pastoralists, tending to their buffaloes, which play an integral part in their religion, lifestyle, and culture. The Kotas are the artisans, and make agricultural implements, tools, pots, and pans. They also make clay cooking pots and water pots. In addition, they are musicians who play traditional music at their own functions, and at those of other indigenous peoples. The Kurumbas (I use the name as an umbrella term to cover the entire Kurumba complex) were hunters, basket-weavers, gatherers of wild fruits, wild honey, berries, and roots. They used to supply jungle wood to the Badagas and the Todas. They were the traditional medicine-men, and cured diseases that the medicine-men of other tribes failed to cure, for, living in the jungles, they had a wealth of knowledge of folk medicines on their finger-tips. Perhaps for this reason they were feared by other communities as sorcerers.

Broadly speaking, the five original inhabitants of the Nilgiris evolved a unique support system based on the division of labour and mutual sharing—the Badagas (Gowdas) provided the grains and vegetables for themselves and the other communities; the Todas, the dairy produce; the Kotas, the tools, pots, and music; the Kurumbas and Irulas, baskets, wild honey, and also herbal medicines.

None of the indigenous peoples have a script; yet all of them have a rich orature, which provides invaluable insights into their credo and culture and fills in some pivotal blanks in their history. Another significant factor that links all the indigenous peoples together is their symbiotic relationship with nature, which in some cases borders on reverence. All of them have their sacred hills and their sacred rivers, their sacred trees and their sacred stones.

Both animals and trees and plants form part of their festivals. At the Uppattua Habba of the Badagas, for example, domestic cattle are led to pits filled with salt water on the maidan of each village. After they have drunk their fill, they are led to the houses of the owners, where they are fed with millets cooked in buttermilk and lentil curry. They are similarly honoured at the festival of Dhodda Habba. At the Badaga festival of Sakkalathi, leaves from several trees and shrubs are collected and strung over the entrance of each house in the village, after the village headman, who collects the leaves, has blessed them.

Similarly, during the seventh month of pregnancy of a Toda woman, the husband presents his wife with a symbolic bow and arrow made from a particular shrub. Needless to say, long before biodiversity became a buzzword in environmental corridors, it was a way of life with these children of the soil.

Many of the tribal elders still tell heartwarming stories of their tribal children playing with bear cubs and panther cubs. Some of the indigenous people believe that animals and birds used to talk in the olden days. In the Badaga legend of Kol Thippe, a crow shows the eponymous heroine the way to the afterworld when her fellow-villagers taunt her, saying that she has no support from her parental side. Subsequently, crows' tongues were cut to prevent them from talking, or so the Badagas believe.

There are other heartwarming stories which illustrate the bond of brotherhood among the Badagas/Gowdas, Todas, and Kotas.

According to one, apparently when a major horde of Badagas/ Gowdas fled from Mysore to join their brethren already living in the Nilgiris during the reign of Tipu Sultan, they rested in a forest/ shola in the Nilgiris. Then, hearing the sound of hoof-beats behind them, they panicked and fled, and in their haste, left a baby boy behind them. The baby crawled into a cave. A Toda man who was passing by saw the baby and held his arms out to it, but the baby was frightened, and crawled further into the cave. He then brought his own baby son, placed him in front of the cave, and sprinkled some roasted buckwheat on the ground before him. Seeing the other child picking up and eating the grains, the Badaga baby crawled out of the cave. The Toda man gathered both infants in his arms, and brought up the Badaga baby along with his own child. Legend has it that the Badaga baby is the founder of the present-day Badaga division or *seeme* of Thothanad.

According to another story, when the ancestors of the Badagas/ Gowdas were taking refuge in the Nilgiri Hills from the oppression of Tipu Sultan in Mysore, the Kotas distributed themselves in the different regions of the Nilgiri Hills to protect them.

Although there traditionally exists a strain of animosity between the Badagas/Gowdas and the Kurumbas, there is one heartwarming story that endorses the symbiotic relationship between them. The story, 'Unige Mada', has been documented by Brenda Beck (see Hockings 1987).

A Kurumba called Unige Mada once lived in the village of Bani with his wife and eight sons. Droughts were very common in Bani, but somehow, Unige Mada and his family managed to survive. But during one particularly severe drought, in which there was not even a drop of water to drink, Unige Mada lost his wife and all eight sons, one by one. Broken, but not beaten, Unige Mada decided to leave Bani and visit a Toda friend who lived near Malladu, and seek help. So he made some bamboo vessels, tied them to the end of a bamboo rod, and set off for Malladu. On the way, he dug up some edible tubers and roots to assuage his hunger, and also collected some wild honey from the bees' nests. But Unige Mada became weaker and weaker, and hardly had the strength to move. However, he dragged himself to a spot near the Badaga village of Kinnakore.

Now, there lived a man called Joghi in Kinnakore, with his wife and eight sons, several grandsons and great-grandsons. He was playing with his grandchildren on the village platform which the village elders used to settle disputes among the villagers, and at one point looked up and saw that the buffaloes, which should have been grazing on the village green, were huddled together in a tight circle. He was very worried—had a tiger attacked one of them? With grave concern, he called out to his wife to take the children inside, and hurrying into the house, grabbed his gun from the top of a cupboard. He hastened towards the group of buffaloes and counted them. To his relief, not a single buffalo was missing. He started driving the herd towards the village and as he was rounding up the last few buffaloes, he saw the unconscious Unige Mada. Joghi was greatly perturbed. Perhaps the man had passed out from exhaustion. He lifted the unconscious Unige Mada gently in his arms and carried him to his house. He then called out to his wife to bring some curds. Husband and wife diluted the curds with water, and poured the liquid into Unige Mada's mouth. Slowly, the exhausted man opened his eyes.

'Ayya, thank you for your extreme kindness to me. God will bless you greatly.'

He then proceeded to tell Joghi about his troubles. He concluded by saying: 'When I have recovered my strength, let me look after your family, and your buffaloes for the rest of my days.'

Joghi was very touched by Unige Mada'a words, and said: 'You are most welcome to stay with us for the rest of your life, and you can help to look after the buffaloes.'

'The past,' said the bard, 'is prologue', in a different context, of course. The past, in the context of the Nilgiris, is indeed prologue. The symbiosis which existed among the indigenous peoples exists miraculously even today, between all the communities living in the Nilgiris. There are people from all over the country living here, even though they belong to different faiths and speak different languages. The local people participate in each other's festivals, visiting one another's homes with traditional dishes. At

Christmas, all the clubs and local associations, not to mention the Christian families, celebrate this festival of goodwill with great bonhomie and generosity of spirit, sharing food, hospitality, gifts, and camaraderie with all. Likewise, at Deepavali, the practice in our home is to make extra sweets and traditional dishes for the neighbours, even after the children grew up and left home. At one time we had a Muslim family working for us, and for Bakri Id, they would bring us mutton biryani. This synergy between all the people, indigenous and others, is all the more significant in the face of the growing intolerance and parochialism in the rest of the country, not to mention the world.

This is not to imply that things are perfect in this 'paradise on earth'. Far from it. Although the symbiotic relationship between the indigenous peoples continues in essence and spirit today, time, changing values and lifestyles, and exploitation have taken their inexorable toll. Many have moved away from their original occupations, and have sought jobs elsewhere. The majority of the Badagas has given up agriculture and chosen other professions and jobs. Hillsides are being cut into to accommodate multi-storeyed resorts, leading to immense soil erosion. Effluents from industrial units pollute the once crystal-clear streams which have been the drinking-water sources for the tribals from time immemorial. Another fallout is the loss of herbal and medicinal plants due to deforestation. Yet another is the conversion of tea estates into real-estate, thanks to the challenges posed by globalisation. Add to that the growing alcoholism among the tribals, and one has the complete picture.

Not long ago, a speech by Pope Francis made waves across the world:

> It is not necessary to believe in God to be a good person. In a way, the traditional notion of God is out-dated. One can be spiritual, but not religious. It is not necessary to go to church and give money—for many, Nature can be a church. Some of the best people in history did not believe in God, while some of the worst deeds were done in his name.

He also noted the unbreakable link between indigenous peoples and the environment. 'For them, land is not a commodity, but rather, a gift from God, and from their ancestors who rest there, a sacred space with which they need to interact if they are to maintain their identity and values.'

In an official letter issued in 2015, Pope Francis called on all people to quickly bring 'the whole human family together to protect our common home'.

Were the Pope to visit the Nilgiris, he may well laud the synergistic way in which the indigenous peoples are attuned to their environment, and their credo of a reverent relationship with Nature, their Devar Bettas, and their Devar Sholas. And missionaries who once came to scoff at the 'tree worshippers' and the 'stone worshippers' and sought to straitjacket them into an alien religion, would do well to stay and pray.

Reference

Hockings, Paul. 1987. 'The Man Named Unige Mada (Nilgiri Hills, Tamilnadu)'. In Brenda E. F. Beck, Peter J. Claus, Praphulladatta Goswami, and Jawarharlal Handoo (eds), *Folktales of India*, 125–129, 305–306. Chicago and London: University of Chicago Press [reprint, New Delhi: Motilal Banarsidass, 1989].

Further Reading

'Badaga Poetry', 'Barter', 'Sacred Peaks', 'Sacred Waters', and 'Toda Song'. In *Encyclopædia of the Nilgiri Hills*, Paul Hockings (ed.). New Delhi: Manohar, 2012.

Hockings, Paul. 1968. 'On Giving Salt to Buffaloes: Ritual as Communication'. *Ethnology* 7, 411–426.

A Brief Bibliography for Readers

NOTE: The bibliography for the Nilgiris is massive, for this seems to be the most extensively studied small rural area anywhere in South Asia. The bibliography that was published over twenty years ago already contained 6,786 items—books, articles, pamphlets, manuscripts, and maps—and could doubtless be expanded to 8,000 items by now; see Hockings (1996), below. The Badaga-English Dictionary *is also listed below, as it provides the most accurate phonetic spellings for placenames, of which about 2,000 are analysed there. Below, we are only listing some books that are directly relevant to the chapters in this book.*

Emeneau, Murray B. 1971. *Toda Songs.* Oxford: Clarendon Press.

Francis, Walter (ed.). 1994 [1908]. *Madras District Gazetteers. The Nilgiris*, Vol. I. New Delhi: Asian Educational Services.

Gopalakrishnan, M. 1995. *Gazetteer of India. Tamil Nadu State. The Nilgiri District.* Madras: Government of Tamil Nadu.

Hockings, Paul (ed.). 1989. *Blue Mountains: The Ethnography and Biogeography of a South Indian Region*. New Delhi: Oxford University Press.

____. 1996. *Bibliographie générale sur les Monts Nilgiri de l'Inde du sud 1603–1996/ A Comprehensive Bibliography for the Nilgiri Hills of Southern India, 1603–1996/ Eine umfassende Bibliographie der Nilgiri-Berge Südindiens, 1603–1996*. Bordeaux: Université Michel de Montaigne (Espaces Tropicales 14).

____ (ed.). 2012. *Encyclopædia of the Nilgiri Hills*. New Delhi: Manohar Publishers & Distributors.

____. 2013. *So Long a Saga: Four Centuries of Badaga Social History*. New Delhi: Manohar Publishers & Distributors.

Hockings, Paul, and Christiane Pilot-Raichoor. 2023. *A Badaga and English Dictionary—Glossary and Gazetteer*. New Delhi: Manohar Publishers & Distributors.

Keystone Team. 2007. *Honey Trails in the Blue Mountains: Ecology, People and Livelihood in the Nilgiri Biosphere Reserve, India*. Kotagiri: Keystone Foundation.

Penn, Christopher. 2014. *The Nicholas Brothers and A. T. W. Penn: Photographers of South India 1855–1885*. London: Bernard Quaritch Ltd.

Price, J. Frederick. 2002 [1908]. *Ootacamund. A History*. Compiled for Government. Calcutta: Rupa and Company, 2 vols.

Reddy, Ramya. 2019. *Soul of the Nilgiris: A Journey through the Mountains*. Kotagiri: Keystone Foundation.

Walker, Anthony R. 1986. *The Toda of South India: A New Look*. Delhi: Hindustan Publishing Corporation [2nd edn., 2003, titled *The Toda People of South India: Between Tradition and Modernity*. New Delhi: BRPC].

Zickgraf, Jens M. 2018. *Rupien in der Dollar-Zone: Geld als Prozess und Medium gesellschaftlicher Teilhabe. Eine Ethnographie (Badaga, Nilgiris District, Indien)*. Berlin: Lit Verlag.

Notes on the Contributors

Tarun Chhabra is a practising dentist in Ootacamund, and also an activist for the Toda community. He is among a tiny handful of outsiders who speak Toda fluently (and is perhaps the only one at present to do so). Dr Chhabra is also an environmental activist, and a founding trustee of the Toda Nalavaazhvu (Welfare) Sangam. In 2003, he established an environmental NGO called the Edhkwehlynawd Botanical Refuge (EBR) Centre Trust, which also works on ecological restoration in the Toda heartland. He authored numerous papers on some unique aspects of Toda culture and ethnobotany, and has also lectured widely. He is the author of *The Toda Landscape: Explorations in Cultural Ecology* (2015).

R. J. Ranjit Daniels is an ecologist by training. He has worked extensively on ecology and the conservation of vertebrates, particularly birds and amphibians, both in India and abroad. He was a member of the first team to survey the Nilgiri Biosphere Reserve in the 1986. In 2000, he co-founded Care Earth, and is currently a Trustee of the Care Earth Trust, based in Chennai.

Frank Heidemann is a social and cultural anthropologist and teaches at the University of Munich. He has conducted fieldwork with the Badaga people and published numerous articles on their social and religious life, the monograph *Akka Bakka* (2016; in German), and the textbook, *The Modern Anthropology of India* (2013; with P. Berger). His main interests include visual anthropology, the anthropology of the senses, of aesthetics, and of atmosphere.

Paul Hockings is Professor Emeritus of Anthropology at the University of Illinois, and also Editor-in-Chief of *Visual Anthropology*. He has published a dozen books on Indian topics, mostly on the Nilgiris, and numerous articles, as well as editing *Principles of Visual Anthropology* and four anthropological encyclopaedias. His latest books are *So Long a Saga: Four Centuries of Badaga Social History* (2013) and (with Christiane Pilot-Raichoor) *A Badaga and English Dictionary—Glossary and Gazetteer* (2023).

HANS J. VON LENGERKE studied at the Universities of Hamburg, Bochum, and Mainz. During 1971–1980 at the South Asia Institute, Department of Geography, University of Heidelberg, he did climatological and hydrological research in India and Sri Lanka. After assignments in development projects in South and Southeast Asia and in Africa, he worked during 1988-2003 in the Volkswagen Foundation in Hannover, where he was in charge of Geosciences and of international collaborative research funding programmes.

MARIE-CLAUDE MAHIAS, a French anthropologist, retired as Senior Research Fellow (Emerita) in the CNRS, Paris. Rooted in long fieldworks carried with the Jains, with artisans, and peasants in northern India, and in the Nilgiris, her researches pioneered in the anthropology of food, of techniques, gender specialisation, and cognitive anthropology. She is the author of several books and articles, including *Le Barattage du monde. Essais d'anthropologie des techniques en Inde* (2002). She also edited *Techniques et culture: Inde* (1985) and *Construire les savoirs dans l'action. Apprentissages et enjeux sociaux en Asie du Sud* (2011).

INDU K. MALLAH is a writer, poet, literary critic, and social activist living in Ooty, south India. Several of her short stories have been broadcast over BBC, two of her screenplays have won national awards, and her novel, *Shadows in Dream-time*, has won wide critical acclaim and been translated into several languages. Her collection of poems, *B(r)oken Moon and Other Poems*, has also been critically acclaimed. Her other publications include *Fly Away Paloma*, *Tell Me A Story*, a collection of folk-tales, *Mrg Trishna and Other Poems*, and *The Last Sigh*. She is currently working on a collection of indigenous legends and folk-tales from the Nilgiris.

Revd. **PHILIP K. MULLEY** is a Presbyter of the Church of South India, a renowned local historian and cultural anthropologist, and has long been associated with leading anthropology researchers on Nilgiri subjects. Revd. Mulley is concerned with the indigenous communities, especially the Badaga community to which he belongs. He has acted as a resource person for several organizations too, as well as for individual researchers and students. He was a contributor to the *Census of India—Salem Gazetteer* and *Kongu Encyclopaedia* (two volumes, in Tamil). He has also served on a panel for the compilation and publication of the trilingual Badaga-Tamil-English Dictionary.

PETER NEUNHÄUSER studied Horticulture at Weihenstephan Technical University in Munich. He had a five-year assignment for development co-operation in the Nilgiris, then three years in Kenya (Machakos), and two years in Tanzania. Peter became the Deputy Director at the Centre for Advanced Training in Agricultural Development (CATAD) at the Technical University of Berlin and Humboldt University, but now lives near Hamburg.

CHRISTOPHER PENN gained an MA in jurisprudence at Oxford followed by an MBA at Harvard Business School. After twenty-one years in industry and twelve years in media, Penn began his career as an author. His principal work is *The Nicholas Brothers & A.T.W. Penn, Photographers of South India 1855–1885* (2014). He now lives in Surrey, England with his wife and family.

PRATIM ROY is the Founder Director of Keystone Foundation, which is based in Kotagiri. He has a degree in Ecology from Pondicherry University, and now dabbles in bees, wetlands, and hill water systems. Roy has been a Hubert Humphrey Fellow at Cornell University and now works on governance, fundraising, and organisational development.

SHARADA SRINIVASAN is a Professor at the National Institute of Advanced Studies (NIAS), Bangalore. Her landmark contributions include archæometric characterisation of bronzes of south India using lead isotope analysis, and archæo-metallurgical studies on ancient mining and metallurgy in the region. The winner of numerous awards for this research, she has also been an accomplished exponent of classical dance (Bharata Natyam) and has given numerous lecture-demonstrations in India and abroad. Her co-authored or co-edited works include *India's Legendary Wootz Steel* (2014) and *Performance at the Urban Periphery: Insights from South India* (2022).

WILLIAM TALLOTTE is an ethnomusicologist researching south Asian classical, folk, and tribal musics, with particular reference to performance analysis, cultural and cognitive anthropology, and ritual studies. He is the author of *Music and Temple Ritual in South India: Performing for Śiva* (2022) and has released several CDs for the well-known collection Ocora Radio France. He is currently Research Associate at the Institut de recherche en Musicologie (CNRS - Sorbonne University).

ANITA VARGHESE is an Ecologist by training and currently Director at Keystone Foundation. Her interests lie in understanding the relationships between tropical forests and indigenous peoples. She is an East West Center Graduate Degree Fellow, Hawaii and is Chair of the Western Ghats Plant Specialist Group of the IUCN-SSC.

ANTHONY R. WALKER, an Oxford-trained social anthropologist, retired as Professor of Anthropology at the University of Brunei Darussalam in 2011 and now lives near Kandy, in Sri Lanka. He has also held teaching positions at the Science University of Malaysia, the National University of Singapore, the Ohio State University, and the University of the South Pacific in Suva, Fiji. He is the author of *The Toda of South India: A New Look* (1986), *Between Tradition and Modernity and Other Essays on the Toda of South India* (1998), *Merit and the Millennium: Routine and Crisis in the Ritual Lives of the Lahu Peoples* (2003), and Śākyamuni *and* G'uị Sha: *Two Essays on Buddhism in the Lahu and Wa Mountains* (2014).

ANDREW C. WILLFORD is a Professor of Anthropology at Cornell University. His previous research has focused upon Tamil displacement, revivalism, and identity politics in Malaysia and India. His recent books include *Tamils and the Haunting of Justice: History and Recognition in Malaysia's Plantations* (2014), and *The Future of Bangalore's Cosmopolitan Pasts: Civility and Difference in a Global City* (2018). His current research focuses on mental health, psychiatry, neurology, and religious healing traditions in India.

JENS M. ZICKGRAF received his doctorate from Ludwig-Maximilians-University in Munich. He has done extensive fieldwork in the Nilgiris, and has specialised in economic anthropology. His major interests include the processes of monetisation and financial inclusion, ecologies of payment and social aesthetics of money. Today he works in the fields of education and non-profit-marketing.

Index